EXPLORING AGRIBUSINESS

Third Edition

EWELL PAUL ROY, Ph.D.

Professor and Distinguished Faculty Fellow
Department of Agricultural Economics and Agribusiness
Louisiana State University – Baton Rouge

EXPLORING

AGRIBUSINESS

THE INTERSTATE
Printers & Publishers, Inc.

Danville, Illinois

Also by Dr. Roy and available from The Interstate:

Collective Bargaining in Agriculture
Contract Farming and Economic Integration
Cooperatives: Development, Principles and Management
Economics: Applications to Agriculture and Agribusiness

——Library of Congress Catalog
Card No: 79-90117

ISBN 0-8134-2098-9

Preface

The primary purpose of this book is to provide a more comprehensive understanding of agribusiness—its nature, scope, importance and relationship to the general economy—and to draw attention to the occupational opportunities which exist in this field.

Many of the nation's junior and senior colleges are adjusting their curricula to provide prospective agricultural graduates with more agribusiness training. *Exploring Agribusiness* has been planned to serve as a ready text for a general orientation course for undergraduates in the agriculture curriculum and to provide these students with the knowledge they will need, regardless of their ultimate vocation, of the relationships between farmers and their suppliers and buyers. It will also give them a broad informational base upon which to make their selection of majors and minors in future semesters and into which they may better incorporate the subject matter of their subsequent courses.

However, as an inevitable consequence to meeting this primary purpose, *Exploring Agribusiness* has values which far transcend the college campus. Teachers of vocational agriculture and county agricultural agents, to whom their communities properly look for the most recent and most complete information about all aspects of agriculture, will find in this book a panoramic overview of this new field, with facts and figures which are not conveniently available in any other source. Forward-looking high school agriculture students, who are already giving thought to their college or vocational careers, will find in it a thorough coverage of the subject that will enable them to think more intelligently in terms of where their own future might best lie.

Almost equally important, the public generally needs a better awareness of how farming and related industries blend together to help provide the people of the United States of America with the highest standard of living the world has ever known. *Exploring Agribusiness* is intended to contribute to this end.

The *third edition* brings up-to-date many of the data in the *second edition* and also provides an entirely new set of more current references in addition to many other improvements.

Ewell Paul Roy

Baton Rouge, Louisiana

Table of Contents

1

Agribusiness—

Its Nature and Importance

DEFINITION

What is agribusiness? Agribusiness is the "coordinating science of supplying agricultural production inputs and subsequently producing, processing and distributing food and fiber."[1] Agribusiness involves both technology and economics: It depends on many technologies, such as plant and animal science, forestry, mechanics and entomology, among many others; and it depends on many phases of economics, such as agricultural, consumer, labor and industrial economics. To all of these disciplines must be added.elements of political science, government, history, education, sociology, and psychology. Thus, agribusiness is an all-encompassing discipline of study applied to food and fiber, the mainstays of all civilizations.

NATURE OF AGRIBUSINESS

To appreciate the full significance of agribusiness, one needs only to reflect a few minutes. At breakfast one may have orange juice from California or Florida, which was produced, processed and distributed over thousands of miles and which passed through many points. Next, the cereal probably came from Michigan or Minnesota and most likely

---

[1]Some authorities exclude "farming" or the "production" of food and fiber from the definition of agribusiness.

was made from corn produced in Iowa or from wheat produced in the Dakotas. The milk probably came from nearby dairy farms, was kept refrigerated and was pasteurized by a dairy and finally was delivered to the home refrigerator. The sugar may have come from the beet sugar areas of the West or from the sugar cane farms of Louisiana, Hawaii or Florida. The bacon may have come from Iowa and the eggs from nearby farms. The bread for the toast probably came from a local bakery, but the wheat and other ingredients came from the Middle West. Finally, the coffee may have come from Brazil or Colombia.

To produce these breakfast foods for today, farmers may have made production decisions many years prior, such as planting orange trees or holding back pigs from the litters to use as breeding stock. Many items had to be brought together to obtain these foods—land, labor, seeds, fertilizer, chemicals, machinery and credit, among other resources. In addition, business plants had to be built to handle and process these foods in their raw material state. Many engineering and technological feats were performed to achieve the quality and standardization required. As these foods left the processing plants, trucks, railroads, airplanes and barges may have been used for transportation, requiring roads, tracks, runways, waterways, communications and personnel. As they arrived in the city, a receiving terminal, depot or warehouse was needed to store these goods for later distribution in smaller lots to retail food stores. When the housewife enters the food store to purchase foods for family use, the final destination is rapidly being approached—the day of judgment has arrived. Will she buy? What and how much will she buy? Which kind of orange juice will she buy? Will she take fresh oranges and squeeze them for juice, or will she buy orange concentrate from the frozen food counter? We depend on the consumer finally to cast a vote—to tell us which of all the thousands of decisions that have been made all along the line she is impressed with and to what extent. Many will be disappointed by her decisions because she cannot buy everything and she can pay only so much. These disappointments will be reflected in some persons' suffering losses, quitting production or shifting to something else. Others are overjoyed because their products are accepted for purchase again and again.

It is evident, then, that any success at the job of agribusiness will depend upon how nearly correct and how well coordinated these thousands of decisions are (Figure 1-1).

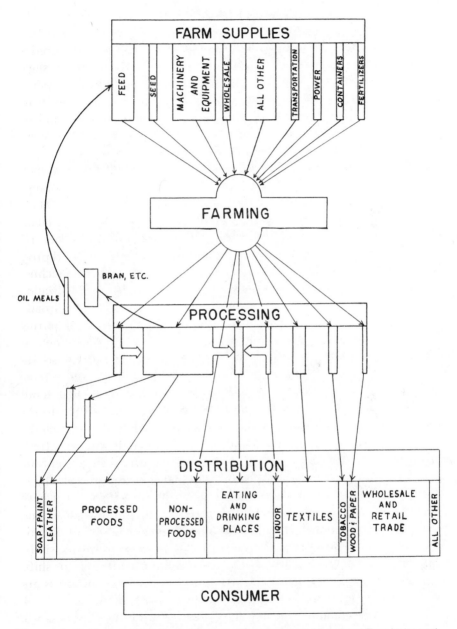

Figure 1-1. Agribusiness flow chart. (Courtesy, Department of Agricultural Economics and Agribusiness, Louisiana State University, Baton Rouge)

DEVELOPMENT OF AGRIBUSINESS

As the United States of America became settled from east to west, farmers were largely self-sufficient. They grew most of the food and fiber they consumed, with any surplus sold locally to those not engaged in farming. In George Washington's first term as President, more than 90 per cent of Americans were engaged in farming, and fewer than 10 per cent were engaged in other occupations. No complex distribution system was required in his time, because the food and fiber supply was largely produced and consumed locally. As the country grew, specialization began to develop. People found that they could move away from producing their own food and fiber because these necessities could and would be produced by others. They exchanged money earned from other occupations for food and fiber. This process has continued, and presently a reversal of Washington's time has occurred—only about 4 per cent of Americans are farmers, while about 96 per cent are non-farmers.

Agribusiness evolves from changes occurring in agriculture. These changes have the effect of reducing the number of operations on the farm. The farmer's main supplies such as feed and fertilizer are secured from off-farm manufacturers or processors. The farmer reduces his processing operations (e.g., manufacture of butter) and discontinues retailing his surplus food and fiber in cities. For all practical purposes, the commercial farmer is a specialist in the production of agricultural commodities. Other industries develop to specialize in manufacturing and distributing farm supplies and in processing and distributing farm products.

Specialization, including the development of specialists in feeds, fertilizers, insecticides and farm machinery, quickly evolves within the farm supplies component. Within the storage-processing-distribution component, specialists begin operating wheat elevators, food processing and other types of firms to handle and/or process farm products. Specialists even develop within farming itself. For example, we have specialized rice farms, wheat farms, cattle farms, etc. This process of specialization occurring within agribusiness is a process of decentralization and segmentation. Agribusiness, then, is the sum total of these segments engaged in supplying agricultural production inputs and producing, processing and distributing the resulting food and fiber.

IMPORTANCE OF AGRIBUSINESS

Man's first concern is food, followed by clothing and shelter. Without these basic necessities, everything in the world would come to a halt. Yet, many people tend to overlook this fundamental fact. Over time, people tend to take food, clothing and shelter for granted. They tend to believe that these necessities are crude or unimportant, probably because of their abundance, at least in our Western civilization.

In the Eastern civilizations, especially Asia, such necessities are not taken for granted, probably because of their scarcity. Every day, man's life may hang in the balance, depending on whether food will be available or not. Even if food is produced and available, it does not necessarily follow that citizens of a densely populated city in India, for example, will get it. Faulty distribution systems are as much a cause of hunger and starvation as is inadequate food and fiber production. Therefore, the distribution of food and fiber may be as critical as their production.

FARMER EFFICIENCY AND AGRIBUSINESS PROGRESS

Without doubt the most far-reaching benefit accruing from the evolution of agribusiness has been the release of workers from farming for employment in other occupations—a development made possible by the increased efficiency in the production and marketing of food and fiber. Specialization brings more productive efficiency. But, widespread specialization is not possible without free exchange. In developing greater specialization with the resulting increases in production, we have in effect substituted town or city labor (and capital) for on-farm labor and tools. Since food, shelter and clothing are primary human needs, it is essential that man first allocate that time and effort required for the production of these items, leaving for other pursuits the residue of his labor force. Thus, increased efficiency in agriculture and the release of manpower for other work are prime prerequisites for increasing industrialization. Moreover, the rate of progress toward increased farm productivity serves to set a ceiling on the rate of industrial development by governing the total manpower available for off-farm work. Fortunately, this ceiling has advanced progressively until today more than 90 per cent of our working force is available for off-farm jobs and approximately 65 per cent for work entirely outside agribusiness. Also, it is fortunate that we have people with the corresponding ingenuity, courage and industriousness to venture into new enterprises that provide productive jobs for the labor force released from farming.

These twin products of research and technology—the release of farm manpower and the corresponding creation of new off-farm jobs—have provided the basis for our tremendous economic growth and development. Of course, the key to such growth and development is increased productivity per worker, providing the basis for the creation of new products and wealth. This, in turn, becomes translated into new risk capital, new factories, new jobs and increased consumer purchasing power; together, all of these provide the basis for further economic progress.

The important result of this progress has been the gradual elevation of the standard of living of all economic groups—both on-farm and off-farm. In the case of food, the public has been offered improved quality, greater variety, wider selection and, in short, greater food values in terms of both the larger quantities that can be purchased with an hour's wages with less drudgery and the time required in the preparation of food in the home. Technology also has increased the mobility of people by freeing them from their own local food supplies; eliminated the fear of famine from the American continent; and given us promise of being able to feed well, for decades to come, a rapidly growing population.

In the case of fibers, agribusiness technology has reduced the price of clothing in terms of what an hour's wages will purchase, increased the variety of fabrics from natural and synthetic sources, made possible popular-priced ready-made clothing and provided fabrics for numerous industrial uses. In addition, living standards for rural people have been further improved through the reduction of back-bending labor, increasing the time available for education and recreation, among other pursuits.

SUCCESS OF U.S. AGRIBUSINESS

The agribusiness complex in the U.S. economy is the marvel of the world. Probably no nation, past or present, has been better fed itself and contributed so immensely to world food supplies as well. Besides providing each American with some 1,500 pounds of food annually, the U.S. agribusiness complex also exports huge quantities of grains, vegetable oils and fats, cotton, tobacco and many other products. This is not all. The U.S. agribusiness complex is so efficient and productive that the federal government has had to institute controls of various kinds to see that overproduction is held back! Some economists believe that if U.S. farmers and agribusinessmen were allowed to produce what they are capable of producing, much of the world would not want for food, clothing and shelter. Such is the success and power of U.S. agribusiness and also its potential for world peace and security. Ill-fed, ill-housed and ill-clothed citizens in any part of the world are a threat to the peace and security of all.

But, food and fiber production problems are one thing, and distribution is another. Impediments to trade and to the movement of goods can frustrate an otherwise good farm production job. Even in the United States, with its modern and efficient production and distribution system, defects still exist. Continuous and vigorous effort has to be maintained daily to oil the production and distribution machinery to minimize the squeaks. The point to remember is that the whole agribusiness process is not automatic. People and resources have to be brought together under a set of rules, formal and informal, and each person must put his or her shoulder to the wheel.

● ● ●

In the next chapter, the scope and size of agribusiness in the United States of America are discussed more specifically.

TOPICS FOR DISCUSSION

1. Define "agribusiness."
2. Discuss the transition from a rural to an urban America.
3. What has made U.S. agribusiness so successful?
4. Make a distinction between "production" and "distribution" of farm products.
5. Describe the "flow chart" for agribusiness.

SELECTED REFERENCES

1. Davis, John H., and R. A. Goldberg, *A Concept of Agribusiness*, Alpine Press, Boston, Mass., 1957.

2. Goldberg, R. A., *Agribusiness Coordination: A Systems Approach*, Graduate School of Business, Harvard University, Cambridge, Mass., 1968.
3. Roy, Ewell P., *Contract Farming and Economic Integration*, The Interstate Printers & Publishers, Inc., Danville, Ill., 1972.
4. Staff, *The Changing Structure of U.S. Agribusiness*, U.S. Chamber of Commerce, Washington, D.C., 1974.
5. Staff, *The Food and Fiber System—How It Works*, Agr. Info. Bul. 383, ERS, U.S. Dept. of Agriculture, Washington, D.C., Mar. 1975.
6. Weyant, J. Thomas, and others, *An Introduction to Agricultural Business and Industry*, The Interstate Printers & Publishers, Inc., Danville, Ill., 1971.

2

Agribusiness—

Its Scope and Size in the United States of America

Various measures may be used to ascertain the scope and size of agribusiness in the United States of America (Tables 2-1 and 2-2). It is estimated that agribusiness expenditures for end products at the final consumer level in 1976 were $312 billion or 18.3 per cent of the Gross National Product (GNP), 26.3 per cent of Disposable Personal Income (DPI) and 28.5 per cent of Personal Consumption Expenditures (PCE). For 1983, final agribusiness expenditures are projected at $520 billion or 17.3 per cent of GNP, 25.5 per cent of DPI and 27.3 per cent of PCE (Table 2-1).

In addition, it is estimated that if other types of agribusiness expenditures were added to those shown in Table 2-1, the agribusiness expenditures percentage of PCE could rise another 3 per cent. Thus, agribusiness is a formidable part of the U.S. economy now and in the future. Note that in the earlier years (1929 to 1967) agribusiness expenditures were even a larger percentage of PCE. The reason is that as the economy grew, relatively less of the total was devoted to foods and fibers while more was devoted to all other items which went to make up a higher standard of living for all U.S. citizens (Table 2-1).

Data in Table 2-2 indicate that the *value added* by the *farming* sector, although it is the most critical sector, has declined as a percentage of total value added, because not only are U.S. citizens buying food and fiber but also services that go in and with the food causing the *value*

Table 2-1. Determination of Value Added by Agribusiness Sectors, USA, for Selected Years

Line no.	Item	1929	1945	1955	1967	1976	Estimated 1983
	I. FARM INPUTS ($ billion)						
(1)	Purchases of manufactured inputs[1] (9 − 10) − (2) or (4) − (2) + (3)	2.0	6.7	11.6	19.5	42.0	78.4
(2)	Other expenses[2]	2.2	2.1	3.1	6.5	16.0	21.8
(3)	Paid to farm sector	3.5	4.2	7.5	12.3	31.2	45.2
	(a) Hired labor[3]	(1.3)	(2.3)	(2.5)	(2.8)	(7.4)	(10.7)
	(b) Materials[4] (4) − (1 + 2 + 3a)	(2.2)	(1.9)	(5.0)	(9.5)	(23.8)	(34.5)
(4)	Total farm production expenses (1) + (2) + (3)	7.7	13.0	22.2	38.3	89.2	145.4
(5)	Value added in supply sector[5] (9 − 10)	4.1	8.7	14.7	28.0	58.0	100.2
	II. FARM OUTPUTS ($ billion)						
(6)	Sales to other farms (3b)	2.2	1.9	5.0	9.5	23.8	34.5
(7)	Sales to nonfarm sector[6] (9) − (6 + 8)	9.0	19.3	24.7	33.7	70.5	110.8
(8)	Other income items[7]	2.6	3.4	3.4	4.2	8.6	13.2
(9)	Total gross farm income[8] (6 + 7 + 8)	13.8	24.6	33.1	47.4	102.9	158.5
(10)	Value added at farm[9] (9) − (1 + 2) or (9) − (4) + (3)	9.6	15.8	18.4	21.4	44.9	58.3
	III. SALES OF FINAL PRODUCTS						
(11)	All food, beverages and tobacco ($ billion)	21.2	43.5	72.2	118.6	274.5	461.2
(12)	Clothing and shoes[10] ($ billion)	9.1	12.7	15.7	23.0	25.5	39.2
(13)	Net agricultural exports[11] ($ billion)	(−)0.3	0.5	(−)0.6	2.3	12.3	20.0
(14)	Total sales of end products ($) (11) + (12) + (13) ($ billion)	30.0	56.7	87.3	143.9	312.3	520.4
(15)	Value added in processing and marketing[12] (14) − (5) − (10) ($ billion)	16.3	32.2	54.2	94.5	209.4	361.9
(16)	Gross national product ($ billion)	103.4	212.3	399.3	796.3	1,706.5	3,000.0
(17)	Agribusiness[13] of GNP (14 ÷ 16) (%)	29.0	26.7	21.9	18.1	18.3	17.3
(18)	Disposable personal income (DPI) ($ billion)	82.3	149.0	273.4	544.5	1,185.8	2,040.0
(19)	Agribusiness of DPI (14 ÷ 18) (%)	36.5	38.1	31.9	26.4	26.3	25.5
(20)	U.S. population (million)	121.8	139.9	165.3	197.8	215.1	234.5
(21)	Per capita GNP (16 ÷ 20) ($)	849	1,518	2,416	4,026	7,934	12,793
(22)	Agribusiness expenditures per capita (14 ÷ 20) ($)	246	405	528	728	1,452	2,219
(23)	Personal consumption expenditures (PCE) ($ billion)	77.3	119.5	253.7	490.4	1,094.0	1,903.0
(24)	Agribusiness of PCE (14 ÷ 23) (%)[14]	38.8	47.4	34.4	29.3	28.5	27.3

¹Gross farm expenses.

²Interest, taxes and net rent to nonfarm landlords.

³Hired labor wages including value of perquisites.

⁴Total paid to farmers for input items such as feed, feeder cattle, seed, baby chicks, etc.

⁵Total value of farm output less value added at farm.

⁶Gross farm income less sales to other farms and other income items (nonmoney income).

⁷Nonmoney income—products directly consumed in farm households plus rental value of farm dwellings.

⁸Excludes government payments.

⁹Total value of farm products less farmers' purchases from nonfarm sources.

¹⁰Allocated to agribusiness on basis of consumption of cotton and wool to total fiber, or natural fibers 33% of total fibers (higher in years before 1967).

¹¹Farm commodities only. Exports and imports of processed farm commodities assumed to be offsetting.

¹²Total sales of end products less "value added" in supply and farm sectors.

¹³Excludes wood furniture, flowers and shrubs, lumber and wood for paper products. These would add another 2.0% of DPI.

¹⁴Other agribusiness expenditures not specifically included here could include floral and nursery plants sold to consumers, wood furniture and furnishings, agricultural-based recreation and wood used for housing and buildings. It is estimated that all these items could add 3% to the data shown here for 1976 and 1983.

Source for: Items (2), (3a), (4), (8), and (9), from USDA *Farm Income Situation*; (10) from annual *Economic Report of the President*; (11), (16) and base data for (12) from USDA, *National Income and Product Accounts of the United States*, and *Survey of Current Business*; (12) allocated to agribusiness on basis of data from USDA, *Statistics on Cotton and Related Data*; (13) (16) (18) (20) and (23), annual *Statistical Abstract of the United States*.

Source for Table 2-1: Luttrell, C. B. "Agribusiness—A Growth Analysis," *Business and Government Review*, University of Missouri, Columbia, Nov. 1969, p. 33 for 1929-1967. 1976 and 1983 updated by author.

Table 2-2. Value Added by Agribusiness Sectors, USA, for Selected Years

Sector	1929	1945	1955	1967	1976	Estimated 1983
A. Value Added ($ billion)						
Supplies/inputs	4.1	8.7	14.7	28.0	58.0	100.2
Farming	9.6	15.8	18.4	21.4	44.9	58.3
Processing and marketing	16.3	32.2	54.2	94.5	209.4	361.9
TOTAL	30.0	56.7	87.3	143.9	312.3	520.4
B. Value Added (Index – 1929 = 100)						
Supplies/inputs	100.0	212.2	358.5	682.9	1,414.6	2,443.9
Farming	100.0	164.6	191.7	222.9	467.7	607.3
Processing and marketing	100.0	197.5	332.5	579.8	1,284.7	2,220.2
TOTAL	100.0	189.0	291.0	479.7	1,041.0	1,734.7
GNP	100.0	205.3	386.2	770.1	1,650.4	2,901.4
Population	100.0	114.9	135.7	162.4	176.6	192.5
C. % of Total Value Added						
Supplies/inputs	13.7	15.3	16.8	19.4	18.6	19.3
Farming	32.0	27.9	21.1	14.9	14.4	11.2
Processing and marketing	54.3	56.8	62.1	65.7	67.0	69.5
TOTAL	100.0	100.0	100.0	100.0	100.0	100.0
D. Value Added as % of GNP						
Supplies/inputs	4.0	4.1	3.7	3.5	3.4	3.3
Farming	9.3	7.4	4.6	2.7	2.6	1.9
Processing and marketing	15.7	15.2	13.6	11.9	12.3	12.1
TOTAL	29.0	26.7	21.9	18.1	18.3	17.3

Source: Luttrell, C. B. "Agribusiness—A Growth Analysis," *Business and Government Review*, University of Missouri, Columbia, Nov. 1969, p. 33 for 1929–1967. 1976 and 1983 updated by author.

added in processing and marketing to increase as a percentage of the total. Also, the *farming* sector is more perfectly competitive than other sectors which causes greater pressure on efficiency levels and lower returns on equity. An individual farmer alone cannot pass his costs on to the next level in the economic system (Table 2-2).

Each of these categories or segments in the agribusiness chain is discussed briefly.

FARM PRODUCTION SUPPLIES AND SERVICES

In past years, farmers relied primarily on home-grown inputs for their production supplies. For example, chicks were hatched from eggs set at the farm rather than purchased from commercial hatcheries. Cottonseed meal and barnyard manure were used as fertilizer materials rather than purchased commercial fertilizers. Seed corn was obtained right out of the corn crib. Horses and mules were used instead of tractors. Many other examples could be cited.

The present-day commercial farmer is a far different type of operator, relying more and more upon purchased rather than home-grown inputs. For example, farmers use enough steel products to make almost 6 million compact cars, sufficient rubber to put tires on more than 8 million cars and enough electricity to power the six New England States. They use the equivalent of 15 billion gallons of crude oil—more than any other single industry uses—and about 41 million tons of fertilizer and lime annually. Credit is needed in most instances to facilitate these transactions.

As agriculture increases its specialization and commercialization, these purchased inputs will increase in relative importance.

PRODUCING THE FOOD AND FIBER

The production of food and fiber is still largely a family operation, although hired labor is often used seasonally. The total value of farmers' marketings has stayed about the same for several years, but as the number of farmers has decreased, sales per capita have increased. That is, the same pie is divided among fewer people. This is a good trend, because it means that per capita farm incomes are trying to keep pace with higher per capita incomes in nonfarming occupations. Even the amount of hired labor used for seasonal farm work is declining as farmers substitute machines for hand labor.

Another factor in farmers' income has been the increasing size of federal payments under various agricultural programs, which have had the effect of stabilizing farm income. However, farmers are not all agreed on the wisdom of such payments as a stabilizing factor in their farm income.

In addition to the billions of farm product sales and government payments received, farmers earn additional income each year from off-farm income sources. The average farm family in the United States earns more than half of its net total income from off-farm sources. Of this amount, about 60 per cent is spent on farm family living expenditures, leaving 40 per cent for investments in real estate, machinery and cooperatives, plus savings of various kinds and payment of debts and obligations.

RECEIVING, HANDLING AND PROCESSING FARM PRODUCTS

Many functions and services are involved between the time the raw products leave the farm gate and the time they leave the processor. The goods have to be assembled, transported, stored, insured, financed, graded and processed. The costs of performing these functions and services have been rising and continue to rise. These marketing steps are vitally necessary, because the farmer's raw products have to be converted into a more usable form. There are also losses and shrinkage in moving these products from farmer to processor, for not all that is assembled and delivered can be processed.

For many years farmers have tried to eliminate some of these middlemen but, in most instances, to no avail. Their functions and services cannot be replaced, because they are necessary and useful. In some cases, however, farmers have replaced some middlemen with their own cooperatives.

WHOLESALING AND RETAILING PREPARED FOODS AND FIBERS

After food and fiber products have been processed, they must enter the wholesale and retail trade channels. Many important steps are involved as products are moved from their processing stage closer to the consumer for final sale.

The *wholesaling* segment's primary function is to serve as a link between the food and fiber processor and the retail stores or shops. However, in many cases, the wholesaling and retailing segments are combined into one; that is, they are under one common ownership.

The *retailing* segment, consisting of food stores, restaurants, cafes, clothing shops, shoe stores, tobacco shops, hamburger and sandwich shops, among many other establishments, represents the final stage of distribution to consumers.

Like farmers, wholesale and retail food marketing firms have also experienced a downward trend in their profits as a percentage of sales and stockholders' equity. This segment of the agribusiness chain is a very competitive one.

CONSUMING THE FOOD AND FIBER

The end purpose of all production is consumption. The farm production job is not finished until food and fiber products are consumed.

Consumption of food and fiber per capita in terms of pounds does not change much over the years. The gains in total food consumption are mostly related to the growth in population. Although per capita food consumption in pounds stays approximately the same, as population grows, the market for food and fiber grows in about the same proportion.

What does change are the kinds of foods that are consumed. People today are eating more salads, proteins and highly processed foods and less "heavy" foods, and they are eating more meals away from home. Also, as persons become wealthier, they tend to eat better in terms of more expensive, convenient foods and to consume a greater diversity of foods outside the home.

These factors and an increased world demand are important to farmers and others involved in the growth and production of food and fiber.

JOBS IN AGRIBUSINESS

Another measure of the size of agribusiness is in terms of employment provided. Although the exact number of all agribusiness jobs is difficult to ascertain, certain measures are available which provide a reliable estimate (Table 2-3). There were an estimated 17.057 million agribusiness jobs in the USA in 1976, or about 19.5 per cent of all jobs. *Manufacturing and mining* jobs connected with agribusiness supplies, machinery and food/fiber processing account for about 24.5 per cent of the jobs while *wholesale and retail* trades comprise about 42.5 per cent of the jobs. *Service* jobs in agribusiness comprise 4 per cent and *construction* jobs associated with wood and wood products add another 3 per cent. *Farming, forestry and fishery* jobs comprise about 26 per cent of all agribusiness jobs (Table 2-3). Thus, in 1976, about one out of five U.S. jobs was in agribusiness.

Another method for classifying agribusiness jobs is shown in Table 2-4, or by *sector* of agribusiness, each containing manufacturing, service and/or distributing jobs as the case may be for both 1976 and estimates for 1983. While the total number of agribusiness jobs will continue to grow by 1983, agribusiness jobs as a percentage of total jobs is expected to decline to about 17 per cent from 19.5 percent in 1976. This is due to the relative decline of food and fiber employment relative to the overall growth in jobs of the economy. Note, however, that only the *farming* sector shows an absolute decline in jobs while other agribusiness sectors indicate job expansions (Table 2-4).

Farm Supplies and Services

The total number of jobs related to the supply of agricultural inputs is increasing as shown in Table 2-4. It is expected that although the number of farm supply jobs will continue to increase, the percentage of the total U.S. labor force required to fill these positions will stay about the same or will increase slightly. The main reason is that added output of feed, farm supplies and machinery items can be obtained by substituting capital for labor, increasing output per worker under industrial-type operations.

Farm Production

In 1890, the number of industrial workers equaled the number of farm workers in the United States. By 1910, only 3 American workers in 10 were on the farm. Then, each farmer supplied food and fiber for 7 people; presently, he supplies over 56 people. Farmers are among the most productive workers in the world, and the United States has become the world's leading agricultural producer. The gain in farm output has come largely by substituting machinery for labor and by using purchased inputs while holding land about constant.

Table 2-3. Estimated U.S. Employment in Agribusiness and Related Agribusiness Share of Total Employment, United States, 1976

Sector	Total agribusiness employment	Sector	Total agribusiness employment
Manufacturing and Mining:		**Services:**	
Stone, clay and glass	6,260	All transportation, utilities and communications	225,450
Primary metals incl. iron/steel	35,700	Banking	38,970
Fabricated metals	13,870	Other credit agencies	13,890
Farm machinery	146,000	Securities and brokers	1,760
Other machinery excl. electrical	19,280	Insurance carriers	11,110
Electrical machinery	18,320	Insurance agents	10,260
Transport equipment	51,990	Real estate	8,090
Instruments and rel. products	5,090	Other finance institutions	1,160
Misc. industries	4,210	Personal	8,210
Food and kindred products	1,710,000	Misc. business services	21,190
Tobacco	76,000	Motion pictures	6,090
Textile mill products	483,000	Medical/related health	44,410
Apparel	650,000	Federal govt. agr.	60,000
Paper and allied products	676,000	State/local govt. agr.	240,000
Printing and publishing	32,400	Sub-total	690,590[3]
Agricultural chemicals	56,000		
All chemicals excl. agr.	29,340	**Construction:**	
Petroleum and coal	10,150	Residential and commercial buildings/lumber and wood product employment (10% of total construction employment):	
Rubber and plastics	18,420		
Leather tanning	24,000		
Footwear excl. rubber	85,000	Sub-total	516,200[4]
Handbags and personal goods	18,000		
Sub-total	4,169,030[1]	**Farming, Forestry and Fisheries:**	
Wholesale and Retail Trade:		Farmers/farm workers	3,800,000
Wholesaling	426,300	Fisheries	119,000
Retail general merchandise	100,320	Forestry, logging, sawmilling, millwork and wood containers	510,000
Retail food stores	2,061,000	Sub-total	4,429,000[5]
Retail apparel and acc. stores	402,500		
Retail furniture/home furnishing	159,900	Grand total of agribusiness employment	17,056,740
Retail eating/drinking places	3,624,000		
Hotel/lodging units incl. food	82,900	Total U.S. employment	87,500,000
Retail farm sup./garden centers	115,000		
Retail farm machinery dealers	90,000	% Agribusiness of total employment	19.49
Retail lumber and bldg. materials	190,000		
Sub-total	7,251,920[2]		

[1]24.5%   [2]42.5%   [3]4.0%   [4]3.0%   [5]26.0%
Source: *Statistical Abstract of the U.S., 1977*, with estimates by author of agribusiness share of total employment.

Table 2-4. Employment and Projected Employment in Farming and Agribusiness, USA, 1976 and
1983

Agribusiness sector	1976 Employment		1983 Employment		Estimated % of change 1976-1983
	No.	% of total	No.	% of total	
I. All farm supplies (manufacturing and retailing)	784,770	4.6	885,000	5.0	+12.8
II. Farm operators and farm workers, fisheries and forestry workers	4,429,000	26.0	3,764,650	21.3	−15.0
III. Handling, receiving, manufacturing and processing	3,979,850	23.3	4,393,495	24.9	+10.4
IV. Wholesaling food/fibers	426,300	2.5	464,667	2.6	+9.0
V. Retailing and distributing	7,136,820	41.8	7,872,188	44.5	+10.3
VI. Local, state and federal government employees	300,000	1.8	300,000	1.7	0
Total: Agribusiness	17,056,740	100.0	17,680,000	100.0	+3.7
Total: U.S. employment	87,500,000	—	103,000,000	—	+17.7
% Agribusiness of total	—	19.49	—	17.17	−11.9

Source: U.S. Dept. of Agriculture, U.S. Dept. of Labor, U.S. Dept. of Commerce and *Statistical Abstract of the U.S.*,
1977, with estimates by author of agribusiness share of total employment.

Handling and Processing Jobs

Efficiency is not quite as easy to obtain in handling and processing
jobs, thus, more jobs are required to handle a larger volume of output.
Automation in some type jobs is also limited. There is also greater dispersion of production areas away from consuming areas.

Wholesaling, Retailing and Distributing Jobs

The largest total increase in number of agribusiness jobs as well as
the segment employing the most people is the segment of wholesaling,
retailing and distributing. The main reason is the service and personal
touch required whereby automation is limited and capital invested per
worker is low. Add the trends of eating away from home and the demand for more food and fiber services and the increased job requirements become apparent.

Government

Jobs in government services to agribusiness remain stable (Table 2-4). The same number of government employees serve fewer farmers and agribusiness firms. In other words, government employment is more a function of total agribusiness dollars than of the number of people in agribusiness.

AGRIBUSINESS ASSETS

Another measure of the size of agribusiness concerns money invested. The assets held by agricultural suppliers, farmers and agricultural marketers are estimated as shown in Table 2-5.

Table 2-5. Assets Held by Various Sectors of Agribusiness, 1976

Agribusiness sector	Total assets	% of total	Value added Total	Value added % of assets
	($ billion)	(%)	($ billion)	(%)
Agricultural inputs	63	7.6	58.0	92.1
Farming[1]	558	67.8	44.9	8.0
Food and fiber marketing	202	24.6	209.4	103.7
Total	823	100.0	312.3	37.9

[1]Total assets less 16.2 for household and 11.7 in co-ops. Total liabilities equal $90 billion. Net worth of $468 billion.

Sources: *Balance Sheet of Agriculture*, U.S. Dept. of Agriculture, Washington, D.C., 1976, and various trade sources.

Farmers have about two-thirds of all agribusiness investments.

The second most important group is the handlers and marketers of food and fiber, followed by the suppliers of agricultural inputs.

Land, buildings, machinery, vehicles, etc., employed in agribusiness represent a vital and critical part of America's wealth, power and prestige in world affairs.

The total of agribusiness assets employed in the U.S. approximates $823 billion (Table 2-5).

Note that farmers' value added of assets is only 8 per cent versus around 100 per cent for the two other sectors. This is because farmers have such high overhead investments in earning incomes compared with other segments.

● ● ●

In the next chapter, the role and importance of farm supplies in agribusiness are discussed.

TOPICS FOR DISCUSSION

1. What is the approximate size of each segment of agribusiness in terms of value added?
2. Discuss the job trends within agribusiness.
3. How important are farmers' assets in relation to total agribusiness assets?
4. Why is capital investment per worker higher for agriculture than for industry?
5. Examine the role of agribusiness in your community and its economic importance.

SELECTED REFERENCES

1. Boger, L. L., *Furrows on the Street*, Central Bank for Cooperatives, Denver, Colo., Sept. 1974.
2. Elrod, Robert H., and P. E. La Ferney, *Sector Income and Employment Multipliers*, ERS Tech. Bul. 1421, U.S. Dept. of Agriculture, Washington, D.C., Jul. 1970.
3. Krebs, A. V., *Directory of Major U.S. Corporations Involved in Agribusiness*, Agribusiness Accountability Project, San Francisco, Calif., 1976.
4. Luttrell, C. B. "Agribusiness—A Growth Analysis," *Business and Government Review*, University of Missouri, Columbia, 1969.
5. Roy, Ewell P., and others, *Economics: Applications to Agriculture and Agribusiness*, The Interstate Printers & Publishers, Inc., Danville, Ill., 1980.
6. Schluter, Gerald E., "Food and Fiber Sector Generates Nearly a Fourth of All Business Activity," *Farm Index*, U.S. Dept. of Agriculture, Washington, D.C., May 1974.
7. Staff, *The Changing Structure of U.S. Agribusiness*, U.S. Chamber of Commerce, Washington, D.C., 1974.
8. Staff, *Employment in Agricultural and Agribusiness Occupations*, ERS–570, U.S. Dept. of Agriculture, Washington, D.C., Aug. 1974.
9. Staff, *The Food and Fiber System—How It Works*, Agr. Info. Bul. 383, ERS, U.S. Dept. of Agriculture, Washington, D.C., Mar. 1975.
10. Staff, *Statistical Abstract of the U.S.*, G.P.O., Washington, D.C., 1977.

3

Agribusiness and
Farm Supplies

Modern agriculture consumes vast quantities of farm supplies, machinery and equipment. In an average year, U.S. farmers use the following amounts of supplies:[1]

Item	Quantity
Petroleum products	15 billion gallons
Electricity	32 billion kilowatt hours
Steel	7 million tons
Rubber	360 million pounds
Fencing	277,000 tons
Fertilizer	19 million tons
Feeds	105 million tons
Lime	22 million tons

As agriculture becomes more commercial and specialized, quantities of inputs used will continue to grow.

SCOPE OF THE FARM SUPPLY BUSINESS

The historical pattern of agriculture has changed. Yesteryear's producers farmed for the prime purpose of supplying their own basic needs. They produced their own power, used family labor and produced their own food, clothing and shelter, plus a little extra to purchase off-farm

---

[1]The term "farm supplies" as used here also includes all "production expenditures."

produced items. As population increased, new lands were brought into production by new farmers.

Today, we use a smaller acreage than in 1940 and have fewer, larger and more specialized farms. Production has more than doubled in four decades. Our rapidly expanding population has a greater abundance and variety of food than any in history.

This increased production has been accomplished largely by specialization and the purchase of production inputs from other farms and other sections of the economy.

The rise in farm production expenses since the early 1950s, however, has resulted from approximately equal percentage increases in the volume of purchased inputs and in the level of the prices paid for them.

The scope of the farm supply business is shown in Figure 3-1. Feed for livestock and poultry is the most important single item. As commercial feeding expands, the share of the total attributed to feed will prob-

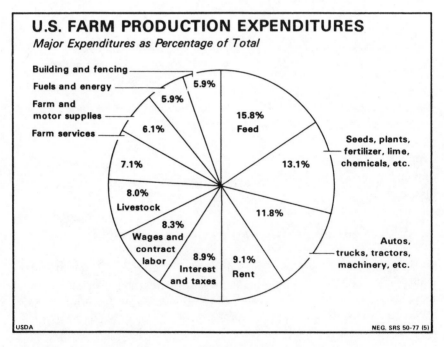

Figure 3-1.

ably increase. Also important are purchases of motor vehicles, farm machinery, equipment, livestock and poultry, various inputs and wages for hired labor. Two of these items of expenditure (machinery and labor) are inversely related; that is, as one goes up, the other usually comes down. Both are substitutable expenses.

CHANGE IN FARM INPUTS

When we consider land, labor and capital as the prime factors in farm inputs, it is evident that *land* remains constant. Its contribution is about 8.5 per cent of the total. *Labor*, on the other hand, has dropped by more than half, contributing about 26 per cent at present, compared with 75 per cent in 1910. *Capital* items (buildings, livestock, machinery, equipment, credit funds, etc.) have about quadrupled, contributing 65 per cent at present, compared with only 17 per cent in 1910. This shows that farmers are substituting *capital* for *labor* and that *land* is remaining constant.

PRICE TRENDS FOR FARM SUPPLY INPUTS

Prices paid for farm inputs vary. Those items which now cost about the same per unit or slightly more are seeds, fertilizers, feed and livestock for feeding. These have a *farm* origin. On the other hand, those input items which have basically a *nonfarm* origin cost more per unit now than formerly. These include items such as motor vehicles, motor supplies, machinery and equipment. Others that cost more per unit now are petroleum products, interest on money, waged labor, chemicals, insurance premiums, lumber and building materials and taxes of all kinds. Electricity cost per unit has risen.

The items of production costs which farmers purchase, rather than furnish themselves, have increased from 54 per cent of gross farm income in 1947–1949 to 80 per cent at present. This increase is expected to continue and is consistent with the trends toward (1) the substitution of machinery for hired and family labor, (2) the decreasing role of land as a factor in total production and (3) an increase in farm technology which puts more emphasis on specialization and research findings rather than on farmer-discovered technology.

DISTRIBUTING FARM SUPPLIES

As shown in Table 3-1, each farm supply item has a distribution system unique to it. This accounts for the wide diversity and complexity of the farm supply business. However, this diversity offers opportunities for farmers and others to effect economies and improvements in the distribution system itself. It also offers many job and employment opportunities.

Table 3-1. Major Channels for Distributing Farm Supplies to Farmers in the U.S.

Type of farm supply	Description of distribution channels

Feed	A. Grain, oilseed meal and other ingredient suppliers sell to feed mills.
	B. Feed mills prepare feeds and distribute them to:
	  1. Farmers directly, or
	  2. Feed mixers and custom mills that combine the farmers' grain with purchased concentrates, or
	  3. Farm supply stores that sell to farmers.
	C. Feed outlets may distribute feed in bags or in bulk—for cash or on credit terms.

Fertilizer	A. Manufacturers of basic materials (nitrogen, phosphorus and potash) supply other fertilizer manufacturers and mixers.
	B. Manufacturers and mixers prepare fertilizers and distribute them to:
	  1. Farmers directly, or
	  2. Bulk blenders of liquid or dry fertilizers who sell to farmers, or
	  3. Company-owned fertilizer outlets that sell to farmers, or
	  4. Farm supply stores that sell to farmers.

Petroleum and petroleum products	A. Crude oil producers sell to refineries.
	B. Refineries sell to bulk petroleum outlets.
	C. Bulk petroleum outlets sell to:
	  1. Farmers directly, or
	  2. Gas and oil service stations, either company-owned or franchised, that sell to farmers, or
	  3. Farm supply stores that sell to farmers.

Farm machinery and equipment	A. Basic manufacturers of steel, rubber, etc., sell to farm machinery and equipment manufacturers. B. Farm machinery and equipment manufacturers distribute through factory branch houses, independent merchant wholesalers or manufacturers' agents. C. Branch houses distribute machinery to franchised dealers or company-owned sales outlets. D. Independent wholesalers or manufacturers' agents distribute farm equipment to dealers,

(Continued)

Table 3-1 (Continued)

Type of farm supply	Description of distribution channels
	such as franchised equipment outlets, farm supply stores or hardware stores.
	E. Dealers in farm machinery and farm equipment sell to farmers and operate repair and service shops.
Agricultural chemicals and veterinary supplies	A. Suppliers of basic materials and ingredients sell to manufacturers and preparers of agricultural chemicals.
	B. Manufacturers and preparers sell to wholesalers and distributors, either franchised or company-owned.
	C. Wholesalers and distributors sell to:
	1. Farmers directly, or
	2. Farm supply stores that sell to farmers, or
	3. Various retail store outlets, or
	4. Organized buying groups.
Containers, bags, sacks, cartons, crates	A. Basic suppliers of wood and other materials sell to container manufacturers.
	B. Container manufacturers sell to wholesalers and distributors.
	C. Wholesalers and distributors sell to:
	1. Farmers directly, or
	2. Company-owned outlets, or
	3. Franchised dealerships, or
	4. Farm supply stores.
Lumber and building materials	A. Basic suppliers of lumber and building materials sell to manufacturers.
	B. Manufacturers sell to company-owned or franchised retail dealers and distributors. Retail dealers and distributors sell to lumberyards and building material dealers, farm supply stores, hardware stores and paint stores.
	C. Dealers sell directly to farmers.
Hardware, iron, steel and related products	A. Basic material suppliers sell to manufacturers and fabricators.
	B. Manufacturers and fabricators sell to wholesalers and distributors, either independent or company-owned.
	C. Wholesalers and distributors sell to:
	1. Farmers directly, or
	2. Farm supply stores, or
	3. Hardware stores.
Autos, trucks and trailers	A. Basic material suppliers sell to manufacturers.
	B. Manufacturers sell or transfer inventory to company-owned or franchised wholesalers and dealers.
	C. Dealers sell to farmers.
Seeds, plants and trees	A. Basic plant breeders and producers sell to wholesalers and distributors.
	B. Wholesalers and distributors sell to:
	1. Farmers directly, or
	2. Farm supply stores, or

(Continued)

Table 3-1 (Continued)

Type of farm supply	Description of distribution channels
	3. Home and garden stores, or 4. Nursery and greenhouse outlets.
Utilities (electricity, water, gas and telephone)	A. Utility companies are franchised by governmental authority and sell service to farmer-users. B. Utility companies (rural electric and telephone co-ops) are organized by farmer-users directly. C. Utilities are supplied by government-owned and -operated facilities.
Capital and credit funds	A. Money markets, investors' funds or public funds are supplied to capital and credit agencies. B. Private capital and credit agencies operated for profit (commercial banks, finance companies, trusts, syndicates, insurance companies) or individuals, merchants and dealers extend capital and credit to farmers, or C. Cooperative capital and credit agencies (credit unions, production credit associations, federal land banks, banks for cooperatives) extend capital and credit to farmers or businesses owned by farmers, or, D. Government capital and credit agencies (Farmers Home Administration and Rural Electrification Administration) extend capital and credit to farmers and businesses owned by farmers.

IMPORTANT SUPPLY SOURCES

Besides manufacturing plants or company-owned dealerships, which may sell directly to farmers, the four most important supply outlets in the farm supply business are: (1) feed mills, (2) farm supply stores, (3) farm machinery dealerships and (4) retail lumber dealerships.

Feed Mills

There are about 11,500 feed mill and mixer establishments in the United States. These mills range from small custom mills, where local grain brought by farmers is mixed with purchased concentrates, to large-volume mills, where many different feed formulas are prepared. Slightly more than half, or 6,340 feed mills, produce formula feeds.

A majority of feed mill operations are of the corporate or co-op type. The smaller mills, usually noncorporate, confine their operations to one or a few counties, selling directly to farmers, while the larger

Figure 3-2. Feed mills comprise a major part of the agribusiness supply industry. (Courtesy, Gold Kist, Atlanta, Ga.)

mills operate over several states, selling to retail outlets mostly. A small mill may have an average investment of $50,000, while a large mill may have several million dollars invested and require considerable grain and ingredient storage facilities. Small mills may also be operated in conjunction with farm supply stores.

There is a tendency to locate feed mills closer to the point of feed consumption rather than to locate them in grain areas and then ship the feed as was done previously.

A majority of feed mill operators develop brand names for their feeds, some of the national feed companies being very successful in this respect. Market competititon among feed millers is very strenuous, price competition is formidable and service competition is an increasingly important factor.

Factors affecting net profits of feed millers are as follows: (1) volume of business, (2) labor efficiency in the mill, (3) transportation costs, (4) type of customers for feed, (5) balancing of feed sales with mill capacity and (6) ability to operate year-round instead of seasonally.

Problems of concern to feed mill operators include (1) growth of contract farming and vertical integration, (2) collection of credit accounts, (3) fast-changing technology in feed milling and distribution, (4) seasonality of operations, (5) low-profit margins, (6) trend toward bulk feeds, (7) development of grain banking, (8) development of on-farm feed mixing, (9) development of mobile feed milling, (10) sale of feeds by manufacturers directly to farmers and (11) least-cost formulation.

Fertilizers

U.S. farmers are using increasing amounts of fertilizer primarily because of the large added returns from fertilization in relation to its cost. Fertilizer prices generally have remained relatively stable in relation to other inputs. Nitrogen fertilizer production has increased in recent years with the construction of large anhydrous ammonia plants.

There are approximately 2,500 fertilizer-mixing plants in the United States preparing over 3,000 grades of mixed fertilizers, although only 155 grades are prepared in amounts of 10,000 tons or more annually. In addition, there are over 2,600 bulk-blending plants that blend two or more fertilizer ingredients in certain combinations according to farmers' needs and specifications.

Sources of nitrogen fertilizer include primarily synthetic ammonia and some imported nitrates. Since ammonia-producing facilities have expanded rapidly, there appear to be ample nitrogen supplies for future needs. Oil companies have been in the forefront in ammonia production.

Phosphorus sources are primarily from phosphate rock in Florida and supplies appear ample for future needs. Potassium sources include primarily New Mexico mines and Canadian deposits, which are vast in nature and ample for future needs.

Technology in the fertilizer industry has been innovative and has led to increased production and use of liquid fertilizers; increased use of nitrogen materials; use of high-analysis and pelleted fertilizers; increased emphasis on micronutrients; and shorter distribution channels between the manufacturer and the farmer. Farmer-owned fertilizer distribution facilities account for 34 per cent of all fertilizer retailed.

For example, mixed fertilizers today in the dry bulk form account for 57 per cent of the total primary nutrient mixtures and consumption of fluid mixtures represents 17 per cent of the total mixed fertilizer sold today. Unlike in the past, today, direct application of straight materials in dry bulk form makes up 46 per cent of all direct application materials.[2]

Agricultural Chemicals

Agricultural chemical sales have expanded rapidly because of greater volume and higher unit prices. This market is divided about as follows: herbicides, 60 per cent; insecticides and rodenticides, 34 per cent; and fungicides, 6 per cent.

Feed and Farm Supply Stores

There are an estimated 11,600 farm supply stores in the United States and about 6,900 home and garden supply stores. Their sales consist primarily of feed, seed, fertilizer, chemicals, veterinary supplies and hardware. The majority of these stores are organized as either sole proprietorships or partnerships. Operators of farm supply stores tend to locate within well-defined farming areas, although, in many cases, there is more than one such establishment per locality. Stores located in larger urban areas have tended to shift to home and garden sales in recent years as the number of farmers declined. Dollar sales per supply store vary considerably from as low as $50,000 to several million dollars per year. The smaller stores are usually husband-wife managed, with some help during busy seasons. The larger stores usually depend on much more hired management and labor. Net profits among farm supply stores also vary considerably. Markups on merchandise have been decreasing due to more intense competition, while costs of operating stores have been increasing. Therefore, net profits per dollar of sales have trended downward. Smaller stores have suffered relatively more than the larger stores. Studies have shown that stores with yearly sales of less than $300,000 will have difficulty staying in business in the years ahead.

One increasingly important factor in retailing farm supplies is the "one-stop shopping center," where a complete line of farm supplies and services is made available to farmers. For example, bagged and

---

[2]*Fertilizer Progress*, Washington, D.C., Jan.–Feb. 1978, p. 32.

Figure 3-3. Farm supply stores are an integral part of the retail business in the United States. (Courtesy, Midcontinent Farmers Association, Columbia, Mo.)

bulk fertilizers are offered, together with bulk-blending services. The center may provide a feed mill operated to prepare complete feeds and/or a concentrate-grain mix or a custom mixing service. Technical information is dispensed, credit is allowed and other services are provided. Often soil tests, seeds, fertilizers and chemicals are combined and offered in one complete farm supply program. Gasoline, oil, tires, batteries and accessories may be sold also. It is believed that this method of farm supply distribution will increase in importance.

While most farm supply operators own only one store, there is a tendency to open branch supply stores. Of course, in other cases, a firm may be operating a chain of retail stores over one or several states.

Another factor in the retail farm supply business is the increasing importance of marketing raw products. Having supplied the inputs for farm production, the store operator often finds that his customers also expect help in marketing produce. If marketing is added, the supply store operator offers a still more complete type of product and service program. Some farm supply store operators have expanded into home and garden supplies, including nursery or horticultural operations, to meet the needs of urban and suburban customers.

Still another factor in farm supply retailing is a tendency for some operators to engage in livestock and poultry feeding themselves or by use of contracts.

Operators of farm supply stores are increasingly concerned about the trend to fewer but larger farms; direct selling to farmers by manufacturers and wholesalers; the growing number of sales on credit; obtaining well-trained personnel; providing farmers with more complete product and service programs; contract farming and vertical integration; and federal farm programs.

More and more store operators are faced with providing discounts to farmers who buy in large quantities in order to hold or obtain their supply business. Farmers are now generally as concerned with services provided and product quality as they are with prices of farm supplies.

Farm Machinery and Equipment Dealers

Slightly over 1,500 firms operate 1,618 manufacturing plants in the continental United States. About one-half of industry output is from seven long-line companies. Some 200 additional firms are significant producers of specialized equipment. Industry output consists of about 115 end-product items classed into about a dozen product groups. There are two basic types of farm machinery and equipment manufacturers: (1) the tractor and other large machinery manufacturers and (2) the specialized machinery and equipment makers. The former group operates regional branch houses, which in turn supply and service local farm machinery dealers. The latter group sells to wholesalers, who then sell to local dealers. In most cases, the two groups are not directly competitive. Each group has its own sphere of operation and market influence. The local dealer may handle products manufactured by both groups when not directly competitive.

About 12,500 farm equipment retailers are scattered throughout the nation's 3,000 agricultural counties. Most represent a single tractor manufacturer and, in addition, sell a wide variety of equipment and supplies and service equipment suited to the farm trade in the territory served (usually a radius of 25 miles). They employ close to 90,000 persons.

A typical dealer has a net worth of around $200,000, on which he earns about 20 per cent. Annual sales volume per dealer averages about $950,000, on which he earns about 3.5 per cent. Two-thirds of his volume is derived from new and used machinery sales. Parts, service and farm supply items are the other major sources of income. An average dealer employs 12 persons.

Because of the rather high capital requirements, a majority of the dealerships are of the corporate type. Most dealers are franchised directly by basic farm machinery manufacturers, who are careful to locate franchises in an optimum manner so that a sufficient sales area is allowed. Of course, several different manufacturers may each locate a franchise in any one area. Therefore, many farming communities may have several local franchised farm machinery dealers. Brand-name advertising by manufacturers is commonplace.

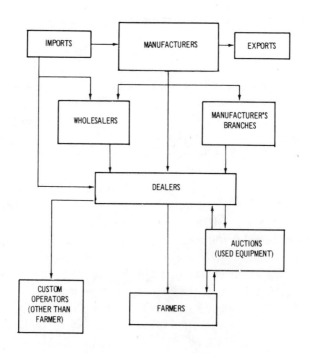

U. S. DEPARTMENT OF AGRICULTURE   NEG. ERS 5355-67 (9)   ECONOMIC RESEARCH SERVICE

Figure 3-4.

A farm machinery dealership is a very complex type of business because of the many different pieces of equipment handled, the number of different parts to inventory and the servicing and repairing of this equipment. Besides the large amount of funds required to start a dealership, funds are also tied up in extending credit and providing other services. Farmers regard the dealers' service programs as being a critical measure of the dealers' business efficiency. Manufacturers of farm equipment, however, provide dealers with credit and service programs.

Net profits for a farm machinery dealer are dependent upon the types of farming characteristic of the area and the subsequent dollar sales potential for machinery and equipment, extent of the trade area, merchandise turnover, adequacy of the repair and service department, success in collecting on credit accounts and efficiency in use of labor. More specifically, net profits are usually directly related to volume of sales and gross operating margin.

In general, a successful farm equipment dealer is one who has a good cash position or liquidity; has at least 50 per cent equity in the business; is not overloaded with credit sales; has a good sales turnover; and is able to realize, at a minimum, the going rate of interest on his equity capital.

Problems of concern to farm equipment dealers consist of the following: (1) Sales of used machinery affect new machinery sales. (2) There are greater demands for better service and repairs. (3) Credit needs of farmers are increasing. (4) Leasing of farm equipment is gaining popularity among farmers. (5) There is need for more automated livestock production equipment. (6) Specialization in the handling and selling of equipment is increasing.

The existence of good repair and service facilities ranks high in the success of a dealer. As agriculture gets more mechanized, this factor will loom still larger. For example, there are over 4 million tractors in the United States. This large an inventory indicates the need for adequate repair and overhaul facilities.

Lumber and Building Material Dealers

There are about 24,000 lumber and building material dealers in the United States. These dealers cater not only to farmers but to others

as well. Most dealerships are locally owned and operated and very often
are of a corporate type. Franchises are very often utilized between
lumber and building material suppliers and dealers. A franchise tends
to isolate and reduce competition for the local dealer and provides him
with brand-name advertising and other supplier assistances.

In other cases, dealers have formed cooperatives which serve as
at-cost wholesalers for the dealer-members of the cooperative. In this
way dealers remain otherwise independent but are allowed to compete
more effectively with other types of lumber and building material
dealers.

Lumber and building material dealers usually operate within a
small geographic area due to the bulkiness of the products for sale and
the consequent high costs of transportation. Although price markups
are usually good, costs of operating a dealership are high, and the merchandise turnover is rather slow. Competence of management and
labor, as well as adequate capitalization of the business, is important.

In recent years, lumber and building material dealers selling to
farmers have experienced an upgrading in the quality of materials and
services demanded. Services such as blueprinting, house construction
and financing are being increasingly demanded. The retail businesses
are finding more competition from diverse outlets. Farmers are shopping around to a much greater extent than formerly for their lumber
and building materials. The advent of discount lumberyards and building material dealers has increased pressure on the prices charged by
conventional retailers.

The level of expenditure for building materials is influenced by
farm income. During a period of extended low incomes, as during a
depression, capital outlays are postponed.

BUSINESS STRUCTURE OF AGRIBUSINESS SUPPLIERS

The number of agribusiness establishments manufacturing various
kinds of farm supplies in the United States is more than 19,000. Since
many companies own more than one establishment, the number of
companies is less than this figure.

About 45 per cent of the establishments have 20 or more employees. Those industry groups with the highest proportion of large establishments are those connected with glass containers, metal cans,

fertilizers, petroleum refining, tires and inner tubes and paperboard containers.

ROLE OF FARMER COOPERATIVES IN
THE FARM SUPPLY BUSINESS

Cooperatives constitute business organizations which have at least three distinguishing features from regular corporations: (1) voting is usually done on a one-man, one-vote basis rather than on a shares-of-stock basis; (2) interest or dividends paid on equity capital are usually limited, not exceeding 8 per cent; and (3) net margins at the end of a fiscal period are allocated back to each patron in the proportion his business is to the total done by the cooperative.

The role of cooperatives organized and operated by farmers engaged in farm supply businesses is steadily increasing to the point where co-ops now account for about 22 per cent of the total farm supply business in the USA. Farmer cooperatives are especially significant in the areas of fertilizer, lime, petroleum, containers, seed and feed manufacturing and distribution. They are somewhat less significant for manufacturing and distributing agricultural chemicals, building materials and farm machinery and equipment.

"BIG BUSINESS" IN AGRIBUSINESS

A large part of the farm supply business involves major corporations in the United States. This is because many of the farm supply inputs have nonfarm origins and, thus, have characteristics of industrial products which are more economically produced under large-scale conditions.

Among these corporate groups are iron and steel, rubber, petroleum, farm machinery, paints, chemicals, auto and truck manufacturing, fabricated metal products and packaging and containers. Net earnings for these corporate groups are usually above-average for groups with few firms, product differentiation and large-scale establishments. However, for some of these groups, sales for farm usage constitute a relatively small part of their total business volume. For example, 10 per cent or less of the total business for chemicals, iron and steel and general machinery are for farm usage while petroleum, rubber and motor vehicles and parts groups produce about 20 per cent of their total output for farm usage.

FARM CREDIT—AN IMPORTANT INPUT

The business of lending money to farmers is large. Currently, outstanding loans to farmers amount to over $102 billion. The farmers' real estate or mortgage debt is about $56 billion, and the farmers' nonreal estate debt is about $46 billion. Furthermore, the amount of farm credit outstanding is expected to continue to rise. Important sources of farm real estate credit are land banks, commercial banks, insurance companies, individuals and the Farmers Home Administration. Important sources of production credit are production credit associations, commercial banks, individuals, credit corporations, trade credit from merchants and dealers, the Farmers Home Administration and the Commodity Credit Corporation.

FARM INSURANCE

Insurance of various types for agribusinesses is also an important and large business. Besides life, hospital and surgical insurance on farm families, farmers require the following: crop insurance; liability and property damage insurance on autos, trucks and tractors; and fire, hail and windstorm insurance on buildings, equipment and inventories.

FARM SERVICES

Both the volume and the unit cost of farm services are rising at a rapid rate as farmers are hiring more custom services for planting, cultivating, spraying, harvesting and transporting. Farmers are also engaging more professional consultants in many phases of agribusiness.

● ● ●

In the next chapter, the role of farmers in agribusiness is considered.

TOPICS FOR DISCUSSION

1. Discuss the relative importance of various farm supply items.
2. Discuss the changing role of land, labor and capital in agricultural production inputs.
3. Visit one or more retail-type stores handling feed or farm supplies, lumber or farm machinery, and write your impressions of the store or stores.
4. Discuss the role of cooperatives in the farm supply business.
5. Prepare a list of corporations in your area which are engaged in the farm supply business.

SELECTED REFERENCES

1. Dahl, Dale C., "Structure of Input Supplying Industries," *American Journal of Agricultural Economics*, Dec. 1969, p. 1047.
2. Dahl, Dale C., and others, *Purchased Farm Input Markets in the U.S.: A Bibliography*, Minn. Agr. Exp. Sta. Misc. Rept. 103, St. Paul, Jun. 1971.
3. Mather, J. Warren, *Supply Operations of Major Regional Co-ops*, FCS Res. Rept. 40, U.S. Dept. of Agriculture, Washington, D.C., Jul. 1977.
4. Minden, Arlo J., "Changing Structure of the Farm Input Industry," *American Journal of Agricultural Economics*, Dec. 1970, p. 678.
5. Mire, Ronald, and Ewell P. Roy, *Farm Supply Store Operations*, La. Agr. Exp. Sta. DAE 448, Baton Rouge, Nov. 1972.
6. Roy, Ewell P., *Contract Farming and Economic Integration,* The Interstate Printers & Publishers, Inc., Danville, Ill., 1972.
7. Staff, *Cooperatives in Agribusiness*, FCS Educ. Cir. 33, U.S. Dept. of Agriculture, Washington, D.C., Oct. 1972.
8. Staff, "Structure of the Feed Manufacturing Industry," *Feedstuffs*, Minneapolis, Minn., Apr. 2, 1978.

4

Agribusiness and
the Farmer

We have seen how the farm supply segment of agribusiness is organized to provide inputs necessary for successful farming.

Although agricultural production may be distinct otherwise from agribusiness, its key importance cannot be denied. Without farmers to till the soil and create production, agribusiness would be nonexistent. A sound, healthy agricultural economy is vital to agribusiness, to the nation and to other peoples throughout the world who are dependent upon U.S. farm output.

FARMING REGIONS

The 10 major farming regions in the United States differ in soils, slope of land, climate, distance to market, and storage and marketing facilities. Together they comprise the agricultural face of the nation.

The Northeastern States—from Maine to Maryland—and the *Lake States*—the northern tier of states bordering on the Great Lakes from Michigan to Minnesota—are the nation's principal milk-producing areas. Climate and soil in these states are suited to raising grains and forage for cattle and for providing pasture land for grazing. Broiler farming is important in Maine, Delaware and Maryland. Fruits and vegetables are important to New York and New Jersey farmers.

The Appalachian Region—Virginia, West Virginia, North Carolina, Kentucky and Tennessee—is the major tobacco-producing region of the nation. Peanuts and cattle and dairy production are also important.

Farther south along the Atlantic coast is the *Southeast Region.* Beef and broilers are important livestock products. Fruits, vegetables and peanuts are grown in this area. And of course, there are the big citrus groves and winter vegetable production in Florida.

In the *Delta States*—Mississippi, Louisiana and Arkansas—the principal cash crops are soybeans and cotton. Rice and sugar cane are also grown. With improved pastures, livestock production has gained in importance. This is a major broiler-producing region.

The Corn Belt—extending from Ohio through Iowa, has rich soil, good climate and sufficient rainfall for excellent farming. Corn, beef cattle, hogs and dairy products are the major outputs of farms in the region. Other feed grains, soybeans and wheat, are also important.

Agriculture in the *Northern and Southern Plains,* which extend north and south from Canada to Mexico and from the Corn Belt into the Mountain States, is restricted by low rainfall in the western portion and by cold winters and short growing seasons in the northern part. About three-fifths of the nation's winter and spring wheat is produced in the region. Other small grains, grain sorghum, hay, forage crops and pastures form the basis for cattle and dairy production. Cotton is produced in the southern part.

The Mountain States—from Idaho and Montana to New Mexico and Arizona—provide a still different terrain. Vast areas of this region are suited to raising cattle and sheep. Wheat is important in the northern parts. Irrigation in the valleys provides water for crops such as hay, sugar beets, potatoes, fruits and vegetables.

The Pacific Region—includes the three Pacific Coast States plus Alaska and Hawaii. Farmers in the northern mainland area specialize in raising wheat and fruit; vegetables and fruit and cotton are important in the southern part. Cattle are raised throughout the region.[1]

FARMS OF TODAY

The technological revolution in agriculture and other industries has narrowed the function of the family farm. Basically, farming has changed from a subsistence to a commercial status. Now, the progressive farm family consumes only a small fraction of what it grows, the

---

[1]Department of Agricultural Economics, Cornell University, Ithaca, N.Y., 1977.

balance being sold to feed the other 96 per cent of the population living off the farm. Today's modern farmer is a specialist who largely confines his operations to growing crops and livestock. The functions of storing, processing and distributing food and fiber have been transferred largely to highly specialized off-farm business firms. In many instances, these off-farm businesses are owned by farmers through some cooperative or corporate setup.

In some cases, whole industries have come into being to supply the needs of modern agriculture. Illustrative of these are the meat packers, the food canners and the food freezers. The present agribusiness economy has come about by the gradual dispersion of functions from agriculture to business.

FARMING EFFICIENCY GROWS

The efficiency of U.S. agriculture is recognized throughout the world. For example, although total farm employment drops 2 per cent each year, American agriculture has been increasing total farm output about 3 per cent; crop yields per acre, 2.5 per cent; and farm output per man-hour, 10 per cent.

Another way to measure agricultural efficiency concerns the number of persons supplied food and fiber by one farmer. At present, one farmer supplies over 56 persons, compared with only 20 in 1955 and 15 in 1945. Overall output per unit of input is about 70 per cent greater than in 1940. Since 1940, farm output has increased 70 per cent, but the volume of physical inputs has increased a slight 10 per cent. About 5 billion man-hours are now required to produce the food and fiber to meet our needs. This is about 20 per cent of the 24 billion man-hours required back in 1918 to produce requirements for a substantially smaller population.

REASONS FOR AGRICULTURAL EFFICIENCY

Numerous interrelated factors have contributed to the large output and high individual productivity of American agriculture. They include:

1. A large supply of land and water resources.
2. Large investments for education to improve human skills and managerial abilities.

3. Development and diffusion of new knowledge about agricultural technology.
4. Complementary industrial development that supplies capital inputs for agriculture and nonfarm employment opportunities for people not needed in agriculture.
5. A structural organization of farm production and marketing that provides powerful economic incentives for farmers and marketing firms to increase output and productivity.
6. Public and private institutional services that help:
   a. To conserve and improve natural resources.
   b. To increase the fund of knowledge about improved agricultural technology.
   c. To encourage capital formation and investments in agriculture.
   d. To assure farm people that they will share in the economic benefits of increased production.

THE FARMER AND THE LAND

The total area of the United States is 2,314,000,000 acres, of which 2,271,000,000 acres are land and 43,000,000 are water. Of the total land area, 20.8 per cent is cultivated cropland, 26.7 per cent is grassland pasture and range and 31.9 per cent is forest, with the rest put to other uses such as 7.9 per cent for urban areas, roads and recreation and 12.7 per cent for lowlands, deserts and tundra.

Major changes in use of land have occurred in the last three decades. For example, 30 million acres or more of poorly adapted cropland have been shifted to forest and pasture, while at the same time an estimated 20 million acres have been brought into cultivation. Substituting good land for poor has been important in increasing production.

The country's forests are indispensable to many of its basic needs. They provide billions of feet of timber a year for everything from houses to packing boxes. They produce raw materials for the expanding chemical, textile, paper and plastic industries. The forests are nature's refuge for animals and birds and are man's retreat for camping, hiking, hunting and fishing. Most of all, they hold the soil on slopes and hills, prevent floods from sweeping down river valleys and retain moisture in the land.

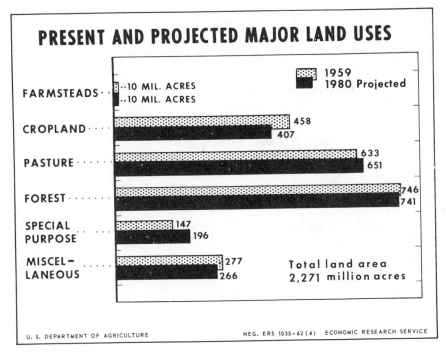

PRESENT AND PROJECTED MAJOR LAND USES

1959
1980 Projected

FARMSTEADS· · ··10 MIL. ACRES
·· ··10 MIL. ACRES

CROPLAND · · · · 458
407

PASTURE · · · · · 633
651

FOREST · · · · · · 746
741

SPECIAL
PURPOSE 147
196

MISCEL-
LANEOUS 277
266

Total land area
2,271 million acres

U. S. DEPARTMENT OF AGRICULTURE   NEG. ERS 1035-62 (4)   ECONOMIC RESEARCH SERVICE

Figure 4-1. (Courtesy, USDA, Washington, D.C.)

In some areas, farm acreage is fast being absorbed by cities and factories. Lands in fringe areas either have been abandoned or lie partly used. About a million farm acres a year are needed for expanding cities, highways, and airports and for other intensive uses.

More than 60 per cent of the land area in the 50 states is privately owned. Most of the country's crop, range, timber and pasture production is on this private land. Federally owned land makes up a third of the land area and is used for timber, grazing, mineral development, recreation, watershed development and wildlife habitat. It constitutes reserves for timber, minerals and water. About 5 per cent of the land area is owned by state and local governments.

With fewer farmers to farm land, the acreage per farm continues to increase, and all signs point to even larger farms in the future. Mechanization and use of better technology in farming allow the number of acres and output per man to increase. Farmers, thus, become more specialized and less diversified.

Despite these trends, however, farm size is still within the means of a farm family to handle; that is, the use of hired labor has not grown in proportion to the increase in acreage per farm.

Moreover, many farmers are becoming farm owners instead of being renters or sharecroppers. About 80 per cent of U.S. farmers own all or part of the land they operate.

FOREST MANAGEMENT

America's forest lands now occupy about one-third of the nation's land. About 500 million acres are classified as commercial timberland which is adapted for the continuous production of trees for commercial use. The Forest Service of the U.S. Department of Agriculture manages 187 million acres in the national forest system. This includes 18 per cent of the country's commercial forest land, which contributes 16 per cent of the nation's total annual timber harvest.

Of the remaining commercial forest land, 59 per cent is owned by several million nonindustrial, private owners; 14 per cent is owned by industry; and 9 per cent is comprised of other public lands. In 1970, private, industrially owned timberlands contributed 26 per cent of the national timber harvest, while small private ownerships provided 52 per cent. Other federal- and state-owned lands provided about 6 per cent of the national timber harvest. About 45 per cent of the nation's timber harvest came from the South, 32 per cent from the Pacific Coast and 23 per cent from the North and the Rocky Mountain area. The South is expected to be the major timber producer in the future.

THE CHANGING FARM STRUCTURE

In the *1974 Census of Agriculture,* a farm is defined as "any establishment from which $1,000 or more of agricultural products is sold or would normally be sold during a year." This differs from the old classification in which a farm was "any place under 10 acres with annual sales of $250 or more of agricultural goods" or "any place of 10 or more acres selling $50 or more of agricultural goods annually."

To further define the blurring distinction of just what constitutes a farm and the different kinds of farms, the overall definition is now divided into four classes:

1. A *primary farm* is any farm on which the operator spends at least half of his work time or any farm operated by a corporation or multi-establishment firm which receives at least one-half of its gross business income from farming.
2. A *part-time farm,* on the other hand, is any farm on which the operator spends less than half of his work time.
3. A *business-associated farm* is any farm operated by a corporation or multi-establishment company that receives less than one-half of its gross business income from farming.
4. An *abnormal farm* is any farm operated by an institution such as a hospital or a school, is operated on an Indian reservation or is operated as an experimental or research farm.

As shown in Table 4-1, there are about 2.680 million farms. As mentioned earlier, the number of farms is declining year by year, especially the smaller ones.

Table 4-1. Number of Farms and Land in Farms, United States

Year	No. of farms	Land in farms	Average farm size
	(thousands)	(thousand acres)	(acres)
1967	3,162	1,123,456	355
1968	3,071	1,115,231	363
1969	3,000	1,107,811	369
1970	2,949	1,102,371	374
1971	2,902	1,096,863	378
1972	2,860	1,092,065	382
1973	2,823	1,087,923	385
1974	2,795	1,084,433	388
1975	2,767	1,081,448	391
1976	2,738	1,078,263	394
1977	2,706	1,075,003	397
1978	2,680	1,072,333	400

Source: U.S. Dept. of Agriculture, Washington, D.C.

Family farms and other-than-family farms have decreased in number and increased in size, but family farms still account for 95 percent of all farms and about 60 percent of all farm products sold, percentages that have not changed much during the last two decades.

Types of Tenancy

In 1880, the census revealed that one of every four farms was tenant operated. The proportion of tenancy increased until in 1930 when about 43 per cent of the farms were operated by tenants. Since 1935 to 1940, the proportion of tenant farms has dropped to one in seven.

There are two basic types of farm renters: (1) cash tenants and (2) share tenants. Cash tenants pay a rental fee per acre of land farmed and have about the same managerial responsibility as owners. Share tenants pay rental by sharing a proportion of their production or returns with the landowner. The specific share depends on the amount of resources and managerial responsibility furnished by each of the two parties. A one-fifth share is a common arrangement paid by tenants to the landlord. Cash tenancy is increasing in importance relative to share tenancy.

Contrary to popular beliefs, farm tenancy is not necessarily a bad arrangement. Tenancy is a good form of tenure especially for young men entering farming: (1) when land prices are extremely high, (2) when capital is limited and (3) when mineral rights in land make it otherwise unavailable for sale.

However, tenancy as a form of tenure may have several adverse effects: (1) may become exploitative in nature with a tendency to neglect soil conservation, (2) may have lease or rental arrangements which may be unfair to one or both parties, (3) may have a tendency to favor row-cropping over other types of farming and (4) may have a tendency not to compensate tenants for any improvements made on rental land and property.

These disadvantages may be overcome by the following methods: (1) agreeing on compensatory payments to tenants who improve land and property; (2) negotiating lease terms longer than for one crop year; (3) arranging for commercial farm management of rented farms by commercial agencies which select tenants, draw up leases, plan the farm program and collect rents for a reasonable fee; (4) negotiating leases in writing and recording them; and (5) adopting more flexible rental rates dependent upon tenants' productive efficiency, farm price levels and incomes generated.

RELATIVE IMPORTANCE OF AGRICULTURAL OUTPUTS

U.S. farm output is very diverse. If all the farm production of the United States were reduced to an index of 100 for any given year, what would be the relative dollar importance of each commodity group?

This can be estimated as follows, based on data from the U.S. Department of Agriculture:

Item	Percentage of total output
Meat animals	39.6
Feed grains	17.9
Dairy products	11.8
Poultry and eggs	6.9
Vegetables	5.3
Food grains	4.7
Other crops	4.0
Fruits and tree nuts	4.0
Cotton	3.0
Tobacco	2.4
Other livestock	0.4
Total	100.0

THE FARMING POPULATION

The rural-farm population numbers about 9 million, or about 4 per cent of the U.S. population. It has been decreasing as a percentage of the total because as production requires fewer and fewer farmers, the nation's population continues to grow. This is a good sign. It means that fewer farmers can produce more and keep the whole nation and others throughout the world well fed and clothed. Day by day, the role of the U.S. farmer becomes more important, because more and more people are becoming dependent upon the U.S. farmer.

One distressing sign about U.S. farmers, however, is that their average age, now about 50 years, is increasing. This indicates that fewer young men are entering the farming profession, which means that more encouragement will have to be given and more opportunities provided for young men to become farmers. If this is not done, then corporation-management of agriculture may have to be used, as one example.

However, there obviously is no scarcity of farm children, because farm people continually reproduce above the number required to sustain the profession. This excess migrates to urban areas, although rural areas have to bear the cost of educating and training these young people. This factor alone causes quite a drain on rural resources, since educating one rural youth costs $10,000 or more.

WHAT ARE FARMERS WORTH?

As a group, U.S. farmers are in sound financial position, owning about 75 to 80 per cent of the assets they have. Perhaps no other economic group in America can match this ratio. Land owned by farmers accounts for two-thirds of their assets, the remainder being comprised of livestock, machinery, motor vehicles, crops on hand, household furnishings and financial investments. Farmers owe only 20 to 25 per cent of the value of their assets. These debts are in real estate mortgages, production credit loans, etc.

While this overall financial picture is very good, it does not mean that each and every farmer is well-off. Many are not, especially the younger ones who are heavily in debt trying to buy land, machinery, etc., and to meet family expenses.

Those fortunate enough to own land have a valuable asset now and in the future. As population increases, land inevitably appreciates in value and also allows farmers a good hedge against inflation.

Because of inflation in land values, all farmers, on the average, who own land, gain about twice as much each year from appreciation in land value than they do from the net income produced by that land.

FARMERS USE MORE CREDIT

In years past, when farmers were more self-sufficient and diversified, they did not require large amounts of capital. The modern farmer, however, faced with specialization and higher farming costs, is increasingly dependent upon credit to buy land and to finance seed, fertilizer and chemicals. To purchase stock in a cooperative, many farmers resort to borrowed capital. Borrowing funds is not necessarily a bad practice, because in most cases there is an asset behind the borrowing or else the farmer's ability to repay is clearly visible to the lender. On the contrary, if farmers use borrowed funds wisely, they grow richer by borrowing instead of using only their own money.

FARMERS' LIVING STANDARDS

As one travels the countryside it is quite obvious that farmers are living more like their city counterparts. Electricity in rural areas has permitted the purchase and use of home appliances and electric tools and gadgets. Farmers' homes are being built more and more to urban specifications. Motor vehicles and better roads have freed the farm family from isolation. Telephones, too, have provided farmers with better connections with the outside world.

In many cases, natural gas and water supply lines have been built within rural areas or have been extended to them from urbanized centers. Fire-fighting measures and facilities have been improved in rural areas to meet those types of disasters.

Schools have been consolidated and improved to the extent that rural schools now compare favorably with schools in urban areas. Rural churches have likewise undergone consolidation and improvement.

More farm families now subscribe to health and medical insurance plans, while rural hospital treatment and facilities have improved. Although the doctor-patient ratio in rural areas is not so good as it ought to be, good roads have provided access to medical specialists located in more urban areas. Dental and drug store services have improved in small towns which radiate these services to rural areas.

Library and newspaper availability to rural areas has increased. Many states now provide traveling libraries on regular routes for farm residents.

Radio and television coverage into rural areas has improved. More civic and cultural programs are now available in small towns.

FARM FAMILY SPENDING

Farm families increasingly spend their money in approximation of urban family spending. For example, farm families are producing less of their foodstuffs and buying more groceries from stores than they did formerly, a factor true for clothing purchases as well. The farm housewife desires and obtains household appliances and furnishings equivalent to those of her city cousin. Farm children develop recreational and educational pursuits in a pattern similar to urban children. More and more, the farm family budget provides for life and health insurance, medical care, recreational allowances, educational materials and a variety of personal services. Farm families now spend increasingly more on housing, building modern, all-electric homes with central air conditioning and heating. Expenditures on transportation are also rising.

NONFARM INCOME

Nonfarm sources of income continue to be an important part of total personal income of the farm population. For small farmers, non-farm income may be the main factor which can keep them in a rural setting. Overall, nonfarm income represents over half of all U.S. farmers' net income (Table 4-2). Half the U.S. farmers earn more than 83 per cent of their income off-farm.

Farmers in every sales volume category receive off-farm income, but the amount received is relatively more important to operators with less than $10,000 in annual sales than to those with larger gross sales. The lower the farm product sales, the higher the proportion of off-farm income to total family income. Farmers with sales of less than $10,000 have off-farm incomes ranging from 75 to 89 per cent of their total family income. But for those with sales of $10,000 or more, off-farm income ranges from 19 to 57 per cent of their total family income.

Noncommercial farmers receive considerably more off-farm income than on-farm income. It is likely that this enables them to continue some type of farming activity (Table 4-2).

Table 4-2. Income per Farm Operator Family by Major Source and by Value of Farm Product Sales Classes, USA

Farm product sales classes	Net farm income plus government payments	Off-farm income	Total family income
	----------------------------(dollars per farm)----------------------------		
$100,000 and over	55,716	13,310	69,026
40,000 to 99,999	16,558	6,906	23,464
20,000 to 39,999	9,622	5,762	15,384
10,000 to 19,999	5,248	7,060	12,308
5,000 to 9,999	3,030	9,124	12,154
2,500 to 4,999	1,725	10,342	12,067
Less than 2,500	1,921	15,630	17,551
All farms	7,885	11,174	19,059
	------------------------------(% of total income)------------------------------		
$100,000 and over	80.7	19.3	100.0
40,000 to 99,999	70.6	29.4	100.0
20,000 to 39,999	62.5	37.5	100.0
10,000 to 19,999	42.6	57.4	100.0
5,000 to 9,999	24.9	75.1	100.0
2,500 to 4,999	14.3	85.7	100.0
Less than 2,500	10.9	89.1	100.0
All farms	41.4	58.6	100.0

Source: U.S. Dept. of Agriculture, Washington, D.C., 1976.

HIRED FARM LABOR

In the farming segment of agribusiness we must not neglect the hired worker, who performs a most valuable role. About half of America's farmers employ at least some hired labor one or more times during the year. Hired labor for harvesting and certain cultural chores is very important, with workers usually paid by the day, by the hour or on a piece-rate basis. Actually, wage rates for hired labor are increasing, but the rising cost of living consumes much of these gains as it does for others. Unfortunately, many hired farm workers and their families suffer from a lack of education and training. Considering this and other limitations, for many, their employment in agricultural-type work is probably their one best choice.

Hired farm workers consist of three types: (1) year-round workers, (2) seasonal laborers and (3) casual workers. On a days-worked basis, the year-round workers are of greatest importance, followed by seasonal and casual workers. On the basis of numbers of workers, casual

Major routes followed by migratory farm workers

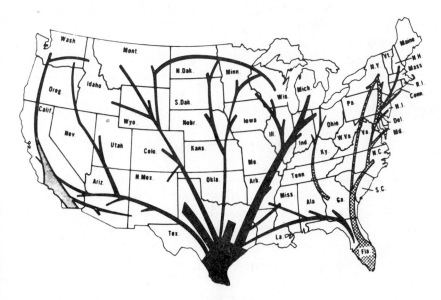

Figure 4-2.

workers are most numerous, followed by seasonal and year-round workers.

Hired farm workers, particularly migratory ones, suffer from low incomes due to seasonal employment, excessive moving costs and lack of community roots in schools and civic life.

Farm wage rates per hour are highest in the Pacific and New England states and lowest in the South Atlantic and South Central states. Recent minimum wage legislation applicable to workers on large farms has tended to narrow somewhat the differentials in hourly wages paid in various regions of the country. It has also caused widespread unemployment for workers not skilled enough to earn these minimum wages. While farm wage rates paid per hour are lower than wage rates paid nonfarm labor, farm workers probably have lower living costs in terms of housing and have other benefits in terms of garden, poultry, etc.

FARMERS' DECLINING POLITICAL POWER

If it is true that farmers have a hand in shaping their own political and economic destiny, then they are faced with an important problem. Farmers are now a small part of the total population, and their proportion is growing smaller every day. This means that farmers may have less potential political power than they had in earlier times. Therefore, it becomes doubly important to farmers that they understand and use their farm organizations with maximum effectiveness. Only if farmers organize themselves for effective group action will their wants and needs be fully recognized in government and in the marketplace.

BECOMING A FARMER

The traditional concept of the "agricultural ladder" by which a youth climbs to ownership and operation of a farm includes most of these steps: (1) obtaining experience on his parents' farm, (2) working on a neighbor's farm to get more experience and enough capital to become a tenant, (3) renting land to earn a down payment on a farm, (4) buying a mortgaged farm and (5) eventually paying off the mortgage.

In 1880, the census revealed 1 in 4 farm operators was a tenant.

The proportion of tenant and sharecropper farmers increased until 1935. Since 1935, the proportion of tenant farms has dropped to less than 1 in 6, that of sharecropper farms to 1 in 30. The proportion of farm laborers increased until 1940.

About 80 per cent of farm operators now own part or all of their farms. There are, however, some 800,000 farm operators renting land in addition to that which they own. The need for larger acreage to make efficient use of expensive farm machinery creates a strong demand for land. Added cropland speeded the decline in numbers of farm workers and farms by making possible more use of larger, expensive equipment.

As farm job opportunities decline, a farm labor surplus is created. As the number of farms declines and capital requirements increase, the traditional "agricultural ladder" is disrupted. Keen competition for available lands, relatively low wages and low net profits make ownership extremely difficult for the young farm worker.

Inheritance and family help are alternatives to the traditional self-help ladder. Neither will usually permit all the children of farm parents to achieve farm ownership. About 80 per cent of the farm-reared youth must find jobs outside farming. Thus, agribusiness employment offers opportunities to farm-reared boys and girls who are not able to enter farming directly and who may wish to enter farming later when enough equity capital is accumulated for a down payment on a farm.

More recently, routes more frequently used by young persons to enter farming consist of contract farming, farm managership and renting or leasing arrangements.

CORPORATION FARMING

Actually there are several different types of corporations involved in farming. The most numerous type is the family farm which has adopted the corporate business structure. A second type is the corporation formed by a group of unrelated individuals for the purpose of owning or operating a farm. These individuals pool their resources and receive their profits in the form of dividends or appreciation in stock value. The third type of corporation is the one that receives the most publicity. It is the nonfarm corporation, already established in manufacturing or other fields, that enters agriculture for purposes of diversification.

The family farm corporation is actually a desirable alternative since it provides the farm family with all the advantages of a corporation and with few of its disadvantages. It can borrow money more readily, retain the farm within the family when the operator dies and may pay less income taxes than it might otherwise have to pay.

CONTRACT FARMING

Contracting between farmers and off-farm businesses for various products, such as broiler chickens, turkeys, eggs, vegetables, sugar beets and other commodities, is developing at a rapid rate in some areas of the United States. Usually, the land, labor and equipment are furnished by the farmer, while the contractor provides the supplies, operating capital and some management and marketing assistance. This type of operation holds promise for young farmers who are short of capital, enabling them to enter farming at considerably less risk.

FARMING AND COMPUTERS

Computers are becoming increasingly important in farm management for purposes such as selecting the most profitable enterprises, keeping farm records and filing tax returns, following proper ration formulations and employing financial and investment strategies, among others. Besides county agricultural extension service offices, private consulting offices are available for advice on computing functions in agriculture. In addition, many banks and the Production Credit Association offer computer services as part of their programs for borrowers.

SUMMARY

Farming has made at least seven specific contributions of major importance to the nation's economic growth since the turn of the century:

1. It has made a direct contribution to industry by its release of workers, which also serves as an indicator of overall economic growth.

2. It has lowered food costs relative to incomes.
3. It has increased its purchases of industrial goods.
4. It has sustained output during economic depressions.
5. It has met wartime demands for food.
6. It has produced high earnings from exports.
7. It has assisted other countries in their economic development.

● ● ●

In the next chapter, the nature and scope of agribusiness marketing is discussed.

TOPICS FOR DISCUSSION

1. Contrast the modern farmer's operation with that of yesteryear.
2. What are some of the reasons for increased farm output?
3. Discuss some of the important aspects of land, timber and water resources.
4. Can the family farm survive in the years ahead?
5. Discuss the living levels and spending patterns of farm people.
6. Discuss the status of hired farm laborers in your vicinity.
7. Discuss some of the problems of youth in becoming farmers.

SELECTED REFERENCES

1. Bailey, Warren R., *The One-Man Farm*, ERS–519, U.S. Dept. of Agriculture, Washington, D.C., Aug. 1973.
2. Gardner, B. D., and R. D. Pope, "How Is Scale and Structure Determined in Agriculture?" *American Journal of Agricultural Economics*, May 1978, p. 295.
3. Reimund, D. A., *Farming and Agribusiness Activities of Large Multiunit Farms*, ERS–591, U.S. Dept. of Agriculture, Washington, D.C., Mar. 1975.
4. Roy, Ewell P., *Contract Farming and Economic Integration*, The Interstate Printers & Publishers, Inc., Danville, Ill., 1972.
5. Staff, *Changes in Farm Production and Efficiency*, ERS Stat. Bul. 581, U.S. Dept of Agriculture, Washington, D.C., Nov. 1977.
6. Staff, *Regional Agricultural Production—1985 and Beyond*, ERS–564, U.S. Dept. of Agriculture, Washington, D.C., Aug. 1974.
7. Thomas, K. H., and M. D. Boehlje, *Farm Business Arrangements—Which One for You?* Minn. Mgr. Ext. Serv. Bul. 401, St. Paul, 1976.

8. Walker, Odell L., and D. L. Minnick, *Resource Requirements and Income Opportunities for Beginning Farmers,* Okla. Agr. Exp. Sta. Bul. 729, Stillwater, Jul. 1977.

5

Agribusiness Marketing of Food and Fiber:

Nature and Scope

Agribusiness marketing is "those processes, functions and services performed in connection with food and fiber from the farms on which they are produced until their delivery into the hands of the consumer." Many steps are involved in marketing, such as buying, assembling, storing, packing, warehousing, communicating, advertising, financing, transporting, grading, sorting, processing, conditioning, packaging, selling, retailing, merchandising, risk-taking, insuring, standardizing, regulating, inspecting and gathering market information (Figure 5-1).

The supply of food and fiber in the United States for any given period reflects not only what is *produced* but also what is *imported* and what remains of the *inventory* from past years. This supply of food and fiber is disposed of in about the following proportions:

Type of outlet	*Percentage of total*
Civilian use	72.9
Military use	.5
Other nonfood use (industrial, etc.)	7.3
Exports	19.3
Total	100.0

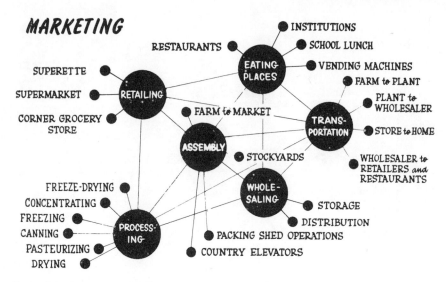

Figure 5-1. Agribusiness marketing is a complex operation involving many agencies and functions. (Courtesy, USDA, Washington, D.C.)

COSTS OF MARKETING

Marketing costs include the payments or charges for items such as labor, transportation, containers, supplies and taxes and provide markups for profits as well. Marketing costs also include services that add value to food. When there is a demand for these services and they can be provided efficiently, consumers will pay the marketing cost. These services cost money and add to the retail price, but they make foods more attractive and reduce the time and cost spent in kitchen preparation. Likewise, higher wages to workers may add to costs, but they also attract more efficient workers. Greater efficiency may offset part or all of the increased wage costs.

Therefore, many food and fiber products in their raw state are not yet ready for market in the sense of being ready to cook or to wear. A long series of steps is involved before some raw products can be termed "marketable."

FARM-TO-RETAIL PRICE SPREADS

Overall, the farmer obtains about 40 per cent of the U.S. food consumer's dollar. But, this ratio varies greatly from one commodity to another. For those products which require minimum processing, the farmer's share is higher; conversely, for those which require considerable processing and handling, the farmer's share is less. For example, the following products indicate this relationship:

Product	Farmer's share of food dollar (%)
Eggs	64
Meat products	58
Poultry	54
Dairy products	51
Fats and oils	33
Fresh fruits and vegetables	31
Processed fruits and vegetables	19
Bakery and cereal products	17

The 60 cents out of each consumer dollar which the farmer does not get goes for varying other costs, such as approximately:

Agribusiness cost	Percentage of	
	Total marketing cost	Consumer's food dollar
Labor	48	28.8
Packaging	12	7.2
Transportation	8	4.8
Corporate profits before taxes	4	2.4
Depreciation	4	2.4
Interest, repairs, etc.	4	2.4
Business taxes	4	2.4
Advertising	3	1.8
Rent	3	1.8
All others	10	6.0
Total	100	60.0

Wages for labor have risen considerably in recent years although labor cost has not risen proportionately because labor has been more productive. Consumers now demand more built-in services and convenience in foods which shift the labor input from the housewife's kitchen to a food processing plant.

Transportation costs have risen due to more expensive equipment, higher driver wages and higher fuel costs.

Packaging costs have increased. Not only have unit costs gone up, but more packages, wrap and containers are being utilized in marketing foods.

Corporate profits of food processors, while substantial, appear to be in line with or below profits made by other industry groups.

Why have food marketing costs risen? There are three reasons: (1) the rise in *prices* of inputs purchased by marketing firms, (2) the increase in *volume* of farm foods handled and (3) the increase in *services* provided.

Rises in the cost level of inputs account for 47 per cent of the increased food marketing bill, growth in the volume of food marketed accounts for another 33 per cent and increased services provide the remaining 20 per cent.

A common error in discussing marketing costs is to assume that a farmer's small share of the consumer's dollar means low farm income and a farmer's large share means high farm income. This is false because it leaves out the effect of quantity sold. Most egg producers find that 100 per cent of the consumer's dollar (from home deliveries) brings less net income than 60 or 80 per cent on a much larger volume of eggs sold at the egg room. Tobacco is a similar case in which the grower receives less than 15 cents of each consumer's dollar spent on cigarettes.

Some of the more specific reasons for high marketing costs are:
1. Most farm goods are bulky, thus adding to the task of marketing and distribution.
2. Most farm goods mature during a short period, thus intensifying marketing tasks such as storage.
3. Farm products are perishable, although the degree of perishability varies among commodities.
4. Farm production is variable—there are years of abundance and years of scarcity.
5. Farm products reach the consumer in various forms, such as fresh, canned, dried, etc. The processed food segment is expanding relative to the fresh.
6. Farm products are often produced in small quantities over a

wide area, and are heterogeneous. They must be assembled, sorted and graded.

7. Consumers in our diverse population demand a wide variety of goods, packages and services, including more processed foods.

Marketing costs do not vary so much as the returns to producers of agricultural products, farmers receiving greater relative returns during periods of prosperity and lower relative returns during periods of depression.

When contemplating the farmer's declining share of the consumer's dollar, remember that the farmer's share is an estimate of the return for the farm product equivalent to the product sold at retail. It does not provide a direct measure of the income position of agriculture nor any basis *per se* for judging the "fairness" of shares going to agriculture or to other groups.

Prices to Consumers and Farmers' Prices

Why is it that prices to consumers do not fall in proportion to the decline in farmers' prices? There are many explanations for this question, among which are:

1. The competitive structure is different. Farmers compete in a more "perfect market" than retailers, the latter having some control over their prices while farmers do not.

2. Middlemen's costs and margins are rather inflexible and slow to change, usually going upwards.

3. Productivity per worker in processing, wholesaling and retailing does not increase very rapidly, and increased wages simply increase the unit cost of labor.

4. Retailers, for example, prefer to keep a steady price on their merchandise rather than to markup or markdown prices daily in line with fluctuations in farmers' daily prices.

5. Retailers and other middlemen price their merchandise on the basis of an overall "target" return to stockholders' equity or invested capital. Therefore, their prices are less responsive to the changes in farmers' product prices. Maximization of stockholders' returns is their prime goal, not maximization of farmers' prices.

6. Policies of a few companies having control over wide segments

of the industry may have a greater influence on prices paid to farmers and prices charged to consumers than policies established by many smaller buyers and sellers. A company which sells in more than one product market need not sell every item at a profit. Rather, it may classify its products into categories such as money-making items, convenience goods and loss leaders and may follow different policies in selling products of the different classes.

7. The farmers' share of the consumers' food dollar drops to a relatively greater extent when supplies are increased because of the less elastic (inelastic) demand for food at the farm level. The converse happens when supplies are decreased. Food demand at retail is more elastic, thus, supply changes affect retailers' share relatively less.

FOOD CONSUMED OUTSIDE THE HOME

More and more consumers are eating outside the home. It is estimated that 65 per cent of the U.S. population eats noon meals outside the home; 35 per cent, evening meals; and 10 per cent, breakfast.

The largest increase in marketing workers has been in the number employed in eating places. The number of eating-place workers has risen 30 per cent, accounting for over one-third of all marketing workers, compared to one-fifth in 1947. Employment in eating places exceeds that in retail food stores.

INDUSTRIAL USES OF FARM PRODUCTS

Farm products with the largest industrial usage are oils from various seeds, by-products of the slaughter and dairy industry and starch from corn. The proportion of the main agricultural commodities used for industrial purposes varies greatly but is increasing generally. However, synthetic materials are making substantial inroads on some food and fiber products used for either domestic food needs or industrial purposes. Synthetic fibers, soap and detergent materials, milk products, ethyl alcohol, leather, sweeteners and proteins, among others, have affected the market for and use of natural agricultural products. Some synthetic products made from nonagricultural sources are whole substitutes for agricultural products while other synthetics are comprised partly of agricultural materials, such as filled milk.

MILITARY DEMAND

The U.S. military demand for food and fiber products consists not only of requirements for personnel stationed domestically but oftentimes at foreign posts as well. In addition, various food aid programs to foreign nations are handled through military channels in areas of military conflict. U.S. food and fiber products are an important military weapon in many situations to say nothing of the rehabilitation value of food and fiber products after military conflict ceases.

EXPORTS AND IMPORTS

Besides the domestic sales of food and fiber, agricultural exports and imports are a booming business, affecting the entire national economy. Almost everyone is touched in some way by the buying, selling and shipping of the $40 billion worth of agricultural commodities moving in or out of our ports every year. About $27 billion worth comprise exports and $13 billion, imports.

To the business world that services it and makes it flow, this trade means profits and jobs. To the farmer who produces for export, it means more buyers. To the consumer, it means coffee or tea on the breakfast table, some of the rubber for tires and many other things taken for granted, such as chocolate, bananas and other tropical fruits. It means the extra things which, when combined with U.S. production, gives U.S. consumers the highest standard of living in the world.

About 20 per cent of U.S. farm workers are engaged in producing agricultural exports. In addition, many thousands of nonfarm workers are involved in manufacturing, assembling, transporting and doing other jobs in exporting farm products.

Major U.S. exports consist of cotton, feed grains, wheat, meats, oilseeds, tobacco, poultry, dairy products, fruits and vegetables.

The major countries importing U.S. agricultural products are Japan, Canada, United Kingdom, the Netherlands, West Germany, India, Bangladesh, Italy, Egypt, Belgium, France and Russia.

The major U.S. imports are tea, coffee, bananas, sugar, vegetable oils, meats, certain fruits and vegetables, tobacco, wool, cheeses, barley, rubber and cocoa products.

About 40 per cent of imports into the United States are complementary products which do not compete with domestically produced goods. The other 60 per cent is supplementary and partially competitive with domestically produced commodities. Brazil, Mexico, Philippines, Australia and Canada are major exporting nations to the United States.

International trade, when no restrictions or barriers are erected, gravitates between and among nations according to the *law of comparative advantage.*

Certain nations will produce those commodities where they have the greatest advantage or least disadvantage comparatively. In total, all nations and people will be better off in so doing than if each nation attempted to be self-sufficient. Another truism is that for any nation to export, it must likewise be willing to import. If the exports of one nation exceed its imports, other nations are in debt to that nation; and, if imports exceed exports, it is in debt to others. A nation must then attempt to rectify this import-export deficit by transfer of funds to nations with surplus positions.

Offsetting the attempts of nations to export are governments that use various methods to restrict imports with: (1) tariffs, or a tax; (2) variable levies, or a tariff going up or down depending on how high an import price is desired; (3) quotas, or a quantity limitation; (4) licenses, or permits enabling the exporter to enter goods; (5) foreign exchange controls, or regulations affecting how importers may convert their funds to other currencies; and (6) embargoes, or complete restriction over imports.

U.S. agriculture, as a whole, stands to benefit more by a free trade policy than one of restriction because U.S. feed grain, food grain, oilseed, poultry, tobacco and cotton exports, among others, are relatively more important than the relatively small amount of farm commodities imported. Also, many of the farm goods imported by the U.S. cannot be produced at all domestically, such as bananas, coffee and tea.

U.S. industry and business, on the other hand, very often favor restrictive trade rather than freer trade. Thus, in protecting some U.S. industrial goods, we tend to restrict other nations from selling in the United States which then tends to restrict these nations from buying

U.S. farm goods. However, even in U.S. agriculture, the voices for restricted trade are many and loud. In addition, the price support activities of the U.S. government, in certain farm commodities, tend to elevate the domestic price above the world price which normally would cause an influx of foreign goods into the United States but which may be conveniently cut off with tariffs and import quotas. Foreign nations may then retaliate by imposing tariffs and import quotas on goods entering their country from the United States. Another adverse effect of abnormally high domestic prices and low export prices is to encourage dumping of U.S. goods abroad which tends to depress world market prices and compounds the trade problem among nations. This "dumping" may take the form of selling: (1) below cost, (2) below world market prices, (3) for foreign currency, (4) for credit and (5) through outright grants. However, the United States is not alone in following these practices. All nations are guilty of one or more restrictive trade practices. For example, the European Common Market nations impose restrictions on U.S. poultry meat to protect their own industry. Other foreign nations subsidize certain farm commodities which make it difficult for the United States to compete. In addition, when U.S. farm policies call for a restriction in production, other nations expand their output to fill the export gap, as has occurred in cotton to the great disadvantage of U.S. cotton exports.

EXTENT OF COOPERATIVE BUSINESS

Farmers have at least three choices for marketing food and fiber. They can: (1) turn their produce over to nonfarm businesses, letting them perform the marketing steps; (2) sell certain produce (rice, cotton, wheat, peanuts, corn, etc.) to the federal government under the various price support programs; or (3) organize cooperatives for marketing their produce.

Cooperatives handle about 30 per cent of all products produced and sold at the farm level. This percentage has been increasing over the last few years. Cooperatives are especially important in marketing milk, 75 per cent; sugar products, 65 per cent; rice, 65 per cent; nuts, 45 per cent; fruits and vegetables, 30 per cent; cotton, cotton products, grains and soybeans, 30 per cent; tobacco, 25 per cent; and wool, livestock and poultry and eggs, less than 20 per cent.

Many observers of the food marketing system believe that cooperatives could be more effective in helping farmers obtain a greater share of the consumers' food dollar.

"BIG BUSINESS" IN AGRIBUSINESS MARKETING

Many of the off-farm corporations engaged in marketing food and fiber are "big business" corporations. These are becoming increasingly important in the agribusiness marketing function.

There is a wide range in the profits reaped by such corporations. Generally, apparel and textile firms are the least profitable when profits are measured as per cent return on equity. Food and kindred product firms are relatively more profitable while tobacco products processing and marketing and beverage firms are the most profitable.

CONCENTRATION IN FOOD PROCESSING
AND MANUFACTURING

Fewer firms are controlling a relatively larger share of total sales in food processing and marketing. The following food groups are especially concentrated: breakfast cereals, vegetable oils, cracker and cookie manufacture, flour milling and livestock slaughter. Relatively moderate concentration is found in fruit and vegetable freezing and canning, baking and fluid milk processing.

● ● ●

In the next chapter, market channels and marketing functions for food and fiber products are discussed.

TOPICS FOR DISCUSSION

1. Define agribusiness marketing.
2. What are the principal cost items in marketing farm products?
3. Discuss the farmer's share of the consumer's food dollar. Do you think the farmer's share will continue to decline?
4. Discuss the export-import of foods.
5. Discuss the role of cooperatives in agribusiness marketing.

6. Prepare a list of corporations in your area which are engaged in marketing food and fiber products.

SELECTED REFERENCES

1. Farrell, K. R., *Market Performance in the Food Sector*, ERS–653, U.S. Dept. of Agriculture, Washington, D.C., 1977.
2. Godwin, M. R., and L. L. Jones, "The Emerging Food and Fiber System," *American Journal of Agricultural Economics*, Dec. 1971, p. 806.
3. Greig, W. Smith, *Profitability and Other Financial Operating Ratios in the Food Processing Industry*, Wash. Agr. Exp. Sta. Bul. 778, Pullman, Jul. 1973.
4. Linstrom, H. R., *Farmer-to-Consumer Marketing*, ESCS–01, U.S. Dept. of Agriculture, Washington, D.C., Feb. 1978.
5. Marion, Bruce W., and C. R. Handy, *Market Performance: Concepts and Measures*, ERS, A.E. Rept. 244, U.S. Dept. of Agriculture, Washington, D.C., Sept. 1973.
6. Minden, Arlo J., "A Systems Approach to Planning Long-Range Marketing Programs," *American Journal of Agricultural Economics*, Dec. 1968, p. 1745.
7. Roy, Ewell P., and others, *Economics: Applications to Agriculture and Agribusiness*, The Interstate Printers & Publishers, Inc., Danville, Ill., 1980.
8. Staff, *Cost Components of Farm-Retail Spreads for Selected Foods*, ERS, A.E. Rept. 343, U.S. Dept. of Agriculture, Washington, D.C., Jul. 1976.

6

Agribusiness Marketing of Food and Fiber:

Market Channels

The movement of food and fiber from farms to processing plants is a complex operation involving many market channels and functions, types of facilities and skilled management and personnel.

The *functional* approach to the study of marketing considers the various activities performed to increase the utility of food and fiber products from farmer to consumer. This approach is in contrast with the *channel* approach which focuses on the agencies involved in the movement of goods from farmer to consumer.

MARKETING CHANNELS

We must recognize that each food or fiber commodity has a marketing system unique to it. The channels through which commodities pass are varied and complex. In Table 6-1 is a summary of channels employed in disposing of various agricultural commodities.

Firms involved in the marketing of food and fiber may be classified into at least two groups: (1) assemblers and (2) processors.

Assemblers of Farm Produce

Between the farmer and the processor are found over 10,000 assemblers of farm products.

Table 6-1. Processing and Marketing Outlets (Except Retailing Outlets) for Various Types of Farm Commodities

Type of commodity	Main types of market outlets	
	First handler	Subsequent handlers

Cotton	Gins
	Cotton buyers
	Cotton merchandisers
		Lint: compresses
		       warehouses
		       linters
		       textile mills
		       apparel mfrs.
		       exporters
		Seed: oil mills
		       oil refiners
		       exporters

Sugar cane, sugar beets, maple and honey	Raw sugar factories Processors	Refiners Molasses users Sugar byproduct plants Processors Confectioners Beverage bottlers
Fruits, nuts and vegetables: fresh	Local farmers' markets Shippers Packing sheds Auction markets Terminal markets	Brokers Distributors Wholesalers
processed	Driers Shellers Freezers Canneries Dehydrators Processors Distillers	Brokers Wholesalers Distributors
Beef cattle, hogs and sheep	Terminal markets Auction markets Direct sales markets	Feedlots for further feeding Meat packers Meat slaughterers Renderers Wholesalers Brokers Curers Fabricators Meat locker plants Pharmaceutical mfrs.
Table eggs	Processors Packers	Wholesalers Direct sales markets Brokers
Hatching eggs (chicken and turkey)	Hatcheries	Feed stores Farmers Integrators
Broilers, turkeys and other poultry meats	Processors Renderers	Wholesalers Brokers Distributors Exporters

(Continued)

Table 6-1 (Continued)

Type of commodity	Main types of market outlets	
	First handler	Subsequent handlers
Fish	Canners Freezers Processors Curers	Marine oil refiners Wholesalers Brokers Distributors Exporters Byproduct plants
Feed grains (corn, oats, barley, soybeans, sorghum)	Elevators Driers Oil mills Other farmers	Feed mills Ingredient mills Refiners Manufacturers Exporters Seed houses Wholesalers Brokers
Seeds	Processors Cleaners Driers Handlers	Wholesalers Farm stores Home and garden stores
Hay	Local handlers Wholesalers Other farmers	Retailers Distributors Farm stores
Hides, skins, pelts, mohair and wool	Processors Curers Tanners Finishers	Mills Manufacturers
Milk and milk products	Haulers Processors Bottlers Manufacturers	Distributors Wholesalers Brokers Institutions
Tobacco	Curers Warehouses Dealers Stemmers	Manufacturers Exporters Distributors Wholesalers
Greenhouse, nursery and floral products	Shippers Distributors	Wholesalers
Wood and wood products	Loggers Veneer and plywood mills Lumber dealers/brokers/ assemblers Pulpwood mills Paper mills Sawmills Byproduct processors Planing mills Paperboard mills Naval stores dealers	Preservers Manufacturers Wholesalers Distributors Chippers Processors Brokers

(Continued)

Table 6-1 (Continued)

| Type of commodity | Main types of market outlets | |
	First handler	Subsequent handlers
Food grains (rice, rye, buckwheat, wheat and barley)	Elevators Driers Brewers Malters	Bakeries Brokers Distributors Wholesalers Exporters Millers Processors Seed houses

Assemblers perform a useful function in aggregating many smaller lots of produce into larger, more economical volumes but do not usually process or change the form of the product materially if at all.

The principal assembling agencies include milk and cream receiving stations, egg sorting plants, fruit and vegetable packing sheds, country grain elevators, livestock terminals, other country assembly points and farmers' markets.

Those who move farm products on to wholesale markets include resident buyers, traveling buyers and order buyers.

Resident buyers own or operate local marketing facilities through which they buy products. They operate independently or as representatives of other firms.

Traveling buyers, who operate independently or as representatives of terminal buyers of firms operating at local shipping points, go from one producing district to another as crops mature. Purchases are made in trucklots or carlots from the producers, a procedure followed for fruit and vegetable crops, the produce in which traveling buyers specialize.

In the fruit and vegetable industry, *grower-shippers* have increased in prominence. Many are former cash buyers whose interests as producers have gradually increased. They pack and market products produced by their neighbors, generally for a fixed packing charge and marketing commission. Sometimes farmers form a cooperative to take over the business as it expands.

Order buyers function as shipping-point brokers for chain stores or terminal wholesale buyers at country points. Order buyers, who may be salaried employees or paid on a commission basis, buy for cash the kind and grade of produce that customers demand, mainly for livestock.

Auction markets are important for livestock, fruits and vegetables, tobacco, poultry and eggs. More than 90 per cent of the tobacco grown is marketed through auctions, and the amount of other products sold through auctions is substantial.

Direct marketing by producers to consumers indicate that there are 8,915 roadside stands, 3,069 pick-your-own operations and 541 of the more permanent farmers' markets operating in 41 of the 50 states. Estimates for those states not reporting bring the total estimated outlets to over 13,000. Most items sold through direct marketing outlets are fruits and vegetables. Other items include eggs, dairy products, meat, poultry, baked goods, tree nuts, honey, shrubbery and handicrafts. Farmers view direct marketing as an alternative outlet to increase their income. Consumers see it as a means of getting fresher, higher quality foods at less cost. Consumers also find the markets convenient and friendly places to shop.

Overall, the number of assemblers of farm products is declining as assembly points are bypassed for more direct markets.

In the following section an example of selected agribusinesses enaged in assembling and handling farm produce is presented.

Local Grain Elevators

There are some 6,500 grain elevators in the United States. Most are country elevators and consist of corporations, partnerships and cooperatives. Elevators may handle wheat, corn, oats, rice, soybeans, grain sorghum and other grains, depending upon the type of farming area. Their total bushel storage capacity is about .95 billion. Elevators are usually located on rail or water facilities, although trucking has been taking over more of the transport business. Ownership of two or more local elevators by the same person or firm has been increasing.

Local elevators are subject to seasonal operations in the fall. During the rest of the year, the management may handle farm supplies, mix feed and operate other businesses. Total sales per elevator average about $1 million per year. Investment in a local grain elevator usually ranges from $250,000 to $750,000. Capital for fixed investment is usually harder to obtain than operating capital, which is easier to get be-

Figure 6-1. Grain elevators are an essential and important part of the marketing process from farmer to consumer. (Courtesy, Farm Credit Administration, Washington, D.C.)

cause grains are bought and sold over a short period. Where grain storage is engaged in, more operating capital is required. The average local elevator will have a storage capacity of from 50,000 to 350,000 bushels or more. Hedging is normally utilized in connection with storage operations (discussed later). Many elevators also store grain for the federal government in its price support programs.

Local elevators procure or handle grain from within a rather short radius, then market it to more distant terminal elevators located on rail or water facilities or both. Many also sell direct to exporters or grain processors, such as soybean oil mills. Grain brokers may also be utilized.

The principal problems facing local elevator operators are: (1) seasonality in operations; (2) changes in government grain programs; (3) obtaining enough volume to operate efficiently; (4) transportation problems, especially the availability of rail cars; (5) competition among rail, water and truck transport methods; (6) advent of large grain merchandising firms into local areas; (7) confusion with regard to grain grades and standards; and (8) problems in exporting grains.

PROCESSORS OF FOOD AND FIBER

Processing of food and fiber creates *form* utility. The nine principal types of food processing account for about 22,500 plants. About 42 per cent of them employ 20 or more workers. Canned and frozen food, sugar and beverage plants have proportionally more plants employing 20 or more workers (50 per cent of them), while meat, dairy, bakery, grain mill and confectionery products processors have about 30 to 40 per cent of all their plants employing 20 or more workers.

As examples of food and fiber processing, vegetable canning, textiles and paper manufacturing are discussed briefly.

Vegetable Canning Plants

There are about 1,000 fruit and vegetable canneries of all types in the United States, producing several hundred different items.

Vegetable canning plants are a significant part of this total, varying greatly in size. However, most have a facilities investment of between

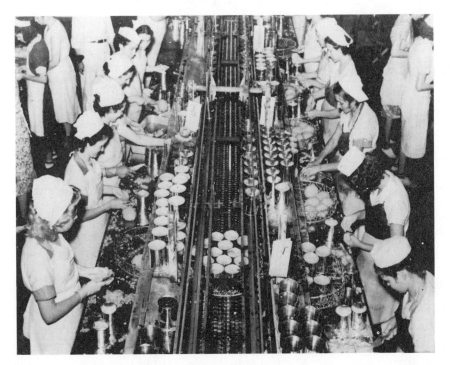

Figure 6-2. Food canning plants are among the oldest types of agribusiness marketing agencies and are increasing in importance. (Courtesy, Cooperative League of USA, Chicago, Ill.)

$300,000 and $1,000,000. As they grow larger, many of them switch to a corporation setup from a single proprietorship or partnership arrangement in order to minimize liability and acquire capital more easily.

Canning plants try to procure most of their supplies from areas close by and often use grower contracts to obtain what they need for their operations.

Seasonality of operation is a problem to most plants. Therefore, plant management tries to diversify by canning several vegetables over the year. This helps also in marketing since such a plant has more than one product to offer buyers.

Warehousing is also a critical factor for canning plants, since they cannot immediately sell all of what they have canned.

One trend in the canning industry deals with canners' packing products for chain food stores and other buyers under the buyers' labels. About one-fourth of the pack is canned in this manner. While some canners are concerned about this trend, others see it as an opportunity to reduce their costs by canning in larger volume.

Although canners may procure their supplies locally, they usually must sell many of the products in distant markets. By the use of food brokers located in large urban centers, canners are able to dispose of their volume at a rather low cost per unit. Besides marketing through food brokers, some canners sell direct to wholesalers or retailers, some bidding on government food contracts and others exporting.

In more recent years, many canners have expanded into frozen food operations which has allowed them to diversify, to extend their operating season and to provide more and better markets for their grower-suppliers.

The main problems faced by canners and other food processors are: (1) obtaining quality raw materials at prices which allow them a profit; (2) operating plants at efficient levels, which requires year-round use, high labor productivity and skilled management; (3) disposing of waste; (4) marketing efficiently, which means productive brokers or salespersons, efficient transportation, stable market outlets and adequate prices; and (5) obtaining sufficient capital to keep facilities up-to-date and maintain plant and sales operations on a sound financial basis.

Textiles and Apparel Manufacturing

There are over 5,000 manufacturing establishments in the textile industry and approximately 25,000 in the apparel industry. Although these plants are widely distributed geographically, they are most heavily concentrated in the New England, Middle Atlantic and Southeastern states. North Carolina, South Carolina and Georgia account for 50 per cent of textile employment, while 30 per cent of all apparel employment is concentrated in New York and Pennsylvania.

Prior to World War II, most textile and apparel firms were small, family-owned, single-establishment organizations, typically specializing in only one of the several manufacturing stages needed to convert textile fibers into finished products. There is a trend to larger firms and vertical integration of manufacturing operations, but even today no single firm accounts for as much as 8 per cent of textile industry sales, and the largest apparel firm accounts for only about 3 per cent of sales in that industry.

The end-use of natural fibers is 40 per cent for apparel goods, 25 per cent for home furnishings, 20 per cent for industrial uses, 10 per cent for other consumer uses and 5 per cent for export.

One of the more significant trends is the continued growth of synthetic fibers in relation to cotton fiber. The relatively high price supports for cotton have made it less competitive with man-made fibers.

Fibers are classified by whether they are produced naturally or synthetically and also on the basis of their chemical composition. There are many natural fibers with wool, cotton and silk being the most common. They are produced seasonally and stored until ready for use. Natural fibers are subject to a lack of uniformity and variation in quality because they are affected by weather, nutrients, insects and disease. Man-made fibers are not subject to the limitations of nature and are quite uniform in quality because the entire production process can be controlled. Besides nylon and rayon fibers are found the polyesters which were first commercially produced in the United States in 1953 and later surpassed nylon to become the most widely used synthetic fiber. This is the result of the great versatility of both the polymer and the yarn. Polyester has a wide variety of end uses and also many desirable properities. About 5 billion pounds of synthetic fibers are used annually in the USA.

U.S. cotton and wool consumption per capita has stayed at about 20 pounds for the last 30 years. In the same period, however, fibers other than cotton and wool have increased from 2 to 36 pounds per capita. Thirty years ago cotton and wool had 92 per cent of the market but now have only 35 per cent. Innovation of other fibers has caused total consumption of fibers to increase from 27 to 56 pounds per person.

This is not to say that cotton and wool have been eclipsed. Cotton still accounts for three-fourths of the fibers used in men's and boys' clothing, four-fifths of those used for girls' and infants' wear. New methods of treating cotton fabrics so that they dry quickly and require little ironing have helped cotton meet the competition of synthetic fibers. Also, man-made fibers are dependent on petroleum stocks which have become more expensive.

Paper and Paperboard Manufacturing

About 500 pounds of paper per person is used each year, requiring the net annual wood growth from about ¾ of an acre of commercial forest. A large New York newspaper uses the equivalent of the yearly growth from 6,000 acres of commercial forest land for its Sunday edition alone. The major producing areas are located in the South, Middle Atlantic, East North Central, New England and Pacific areas. Principal paper products include paper for printing, fine and coarse paper, industrial and tissue paper, container boards, boxboard and construction paper.

Paper has already captured portions of the markets once exclusively held by steel, glass, wood and textiles. With research the industry expects to utilize present-day films, foils and plastics to extend its markets further, by employing these items to complement and fortify paper products.

MARKETING FUNCTIONS

Nine principal *marketing functions* are discussed as follows.

1. Standardizing and Grading

Standardization, as the term implies, includes the setting up of recognized standards for matters such as quality, size, weight and color. Standardization, of course, makes grading possible, for once the criteria are determined, products can be properly classified. In food markets, for example, certain eggs can be graded as Grade A, certain meat can be graded as Prime, etc.

This merchandising function of standardization and grading makes for efficiency in marketing. A buyer can order from his supplier by mail, wire or telephone without the necessity of going to the seller's storage facilities to inspect the products which he as buyer wishes to purchase. This is so because the mention of Grade A or B or C spells out distinctive characteristics which are understood and accepted by both buyer and seller. Standardization and grading, therefore, make for easier contractual and exchange agreements between marketers.

The use of these quality standards is, in most cases, voluntary. They are used in many instances by manufacturers or by packers in quality control work and as the basis of the federal and federal-state grading services.

2. Packaging

The packaging function is an increasingly important one in food and fiber marketing. Packaging serves not only to preserve contents but also to merchandise and advertise products. With the dominance of self-service retailing, displayed packages become their own salesmen with their color, shape, label and other characteristics.

Packaging, a multi-million dollar industry, offers many innovations, such as aluminum containers, tab-pull can openers, paper cans, fiberboard boxes with plastic inner liners and plastic containers and bottles, among many others.

Considerably more of the packaging of foods is being done on the farm or at nearby processing plants. Thus, fewer unsalable products are transported and better product quality is maintained. Automated machinery has also stimulated the advance to packaging. Research and development expenditures have been large.

Figure 6-3. Packaging is becoming an increasingly important function in agribusiness marketing. (Courtesy, Hawaii Agricultural Experiment Station, Honolulu)

3. Storing

Storage provides *time* utility by making goods available at the time they are needed. Storage has a beneficial effect on prices since it removes a portion of the supply from market at harvest time and allows it to enter the market later when prices are more favorable. Thus, storage leads to greater price stability.

The agricultural products stored may consist of two types: (1) unprocessed or raw farm products and (2) processed products. The type of storage may involve elevators, warehouses, bins, sheds, open storage warehouses, kilns, tanks, ships, barges, coolers and freezer lockers, among other facilities.

Storage of farm products may be classified as (1) on-farm storage or (2) off-farm storage. Off-farm storage may involve types of facilities

Figure 6-4. Storage provides time utility by withdrawing excess supplies at harvest and releasing them subsequently. (Courtesy, California Almond Growers Exchange, Sacramento)

such as private or public warehouses; bonded, licensed warehouses or nonbounded, nonlicensed ones; and refrigerated or unrefrigerated storage warehouses. Moreover, farm products may be stored in bulk, in packages or in loose form.

On-farm storage has increased in importance because farmers often desire to hold their products for later sale at a higher price and/or to take advantage of federal price support programs where certain commodities are placed in loan. If prices should rise above the support price, farmers can redeem the commodity on loan and sell on the open market. If prices should fall below the support price, the commodity passes to the federal government in repayment for the loan previously made to the farmer.

Storage facilities have undergone many improvements in recent years, including (1) better construction materials; (2) better, more efficient structural designs; (3) better mechanical and physical methods,

such as the use of mechanical lifters, power trucks, palletizing con-
veyers and unitized loads; (4) improved in-plant efficiency; (5) better
humidity and temperature controls; and (6) better pest and insect control to reduce storage losses.

4. Transportation

Transportation costs are taking a higher proportion of the consumer's food dollar. Products have to move from where they are produced to where they are needed and are to be consumed. Transportation provides *place* utility.

Transportation is provided through networks of railroads, high-
ways, waterways, airlines and pipelines. The total freight shipments in
the United States are handled as follows: railroads, 37 per cent; trucking and pipelines, 25 per cent each; inland waterways, 12 per cent; and
airlines, 1 per cent.

Farm products, which account for about 40 per cent of all goods
transported, are carried mostly in railroad cars and motor trucks, but,
for some purposes, ships, barges and airplanes are used.

For the greater part of freight transportation, the federal or state
government decides matters such as whether a firm will be allowed to
enter the business, what routes it may serve and what rates it may charge.
Such control applies to all of railroading and air transport and to a great
deal of transportation on the highways and waterways.

The general pattern of transportation of farm products is in three
steps: first, from the farm to the local market, which serves as an assembly point for the area's produce; second, from this local market to
one in the consuming area; and third, from this market in the consuming area to the retailer. The first and last phases of this movement are
almost always performed by trucks. The longest movement, the haul
from the local assembly point to the terminal market, may be by rail,
truck, water or even air. Thus, we find rail and motor carriers supple-
menting each other in the transportation process in some situations and
competing with each other for the same traffic in others.

Of course, many products are grown a short distance from the
consuming market; hence only a single step is involved in hauling them
from farm to market. This type of haul is usually done by trucks.

TRUCK.—Truck transport has increased relative to other forms in hauling both raw and processed foods and fibers. Better trucks, larger capacities and better roads have contributed to this increase. Also, in hauling raw or unmanufactured farm products, trucks are exempt from the Interstate Commerce Commission regulations, except for safety and driving regulations. Trucks owned by farmer cooperatives are likewise exempt, allowing much more flexibility and lower hauling costs than would otherwise be the case.

However, trucks are still controlled in other ways, such as by licenses and taxes, load limits, regulations governing length and height of trucks and by state commerce commissions wherever applicable. In addition, the unionization of most truck drivers has introduced inflexibility in driver costs.

The basic advantages of truck transport over other forms are: rapid movement of perishable foods; flexible schedules; lower costs, especially for small loads; dependability; speed; easier back-hauling; less loss in transit; and faster, more efficient loading and unloading. Grain, livestock, milk, vegetables and fruits account for about 85 per cent of the truck

Figure 6-5. Truck transport is gaining over other methods of shipment. (Courtesy, Midcontinent Farmers Association, Columbia, Mo.)

haulings of farm produce in the United States. Improvements in high-
ways (such as the interstate highway system) and the use of refrigerated
trucks and piggy-back arrangements with railroads have increased the
advantages of trucks over other forms. Truck transport continues to
suffer from varying regulations and restrictions imposed by different
states.

RAIL.—Rail is the oldest form of general transportation. Initially
railroads were given land ·grants to assist them in developing. Later,
they became highly regulated under the Interstate Commerce Commission and state agencies in both their rates and their schedules. This
regulation is now causing pain in adjusting to competition, and railroads continue to lose their share of the business. Railroads are also
heavily taxed by local and state authorities.

The advantages of rail transport are the efficient movement of large
volumes of bulk commodities and the safety and economy of hauling

Figure 6-6. Although rail transport has lost some of its eminence, it is still the most economical for long-distance hauling of bulky commodities. (Courtesy, California Almond Growers Exchange, Sacramento)

over long distances. Railroads obtain about one-fifth of their revenues from hauling farm products. Grains, animal feeds and canned goods are the principal items moved by rail.

Railroads, in recent years, have made progress in improving transportation by using larger freight cars; specially designed cars; unit trains; piggy-back systems; improved rail communications; and computerized central traffic stations, yards and makeup of trains.

Other improvements have consisted of railroad mergers to reduce overhead costs, lower labor costs and improve services.

Problems remain, however, such as the increasing shortage of cars to transport crops and congestion at ports.

WATER.—Water transport, by both river and ocean, has increased its share of the total business. This method is especially adapted to grains or to large-volume, bulk-commodity shipping, where speed is not critical. It is also a low-cost method. Interstate water traffic is exempt from regulation when bulk commodities, such as grains, are being shipped. Also, public development of waterways has helped water traffic become more competitive. Water transport will become even more important in the future.

Figure 6-7. Water transport is increasing in importance for many agribusiness commodities. (Courtesy, Baton Rouge Chamber of Commerce, Baton Rouge, La.)

AIR.—Air transport is especially adapted to conditions requiring speed and dependability and for commodities having a high value per unit, such as flowers, nursery items, fruits, seafood and specialty crops. Otherwise, it is still too costly for bulk commodities.

Air cargo transport has had most of its development since World War II. Although it did not appear too promising in the beginning, recent developments indicate that it has significant potential. Planes built especially for cargo promise line-haul cost reductions which should permit lower rates and wider markets. While air cargo accounts for only a small proportion of total intercity ton-miles, it has increased significantly in recent years, and the list of commodities which move by air is growing. It is expected that the use of helicopters for hauling cargo will increase also.

PIPELINE.—Pipeline transport is confined primarily to petroleum, petroleum products and natural gas. There are about 160,000 miles of pipelines in the United States.

5. Market Communications

The subject of communications is twofold: (1) the types of media and the relative importance of each and (2) the use of the media to achieve a certain purpose, such as advertising, which is reserved for fuller discussion later.

Principal types of communication media are newspapers, mail, magazines, telephone, word of mouth, radio, telegraph and television.

In distributing farm supplies, agribusinesses employ the use of: newspaper advertising or articles; magazines for more general information (used primarily by large companies); the telephone for answering customers' questions, requests or complaints; radio for advertising and for farm broadcasts; television for advertising and for farm telecasts; and direct mail for the distribution of price lists, circulars or other materials.

Farmers in their production activities may utilize newspapers to obtain farm stories, advertising and general farm news. Mail sources may provide a wide range of market news, bulletins, circulars, etc. Farmers use magazines for educational articles on farm practices and are attracted to general farm advertising as well. Their use of the telephone is varied and increasingly more important. Radio is relied upon mostly for market and farm news reports, as well as for trading posts. Television is used less for market news but is more effective in farm news programming.

In farm product marketing activities, agribusinesses employ all types of media. Newspapers are used for commodity reports, market news, advertising and farm news. Mail pieces are used variously. Magazines attempt to reach consumers of processed farm products primarily. The telephone serves a number of purposes, and teletype facilities are involved in conveying market news reports. Telegrams are often employed in confirming sales transactions. Radio and television, moreover, are used for advertising and for market and farm news programming.

ROLE OF TRADE ASSOCIATIONS.—Trade associations deserve special note in the area of agribusiness communications. Not only do trade associations represent and educate their members, but also they inform the general public concerning trade activities, needs and responsibilities. With dues and assessments collected from members, executives of trade associations, usually with small staffs, wield considerable influence in connection with trade group policies, state and federal legislation and other matters.

Practically every phase of the food and fiber business is represented by one or more trade associations. It is expected that their roles will be more important in the future than they have been in the past.

6. Financing

In the movement and exchange of goods from producer to consumer, there are lags between the time of production and of sale and between the time of sale and receipt of payment. Thus, financing must be provided so that business operations may continue in a smooth manner. If financing were not provided, business firms could not operate the scale of plants nor perform the variety of functions necessary for efficient marketing.

7. Merchandising

Merchandising is a marketing function which is all-inclusive in the sense that it refers to all the characteristics associated with the distribution, display and sale of a product. In a more specific sense, merchandising is making available a product which appeals to a consumer and which satisfies some desire or need of that person or persons.

For example, a product may be very useful to consumers but may not be selling well because of poor packaging, poor display and lack of advertising. Merchandising, as a marketing function, can be utilized to reorganize the entire marketing of the product by changing one or more of the marketing elements to produce a more optimum sum of its parts. Merchandising, in a practical sense, is an art as well as a science. Many marketing failures have been rescued by artful merchandisers.

8. Risk-Sharing and Hedging

A futures market is a specially organized market, often called a commodity exchange or a board of trade, where contracts for future sales or purchases are traded. The exchange provides for standardized methods of trading in contracts. The exchange establishes the rules for trading and the terms of the contracts. Most contracts will specify the commodity and the quantity, quality, price, time of delivery and place of delivery. The exchange specifies who may trade, the time and place trading may occur and the rules and regulations of actual trading. Most of the major agricultural commodities are traded on the various futures markets in New York, Chicago and Kansas City, among other cities.

One economic tool for sharing price risks is *hedging* by an owner of the product being traded in futures. A person trading in futures without an ownership interest is called a *speculator*.

The *advantages* of *hedging* include: First, the hedging operation is regulated by the federal government and everyone trading thereon is financially responsible. This is not always true for other types of marketing and contracting operations. Second, the hedging or futures contract is very detailed and specific so that everyone knows exactly what he is trading in. Third, hedging is a very flexible pricing technique. If an individual thinks he has made a mistake, he can get out of that mistake very quickly and legally. In some other types of price contracting, he may not be able to correct his mistakes until the next crop year, and, the other party to the contract could hold him to a "bad" contract for its duration. Fourth, a person does not have to put up large sums of money initially for a hedging position although if futures go up, he will be called upon for more money, but the cash price of the product will also have gone up. On the other hand, if futures go down, he will be able to draw down some of his profits which are cash in his pocket. Fifth, in world markets, the price risks become so great that hedging is or will become a very necessary pricing technique. Sixth, a lender or creditor will usually loan more money if the crop is hedged than if it is not. This may become a more important factor in the future.

The *disadvantages* of *hedging* include: First, an individual has to have a certain minimum volume of product to hedge. Second, he has to have some basic knowledge of futures trading which means a period of self-education. Third, he has to follow the market to become better informed. Fourth, when futures rise in price, he will not make as much money as his neighbor who did not hedge. If he cannot live with this realization, he had better not hedge. Fifth, he should know all costs, both fixed and variable, so that he can make intelligent hedging decisions. This calls for a modern, accurate and detailed cost accounting system. Sixth, there is rarely a "perfect" hedge in which "losses" or "gains" on the futures offset exactly price increases or decreases in the cash market.

An example of *hedging* is presented as follows:

Suppose a soybean farmer plants in May of one year and is uncertain about bean prices the following October or at harvest. He may reduce this price uncertainty by selling an October futures contract in the month of May for, say $5.50 per bushel, October delivery. When the delivery time arrives in October, the farmer may either deliver the beans for $5.50 per bushel or buy back his contract at some price thus cancelling his October delivery contract. Whether the farmer will deliver the beans or buy an offsetting contract will depend largely upon the price of beans in the cash market in October and the price of October futures contracts.

Assume the following situation:

(A) May — farmer sells 10,000 bushels of beans for
      October delivery at $5.50 per bushel $55,000

(B) October — farmer buys back October futures contract at $5.30 per bushel to offset previous
      contract $53,000

                        Gain on futures transactions $ 2,000

(C) October — farmer sells beans for cash on local
             market at $5.30 per bushel $53,000
                                                               ———————

The farmer could have delivered the beans for $5.50 and not
bothered to buy an offsetting contract, but it's usually better to buy
back the contract.

The farmer has protected his soybean price at $5.50 per bushel
($5.30 cash plus 20 cents gain on futures transactions). If he had specu-
lated, his price would have been $5.30 per bushel (October cash mar-
ket). However, the 20 cents gain per bushel on this particular futures
transactions is a gross amount because the cost of futures trading has to
be paid by the farmer. The cost of futures trading in soybeans is about
½ cent per bushel and cost of money tied up in futures trading may
add another ¼ cent per bushel.

The farmer, under our hedging example, has thus protected his
May sale of beans for October delivery at $5.50 per bushel which he
had considered satisfactory at planting time. If he had not sold futures,
his profit might have been greater but his loss also could have been
very large if beans had dropped to $4 per bushel at harvest. By hedg-
ing, the farmer removed himself from speculation in the cash grain
market. Possible large gains from speculation were sacrificed but possible losses from speculation were reduced also. Hedging then becomes
an economic tool for the farmer to reduce his price risks.

Let us now assume another example or one where the price of
beans rises during the fall cash and delivery futures price:

(A) May — farmer sells 10,000 bushels of beans for
             October delivery at $5.50 per bushel $55,000
(B) October — farmer buys back October futures con-
             tract at $5.70 per bushel to offset previous
             contract $57,000
                                                           ———————
                    Loss on futures transactions $ 2,000
(C) October — farmer sells beans for cash on local
             market at $5.70 per bushel $57,000
                                                           ———————

The farmer obtained $57,000 for cash beans minus $2,000 loss on
futures for a net of $55,000 or $5.50 per bushel price. Thus, the
farmer was successful in locking in his bean price at $5.50 per bushel.
While it is true he would have profited by $2,000 had he not hedged, it

is also true that he could have lost by not hedging. His margin of success, therefore, will depend largely upon the spread between cash and futures prices.

Therefore, the futures market involves two types of traders: (1) speculators, who gamble on price rises, declines and margin spreads and (2) hedgers, who seek to minimize their losses.

Some other commodities eligible for futures trading besides soybeans include corn, oats, cotton, eggs, wheat, broiler chickens, live cattle and hogs, among many others.

Futures markets are regulated by the Commodities Futures Trading Commission and by the commodity exchanges themselves.

9. Advertising

Many food manufacturers attempt to differentiate their product through advertising brand names and to build in more convenience features in their products. These techniques give them better control over the price of their products and isolate their offerings from other competing products.

Food advertising expenditures are $4 billion annually out of a total advertising outlay of $37 billion, retailers having an increasing share relative to manufacturers and wholesalers. Consumers are the main object of advertisers. Use of television as an advertising medium is increasing relative to radio and newspapers, although newspapers are basic to food ads.

Various producer-promotion groups seek, as their ultimate aim, to influence consumers to use their respective products. All producer-promotion groups combined spend about $300 million annually employing various methods and media to achieve their objectives.

The effectiveness of advertising in influencing consumers depends upon the use of media patronized by them, their educational and income levels and the appeal of the advertising technique itself. Some advertisers use their own staffs to develop ads, while others hire advertising agencies.

Advertisers are regulated directly or indirectly by their trade associations, the advertising media, the Federal Trade Commission and other government agencies.

TRENDS IN FOOD AND FIBER MARKETING

Many smaller processors have discontinued operations because they were unable to capitalize and manage needed changes. Others have merged with stronger companies, capitalwise and managementwise, to survive. These larger companies gain a greater share of market power by national advertising, branding and other means. Still others have entered processing because certain consumer needs were not being met by existing firms. However, changes have not been the same for each and every commodity.

In *meat packing,* many smaller firms have entered the business at local levels, tending to lessen the market power formerly held by major packers.

In *poultry and egg marketing,* the advent of vertical and horizontal integration has reduced the number but increased the size of firms, resulting in greater efficiency and increased price competition at the retail level.

In *fluid milk marketing,* the number of firms has decreased and the size of plants has increased. The growth of major firms has been stymied in recent years by government action. On the other hand, price stability for raw milk has been achieved by state-federal marketing orders and agreements. Prices to consumers have become the object of control by many state boards.

In *vegetable and fruit processing,* many small plants have been discontinued and larger, year-round operations have succeeded. The growth in packing vegetables for food stores under their label has increased. Processors also contract with farmers for most of their supplies, bringing stability to that end of the business.

In *grain handling and processing,* the influence of government price support, storage and export programs have influenced competitive aspects of this business. Grain prices to farmers have been stabilized by government action, however. Overcapacity in grain handling is evident in older producing areas and undercapacity in newer grain areas.

In *food fabricating,* suppliers are delivering increasing quantities of food in prepared and semiprepared forms to restaurants or institutions, where the items are served to customers with minimal labor input. Meats are being cut, wrapped and boxed at the packing plant and sent to the kitchen ready for cooking. The operator can buy steaks, roasts or hamburger as needed. Other restaurant or institutional operators are going into the business of preparing main courses or complete meals in a fashion analogous to the process used to prepare the frozen TV dinners available in supermarkets. Furnishing complete meals or the main course in a form which requires only heating before serving has become particularly important for "captive" consumers, such as those on airlines and in school lunchrooms and similar establishments.

OPPORTUNITIES IN AGRIBUSINESS MARKETING

Since marketing is so complex, many opportunities exist to simplify and improve this process. Possible simplifications and improvements might include: first, reducing the cost of performing necessary steps or services; second, eliminating unnecessary steps; third, developing equitable bargaining power between parties in any given transaction; fourth, providing food and fiber consumers exactly what they desire and can afford to pay for; fifth, protecting the health and welfare of the consuming public; sixth, consolidating small establishments to obtain greater economic efficiency; seventh, improving marketing personnel, management and resource use; eighth, improving accounting and cost data; ninth, eliminating interstate trade barriers; and tenth, improving the gathering and dissemination of market news and information.

● ● ●

In the next chapter, agribusiness wholesaling is discussed.

TOPICS FOR DISCUSSION

1. Select one farm commodity, and discuss the main types of market outlets for it.
2. Discuss the assembly of farm produce.
3. Visit one type of marketing facility in your area, interview the manager, and write a summary of what you found concerning his marketing problems.
4. Discuss the importance of marketing functions in agribusiness marketing.
5. What are some of the jobs left undone in marketing?

SELECTED REFERENCES

1. Cain, J. L., and J. J. Ahern, Jr., *Structural Changes in Food Processing in the U.S.*, Md. Agr. Exp. Sta. MP 856, College Park, Jun. 1974.
2. Linstrom, H. R., *Farmer-to-Consumer Marketing*, ESCS–01, U.S. Dept. of Agriculture, Washington, D.C., Mar. 1978.
3. Roy, Ewell P., *Collective Bargaining in Agriculture*, The Interstate Printers & Publishers, Inc., Danville, Ill., 1970.
4. Roy, Ewell P., *Contract Farming and Economic Integration*, The Interstate Printers & Publishers, Inc., Danville, Ill., 1972.
5. Roy, Ewell P., and others, *Economics: Applications to Agriculture and Agribusiness*, The Interstate Printers & Publishers, Inc., Danville, Ill., 1980.
6. Sporleder, T. L., "Market Development for Food Products," *Southern Journal of Agricultural Economics*, Jul. 1973, p. 205.

7

Agribusiness Wholesaling

The movement of food and fiber from processing plants to wholesalers and then to retailers is an important link in the chain of agribusiness distribution.

What is wholesaling? It is the process to facilitate the conveyance of finished or processed goods to the retail outlets. In reality, the wholesaler represents the ultimate consumer, for he buys from the manufacturer or processor only those goods which he believes his retail customers will be able to sell to the final consumer. Despite the fact that he is greatly interested in helping his retailers sell goods, there is little recognition that in his relations with the manufacturer, he actually is a purchasing agent for the final consumer.

The indispensable role of the wholesaler in a free, competitive economy becomes clear if one recalls that the high standards of living in the United States are directly dependent upon mass production, the effectiveness of which is, in turn, dependent upon mass distribution, unattainable without wholesalers.

Modern wholesaling is typified by decreasing numbers of wholesalers, increasing sizes of operations, more products and services handled and increasing integration of the wholesaling-retailing function.

Large retailing has necessitated the growth of large wholesaling operations. The modern wholesale distribution center is an integral part of a major food corporation, or it is an affiliated business of a large group of food retailers. The modern wholesaling facilities may serve as many as 100 stores or more.

The central wholesale facility is usually located in a major marketing center adjacent to an excellent transportation network that includes rail, truck and, at times, air facilities.

In terms of physical facilities, modern wholesale establishments provide a single-story warehouse with floor space of several acres or more. Facilities are being built today with over 300,000 square feet of floor space.

The centralized wholesale operation encompasses many kinds and types of operations. It usually provides quarters for the general offices and administrative functions of the corporate or affiliated group. It houses the buying organization that procures the many thousands of products that are required to stock the modern retail establishment, and it is headquarters for all of the related staff groups that exist to serve the needs of food retailers.

Large-scale wholesaling firms have brought about some important changes in the characteristics of the wholesaling operation. Food wholesaling is no longer a clearly defined marketing function. Rather, it is an integrated manufacturer-wholesaler-retailer business system that exercises strong economic forces in the marketplace. Today, large, integrated wholesaling firms have an important voice in determining quantity and quality of products to be marketed, and they influence greatly the price levels that will exist for these products. Product specifications established by large-scale distribution firms become the market standard by which the majority of the food products are sold. The registered brand names of large wholesaling firms are becoming increasingly competitive with well-established national or regional brands; and this trend is expected to continue in future years.

TYPES OF WHOLESALERS

There are three basic types of wholesalers: (1) merchant wholesalers, who take title to goods and then buy and sell; (2) manufacturers' sales offices and branches or wholesaling operations, which are integrated with manufacturing or processing; and (3) merchandise agents or brokers, who do not take title to goods but act only as agents.

Merchant Wholesalers

Merchant wholesalers are the largest single group of wholesalers, comprising about two-thirds of all wholesalers. Of these, approximately one-third are connected with agribusiness wholesaling. Half of the total business volume is derived from agribusiness products and almost one-half of all employees are involved in agribusiness.

Manufacturers' Sales Branches

Manufacturers' sales branches and offices, which number about one-tenth of all wholesalers, make up the second largest wholesaling group. About 30 per cent of these establishments carry on agribusiness activities. About one-fourth of the total annual sales are derived from agribusiness. About one-third of the persons employed in these branches and offices are involved in agribusiness functions.

Agents and Brokers

Agents and brokers represent the third largest group, accounting for about 10 per cent of all wholesalers, of which some 42 per cent participate in agribusiness. Sixty-two per cent of the total sales can be attributed to agribusiness, and over 55 per cent of the persons employed are involved in agribusiness operations.

The modern *food broker* is a marketing specialist who has become an integral part of the gigantic food and grocery industry in the United States. Devoting his full time to the needs of his market for the products of his principals, the food broker must be the best informed and the most capable food industry representative in that market.

His business is soliciting buyers (wholesalers, chains, supermarkets, industrial users, etc.) and assisting in the negotiation of sellers' (canners, processors, packers, manufacturers, etc.) sales of food and grocery products to buyers in his trade area: (1) in the name of the seller, (2) for the account of the seller, (3) subject to the control of the seller and (4) for compensation in the form of commissions or brokerage based on sales results paid to him exclusively by the sellers. The food broker does not buy and sell in his own name and does not have custody or possession of or other control over the products sold by his sellers.

The food broker legally is an agent of his supplier principals and, as an agent, he acts on behalf of each of his principals without being subject to the control or direct supervision on the manner and details of performance under the sales representation agreement between the parties. The broker is subject to control of his principals as to results but has freedom of judgment and discretion within the terms of the agreement to accomplish the desired results. Being an independent contractor, he engages and controls his own employees and receives his compensation in the form of a commission or brokerage paid by the seller. A food broker is free to represent any number of principals subject to agreement governing the relationship and pursuant to the position of trust he holds with each principal. He must at all times be loyal and faithfully serve each of his principals.

WHOLESALER AFFILIATIONS

When classified by the affiliation of wholesalers with their retailers, wholesaling can be divided into at least three groups: (1) co-op wholesaling, where the retail stores own the wholesaler; (2) voluntary wholesaling, where retail stores work with a wholesaler but have no ownership interest; and (3) unaffiliated or independent merchant wholesaling.

Co-op and Voluntary Wholesalers

Two most significant steps among merchant wholesalers have been the development of (1) the co-op wholesaler and (2) the voluntary wholesaler. With (1), the retailers own the wholesale facility, while with (2), the retailers voluntarily affiliate and agree to work with the wholesaler. These developments have led to closer ties between wholesale and retail units, to decreased wholesaling costs and to improved distributing efficiency and have permitted smaller retail units to survive longer than they would have otherwise. About three-fourths of the total wholesale grocery volume is handled by co-op and voluntary units combined.

Both co-op and voluntary wholesalers provide a number of special services for their retail members, including: (1) merchandising bulletins, (2) equipment procurement assistance, (3) store design and layout assistance, (4) employee training programs, (5) accounting services, (6) advertising, (7) financing assistance, (8) group buying of perishables, (9) merchandising aids and (10) store-level management aids.

It is estimated that there are about 170 co-op retailer-owned grocery wholesalers with about 34,000 member–stores, or an average of 200 grocery store members per co-op wholesaler. There are an estimated 505 voluntary wholesalers.

Independent Merchant Wholesalers

A wholesaler's chief service is to supply the retailer with merchandise. This involves assembling, from a wide variety of sources, the products which the retailer needs to supply his own customer trade. In attempting to make these products available at all times, and in order to do this economically and promptly, the wholesaler buys large quantities of goods and stores them at his warehouse. Here he divides them into small lots of the variety and quantity desired by his individual store customers, and then he delivers them to the retailers. He commonly sells for credit and frequently advises customers on suitable stocks to carry and on up-to-date merchandising methods.

The wholesaler makes it unnecessary for the manufacturer to assume the costly fixed investment of direct sales branches or to carry a large staff of salesmen on the payroll. The wholesaler is a specialist in his field, having close contact with the necessary retail outlets. Since most companies produce a small number of products, their sales to the retailer would be small and the goods would have a high selling cost per unit. The wholesaler can spread his costs over a large number of items, with a resultant selling cost per unit lower than that which the manufacturer normally could achieve.

With very few exceptions, the wholesaler generally must build or rent a warehouse, the design and dimensions of which are governed by the bulkiness, variety and assortment of products that the wholesaler finds necessary to handle and market and by the volume of business expected.

When the wholesaler acquires a warehouse, he must install proper equipment and then order merchandise in bulk from a large number of manufacturers. By handling a heterogeneous assortment of goods, the wholesaler is able to spread the cost of operation, thus reducing the cost of handling each individual product. For example, a tobacco

Figure 7-1. The wholesaler performs a valuable function as an intermediary between the producer or manufacturer and the retailer. (Courtesy, Midcontinent Farmers Association, Columbia, Mo.)

wholesaler, in addition to cigarettes, cigars and tobaccos, will sell pipes and smokers' articles and candy and confectionery products as well as a wide variety of sundries.

To keep the "pipeline" to retail outlets filled, a variety of distributive techniques are employed, and several different wholesaling methods may be used. There is full-line service wholesaling, with salesmen making regular calls, trucking facilities assuring timely deliveries and wholesalers providing credit extension services. Another type of wholesaling includes specialty lines which confine activities to a few merchandise lines where expertness and specialization are developed. "Cash-and-carry" wholesaling is a newer type which eliminates trucking costs and outside sales overhead. It is especially successful in concentrated population areas and where numerous retailers are clustered. Another type of wholesaling is known as "institutional." Firms so engaged specialize in servicing hotels, cafes, restaurants, hospitals and related types of establishments where food is served. Institutional wholesalers specialize in the distribution of large-sized containers at lower cost per unit and counsel on food preparation, menu planning and mass-feeding problems. "Drop shippers" are wholesalers who obtain orders from retailers and forward them to manufacturers, requesting the latter to make shipments directly to retailers. "Rack jobbers" are wholesalers who supply items for side-line operations of retailers, installing display racks or fixtures, replenishing them and billing the retailers for the amounts sold.

VERTICAL INTEGRATION AND THE INDEPENDENT MERCHANT WHOLESALER

The independent merchant wholesaler is being encroached upon by both sides: manufacturers seek to bypass him by establishing their own sales branches and warehouses; retailers, such as the chain and department stores, seek to deal directly with the manufacturers.

The first of these forces began when large manufacturers achieved varying degrees of success from large-scale consumer advertising. The rapid growth of point-of-purchase promotion and the realization of the strategic position of the retailer in dealing with the public were evidences of a desire by manufacturers for greater control over the marketing of their products through manufacturers' branches or sales offices, thus bypassing the independent wholesaler. Thus, integration of production and marketing functions by manufacturers has become one source of competition to the wholesaler.

The other main source of competition has arisen through vertical integration primarily by the large retail chain organizations seeking greater control over their supply sources. This step is comparable to manufacturers seeking greater control of their sales or distribution.

TRENDS IN WHOLESALING

The more important trends in agribusiness wholesaling are: (1) retail food stores have integrated into wholesaling by either the corporate or the co-op method, (2) processors have integrated into wholesaling by developing sales branches, (3) old-line independent wholesalers have lost ground to these two newer organizations, (4) some wholesalers have integrated into food retailing by co-ordinating retailers under a so-called voluntary plan and (5) newer, specialty-type wholesalers have developed.

Independent wholesalers selling to food retailers, for example, are constantly losing sales as retailing itself becomes more concentrated and integrated. General-line wholesalers have, in many cases, given way to specialty-line wholesalers, who, with the advent of specialization and servicing programs, have had a competitive advantage over the general-line wholesalers.

In general, trends point to fewer but larger-sized wholesalers in command of increased capital and management resources.

●   ●   ●

In the next chapter, agribusiness retailing is discussed.

TOPICS FOR DISCUSSION

1. Define wholesaling.
2. Name and discuss the three types of wholesalers.
3. Distinguish between co-op and voluntary wholesalers.
4. Describe the independent wholesaler's method of operation.
5. Discuss some of the trends in wholesaling.

SELECTED REFERENCES

1. Cain, J. L., and A. A. Ahern, Jr., *Regional Changes in Food Wholesaling in the U.S.*, Md. Agr. Exp. Sta. MP 849, College Park, Apr. 1974.
2. Forte, Darlene J., *Wholesaling*, SBA–Bibliography 55, Washington, D.C., Sept. 1973.
3. Jenkins, C. H., *Modern Warehouse Management*, McGraw-Hill Book Company, New York, 1968.

4. Lewis, Edwin H., *Marketing Channels: Structure and Strategy,* McGraw-Hill Book Company, New York, 1968.
5. Mallen, Bruce E., *The Marketing Channel,* John Wiley & Sons, Inc., New York, 1967.

8

Agribusiness Retailing

Agribusiness retailing involves those establishments selling groceries, prepared foods, soft drinks, tobacco and tobacco products, alcoholic beverages, floral products, clothing, shoes, furniture and home furnishings (from agriculturally derived products).

RETAIL GROCERY STORES

The retail grocery is the end of the marketing channel where the products of farm and factory, in a multitude of forms, are placed before the customers. The total number of grocery stores is about 203,000.

The basic task of the food retailer is to provide service. He has to estimate his customers' wants and acquire and price at competitive levels the 3,000 to 10,000 items that the customers might desire. He must display the items attractively—in refrigerators or on suitable fixtures. His store must be handy for his customers. He must provide parking space and other conveniences. The food retailer has to select, train and supervise store personnel. He must advertise often. One big job is to receive the merchandise into the store, prepare it for display, price it, place it on the shelves and finally check it out. Also there are the major tasks of providing the capital, keeping records of transactions and paying operating expenses. The retailer's efficiency in those tasks affects the prices the customers must pay.

Chains Versus Other Grocery Stores

A grocery store "chain" commonly refers to a company operating 11 or more stores. Chains now account for about 54 per cent of present food store sales as against 37 per cent in 1948.

Contrary to popular opinion, the biggest chains have not increased their share of total grocery sales. In fact, the nationwide chains were slow to adopt supermarkets and did so only after their competitors demonstrated their advantages.

The smaller or regional chains have grown more rapidly; therefore, the total chain store share has risen moderately, suggesting that the smaller chains with proximity to local markets and with merchandising flexibility have done remarkably well.

Affiliated stores have grown rapidly, their share of the total grocery business rising from 29 per cent in 1948 to almost 44 per cent at present. They include voluntary groups (wholesaler sponsored) and cooperative groups (retail store sponsored). The share of the unaffiliated independents has declined drastically, or from 34 per cent in 1948 to 2 per cent at present.

Many of the small grocery stores, unaffiliated with a voluntary or co-op wholesaler, are finding it difficult to remain in business. Retail food sales are being made increasingly through larger, well-situated and well-stocked stores.

Vertical Integration

Vertical integration into processing by large retail grocery firms has been most noticeable for milk and other dairy products, bakery products, and coffee. There are also many examples of retail firms establishing their own buying stations for assembling and grading fresh fruit, vegetables and eggs. Some retail firms have integrated into slaughtering and packing operations, but this type of activity has been most erratic. It is notable that much of the integration by retailers back to the assembly and processing levels has occurred in products where there is legal minimum pricing, e.g., milk, or in products with relatively high costs of assembly, processing and/or wholesale delivery.

Horizontal Integration

The entry of retail food firms in recent years into new types of retailing ventures such as discount houses, department stores and drug stores is an attempt to employ their cash flow in areas of opportunity other than supermarkets. One can expect this development to continue in the future as food retailers gain experience and expertise in the fields of retailing still new to them. Retailers are also expanding their merchandising lines into nonfoods within food stores.

Another development in horizontal integration in grocery retailing is the superstore consisting of about 30,000 square feet with relatively large food and nonfood departments handling about 10,000 items and having sales of about $150,000 per week. In these stores are found delicatessens and bakeries as well as household and other consumer products. These superstores are noted for their longer opening hours and higher product turnovers.

Generic or Nonbranded Foods

The development of generic or nonbranded foods and household items is proceeding rapidly. By offering nonbranded products, retailers are passing on the economies of large-scale purchasing plus the elimination of advertising and other expenses to the consumer of food products, sometimes 10 to 35 per cent below nationally advertised products. Generic items allow the customer to pay less for items which are, in most cases, equal in utility to higher-priced, more-advertised products. Generic product quality may be more variable than that of branded products.

Electronic Applications at Grocery Stores

Electronic checkout in supermarkets has attracted considerable attention in the grocery industry in recent years. Electronic checkout is a generic term for several different systems that electronically read item price, ring up the sale amount on a transaction terminal (electronic cash register), print a detailed sales tape, update inventory records and keep track of total sales volume. The typical electronic checkout system utilizes a high-speed optical scanner using a laser light source to read the Universal Product Code (UPC). The UPC is a series of bars representing a 10-digit code that identifies each product with no duplication among the thousands of items merchandised in retail food stores. The scanner reads and transfers product information to the store's own in-house mini-computer and instantaneously searches its memory for the price which has been established by headquarters and fed into the computer's memory, displays the price so that customers can monitor their orders as they are rung up, rings up the price on the checkout transaction terminal and prints a cash register tape that includes the product's description and price. The computer also updates store inventories, keeps track of individual items and store sales volume, remembers whether the item is taxable and whether food stamps can be used.

Potential benefits to the consumer can be summarized as faster checkout, fewer errors in price ring ups, detailed sales receipt, greater accuracy on multiple-priced items and easier check cashing. Consumer complaints have focused on the initial cost of the electronic checkout system. Consumers fear that savings will not be passed on to them and that supermarkets may misuse the computer to cheat them. They don't like the elimination of price marking on each item and the centralization of credit information. In addition, the Retail Clerk's Union is concerned about what the impact electronic checkout will have on membership levels.[1]

Another application of electronics to grocery retailing is a proposal which envisions a "warehouse-to-door" food system in which shoppers either phone orders to a warehouse or place them through an electronic terminal in the home, tied in—possibly through telephone lines—to the store's computer.

Overall costs could be reduced because stores would not have to be built in convenient, usually expensive, locations. The use of cable-television technology, which has two-way communication potential, and the use of automated order filling would reduce labor costs and offset the necessary capital investment.

A second concept is the automated store, which places merchandise "behind the scenes" by centering food shopping around comput-

---

[1]McGinnis, M. A., and L. L. Gardner, "Electronic Checkout and Supermarket Sales Volume," *Akron Business and Economic Review*, Akron, O., Summer 1976, p. 32.

er-controlled selection and a mechanized conveyer-belt "collection and front-of-store delivery system."[2]

PERFORMANCE OF THE RETAIL GROCERY TRADE

One evidence of good performance in the retail grocery business is that high quality foods are abundant in all seasons and are available in

Figure 8-1. The modern food store is bountifully supplied with products, both domestic and foreign. (Courtesy, *IGA Grocergram*, Chicago, Ill.)

---

[2]Greenberger, Robert, "Electronics Promises Grocery Store Efficiency," *Supermarket News*, New York, Apr. 21, 1975.

great variety and in convenient forms. The retail sector has proved to be an active innovator and seems alert in applying new technology. The percentage of consumer income spent on food has declined despite the increase in the number of meals eaten away from home and a variety of added services. Marketing margins, the spread between retail and farm prices, have risen at about the same rate as the general price level. Profits are down from the immediate postwar levels and appear to be moderate. Representative food processors make about 2.5 per cent on sales while wholesalers and retailers average about 1.5 per cent. Profits of all three groups average about 10 to 12 per cent on stockholders' equities. Finally, specific studies of market performance indicate no significant exercise of market power.

There is one practice in the retail food store business, however, which appears unwholesome, namely, the excessive use of advertising, promotional gimmicks, games of chance, trading stamps, etc. Customer traffic is attracted to stores using these devices, but if all stores adopt them, no sales advantages will be realized, and the costs of retailing groceries will go up by the 2 to 4 per cent necessary to cover these promotional expenditures.

OTHER TYPES OF FOOD RETAILERS

In addition to retail grocery stores, there are other types of retail food establishments, which are discussed in the following sections.

Convenience Food Stores

This kind of small store does most of its business when the super-markets are closed, concentrating on essential items and operating at a relatively low sales break-even point. In some areas convenience stores are forcing bigger competitors to stay open nights and Sundays. In some instances, however, large operators are establishing convenience stores of their own so that their big stores can maintain profitable store hours and continue to capitalize on their "low-price" image.

There are over 15,000 convenience food stores in the United States accounting for about 5 per cent of total grocery sales and with a steadily rising share of grocery sales. These stores average 2,500 square feet and handle about 1,500 items.

Specialty Food Stores

Food stores which specialize in selling one or a few food items include: meat markets; fish and seafood markets; farmers' markets; vegetable markets; roadside markets; candy, nut and confectionery stores; dairy product stores; retail bakeries; and egg and poultry dealers, among others.

In general, the number of such stores is declining because of the advent of larger grocery stores and the convenience food stores along with the development of fast-food eating establishments.

Discount Food Stores

In recent years, another type of retailer, the discount food store, has entered the food distribution field. It occupies from 15,000 to 50,000 square feet of floor space, offers a minimum of services, uses less advertising, operates at low cost and prices food at a minimum markup.

Another aspect of the discount food store is that its environment resembles a warehouse where bulk or carton sales of merchandise are made. Customers mark prices, bag and carry their merchandise themselves and accept fewer services and fewer lines of merchandise in return for lower prices, sometimes as much as 20 to 25 per cent below regular supermarket prices. Reports place the retail sales volume of food discounters at about 10 per cent of total retail food sales.

Automatic Merchandisers

There are over 5 million vending machines in the United States.

In the past few years, the vending industry has broadened its merchandising base considerably. Machines now sell everything from nylon stockings to a complete lunch.

Trends in this industry are also in the direction of greater merchandise assortments—within the operational capabilities of available machines situated at more diverse locations.

Eating and Drinking Places

These establishments, which number about 350,000 (based on

available data), include: restaurants; cafeterias; refreshment places; cafes; snack and sandwich shops; hamburger shops; department, drug and variety store lunch counters; supper clubs; ice cream or ice milk stores; fried chicken shops; doughnut shops; and drinking places.

In recent years, such places have gained considerably in their share of the food market, because more people travel and thus eat out, more women are employed outside the home and increasing incomes provide means for people to eat away from home.

Small eating places are declining, while much larger establishments are expanding their share of the market. Chains operating 11 or more eating establishments are increasing their share due to better management, planning, franchising and financing operations on a nationwide or regional basis.

Institutional Food Facilities

Institutional food facilities include all types of eating establishments found in schools, universities and colleges; military posts; prisons; hospitals; plants and factories; transportation media; nursing homes; business offices; golf and country clubs; civic, social and fraternal group centers; sports camps and arenas; and rooming and boarding houses.

This type of food marketing is growing rapidly because of increases in school and college attendance; incarceration of persons; feeding-in operations at industrial plants and factories; the proportion of the population in nursing homes and hospitals; and the standards of living, which lead to increased eating-out expenditures, travel, vacations and sightseeing.

For example, the nation's schools provide an important market for food. During a school year, foods move through lunchrooms in about 80 per cent of all schools in the United States.

The National School Lunch Program encourages schools to serve nutritious, moderately priced lunches. Participating schools agree to serve a lunch which meets about one-third of the daily needs of growing children. The meal must include a protein-rich food, a generous serving of fruits and vegetables, bread and butter and a half-pint of milk. Schools also agree to provide lunches either free or at a reduced price to children from low-income families.

Franchising

The franchise system of distributing goods and services has come of age since World War II. It employs new organizational and marketing techniques which are changing basic distribution patterns and should be of particular interest to almost anyone looking for opportunities in a small business.

In its simplest terms, a franchise is a contract between an independent businessman (the franchisee) and a market supplier of goods or services (the franchisor) in which the businessman is given the exclusive right to sell these goods or services in a specified geographical area. The franchisee has the benefit of the parent company's reputation and established name in addition to its experience and help in choosing a location, financing, marketing, record keeping and promoting products. In return, the franchise holder usually makes a financial investment in the business and agrees to pay a commission on gross sales and to purchase supplies or equipment from the parent company or consents to a combination of these possibilities.

Franchising in agribusiness product marketing has been dramatic as attested to by the development in fried chicken restaurants; hamburger, fish and seafood establishments; doughnut and ice cream shops; and pizza places, among others.

Such establishments are well known throughout the United States through rather heavy advertising schedules. Firms of this type locate near or on highly traveled roadways, in suburbs and in close proximity to centers of population and are easily accessible by car.

Fast-food establishment franchises in the United States number over 47,000 with sales amounting to around $15 billion.

OTHER AGRIBUSINESS RETAILING

Besides food sales, agribusiness retailing also involves the sales of alcoholic beverages, tobacco products, clothing, shoes, millinery, furniture and home furnishings and floral products. These products are, in the main, derived variously from grain, tobacco, cotton, wool, mohair, hides, skins, feathers, wood and nursery and ornamental plants.

As in other lines of retailing, smaller stores are declining in number and losing in their share of the market. Chains operating 11 or

more retail establishments are gaining in their market share. Also, retailers affiliated with wholesalers are faring relatively better than those
that are unaffiliated.

Another factor affecting sales is location. Stores located in downtown
areas of cities have lost sales relative to suburban stores. The difficulty of
finding parking space and the general deterioration of downtown locations have affected seriously stores so located.

TRENDS IN AGRIBUSINESS RETAILING

The more important trends in agribusiness retailing are:
1. Fewer but larger stores under multi-unit management.
2. Increased affiliation of independent retail stores with wholesalers.
3. Increased co-op organization of wholesalers by retailers.
4. Increased development of suburban shopping centers.
5. Increased use of store labels or private brands on merchandise.
6. Increased use of computers in store management decisions.
7. More vertical integration by retailers into wholesaling and manufacturing.
8. Expansion by food retailers into nonfood lines.
9. Growth in automatic merchandising through vending machines.
10. Increased eating-out expenditures by consumers.

● ◗ ●

In the next chapter, the role of the consumer in agribusiness is
discussed.

TOPICS FOR DISCUSSION

1. Discuss grocery store retailing.
2. Are the chain stores gaining in their share of the market relative to
   other types of stores?
3. Discuss other types of food retailing.
4. What are some of the major trends in agribusiness retailing?

SELECTED REFERENCES

1. Cain, J. L., and J. J. Ahern, Jr., *Structural Changes in Food Processing, Wholesaling and Retailing,* Md. Agr. Exp. Sta. MP 851. College Park, Jun. 1974.
2. Dwoskin, P. B., *Foreign and Domestic Prospects for the U.S. Fast-Food Franchise Industry,* ERS, A. E. Rept. 358, U.S. Dept. of Agriculture, Washington, D.C., Nov. 1976.
3. Garoian, Leon, "Grocery Retailing," *Market Structure in the Agricultural Industries,* Iowa State University Press, Ames, Jul. 1966.
4. Nelson, Paul E., Jr., "Price Competition Among Retail Food Stores," *Journal of Farm Economics,* Aug. 1966, p. 172.
5. Pfeiffer, Paul L., *Retailing,* SBA–Bibliography 10, Washington, D.C., Jul. 1975.
6. Schneidau, R. E., and R. D. Knutson, "Price Discrimination in the Food Industry," *Journal of Farm Economics,* Dec. 1969, p. 1143.
7. Stout, T. T., and R. C. Doehler, *Some Conduct and Performance Aspects of Food Specials Retailing,* Ohio Agr. Exp. Sta. Bul. 1082, Wooster, Dec. 1975.
8. Udell, G. G., *The Franchise Agreement Handbook,* Ind. Agr. Exp. Sta. Res. Bul. 889, Lafayette, May 1973.

9

Agribusiness and
the Consumer

The final objective of all production is consumption. The consumer, in a free market economy, is the object of all efforts devoted to production and distribution of products and services. The consumer, with money in hand, holds the votes by which goods are selected or rejected. In the final analysis, therefore, the consumer is supreme in a free market economy. In a government-controlled economy, such as under communism, the consumer is often ignored in favor of what the bureaucrats decide the consumer needs. Needless to say, their decisions are often wrong, because the consumer has complex wishes and desires.

PROFILE OF THE U.S. CONSUMING POPULATION

The U.S. population is becoming increasingly urbanized, with almost two-thirds living in big cities or nearby suburbs.

There is an upgrading of workers, with more people in professional and technical occupations but fewer in manual trades.

Incomes of $10,000 a year now are common with two of every four families earning that much. A decade ago, only 1 in 10 had an equivalent income.

More education and rising incomes create both an expanding demand for goods and services and an upgrading in consumer tastes.

Each year the population grows by between 2.5 and 3 million

people. This rate of growth has slowed in recent years, due largely to a declining trend in the birth rate.

As the population has shifted from rural to urban and suburban, incomes have risen; more homemakers have become gainfully employed outside the home; work has become lighter, permitting more leisure time; knowledge about and developments in nutrition have increased; obesity has become a concern; and technological progress has made many more foods available. These factors will likely continue in the years ahead, causing even more modifications in diets, family living and family spending.

FOOD AND FIBER EXPENDITURES

Consumers in the United States spend about 30 per cent of their total disposable income on *agribusiness* products. The allocation of these expenditures is about as follows:

Item	Percentage of agribusiness expenditures
Food, all	61.7
Clothing	16.5
Alcoholic beverages	8.8
Tobacco products	5.9
Furniture and home furnishings	4.4
Shoes	2.1
Floral products	0.6
Total	100.0

Over the past decade or so, the percentage of disposable income spent for food and clothing by U.S. consumers has declined, due to higher incomes of which proportionally less is spent on food and clothing and relatively more on other goods and services. Also, the retail price per unit for food and clothing has not risen so much as for other goods and services. Thus, these two large components of the agribusiness complex command less of the consumers' disposable income percentagewise than formerly. However, aggregate dollar expenditures for food and clothing have risen and will continue to increase.

For comparative purposes, it is noted that consumers now spend relatively more of their income for housing, transportation, recreation, medical care, personal care and education. Also, the amounts set aside for savings have increased.

However, no two wage earners spend their money in exactly the same way, and yet there are predictable patterns of expenditures for families in various income categories.

Studies have shown that families with low incomes spend most or all of their money for necessities—food, shelter and clothing. Families with high incomes spend more for these necessities. They buy more food, bigger houses, more clothes and more services. They eat out more and shift away from bulky carbohydrates, eating more high-protein foods, fruits and vegetables. Those with high incomes probably "waste" more food than those with less money, and yet, as a proportion of total income, families with high incomes spend less for necessities than do low-income families.

A 19th century Prussian statistician, Ernest Engel, was the first to describe this behavior pattern, which has since been known as "Engel's law of consumption": As family incomes rise, the proportion spent for food declines. Or, as incomes rise, food purchases increase, but not so fast as income. If incomes fall, the proportion spent for food increases.

All food products are not affected in the same way by increases or decreases in incomes. Consumption of some foods increases as incomes rise. These items are called *superior* foods, which has nothing to do with whether they are nutritionally good. The term merely indicates how a change in income affects consumption.

Some other foods are termed *inferior,* which means consumption decreases as incomes increase. Those foods whose consumption is not affected by changes in income are termed *neutral.*

Family disposable income has been trending upward for a good many years. In addition, there is a growing proportion of the population in the middle-income group. These two changes mean that those who produce and sell *inferior* foods will find it increasingly difficult to expand the market for their products.

Of course, there are other factors which affect the market for food and fiber. One of these is the *location* of consumers, i.e., whether they are in urban or rural areas or in warm or cold climates.

Family *size* and *composition* by age and sex are additional factors.

Occupational characteristics have a bearing on food and fiber markets. A case in point is the decline of both farm and blue-collar workers and the incline of white-collar workers.

National origins and *religion* are also significant. These factors, e.g., Jewish and Catholic days of obligation, affect variously the demands for food and clothing.

Educational level of consumers is still another factor, although it is quite correlated with *income.*

PROFILE OF FOOD CONSUMPTION

With a U.S. population of around 220 million and each person consuming 3 plates of food per day, a total daily serving of 660 million plates of food is required. On an annual basis, this amounts to a total of 241 billion plates of food. On a poundage basis, each American consumes about 1,500 pounds annually or a total of 330 billion pounds. These data indicate the tremendous size of the food business and the enormous responsibility which rests on food producers and marketers in the United States.

The American consumer is getting the best buy in the world in food and fibers. Most people of the world spend half their disposable income for food. On the average, Americans spend only 18 to 20 per cent and get a better diet and more built-in services, accounting for a larger farm-retail spread.

It is projected that Americans will eat relatively more beef, chicken, turkey, fish, cheese, margarine, Irish potatoes, vegetable shortening, fruits and vegetables.

It is expected that Americans will eat about the same amounts of veal, pork, frozen dairy products, butter, strawberries, dry edible beans, sugar, coffee and ice cream.

Americans will eat relatively less lamb and mutton, eggs, fluid milk and cream, evaporated and condensed milk, lard, wheat and flour, sweet potatoes and syrup.

Food Stamp Program

Persons are eligible to participate in the program if costs of the foods included in USDA's Thrifty Food Plan exceed 30 per cent of the family income. As the cost of the foods in the plan rises, adjustments are made in the value of the coupon allotment a family receives. However, because eligibility is based on the cost of the plan as a percentage of family income, as that cost rises, so does the maximum level of income a family may earn and be eligible to participate.

Persons on welfare and on the Supplemental Security Income Program are automatically eligible for food stamps. The food stamp program has been liberalized over the years to an extent that no needy person in the United States is excluded from food stamp benefits. However, not all needy persons participate in the program. Some needy persons cannot get transportation to food stamp offices while others choose not to receive such benefits.

ECONOMICS OF FOOD BUYING

There are many misconceptions about food buying and the value of food. Not all high-priced food is of high quality or is highly nutritious. For example, cooked oatmeal, which is very low-cost, is highly nutritious and costs far less per serving than widely advertised cold cereals. However, because housewives are pressed for time in the morning, many cold cereals are served. On the other hand, price-specials and so-called bargains are not always bargains. Whether or not a food represents a bargain is dependent on many things.

1. *Is it offered at a conveniently located store?* Money saved on a food item at a store some distance away might be less than the amount of money used for the gasoline or bus fare it takes to get there and back. Even if the bargain represents a real saving in money, the busy homemaker may find it too costly in time to shop around for food bargains and should choose a convenient and generally low-cost store and stick to it.

2. *Will the family eat and enjoy it?* No food is a bargain if the family will not eat it. However, a little persistence on the part of the meal planner may turn a disliked food into a family favorite. A different method of preparation or special care in serving may do the trick. Ideas, particularly of children, as to what is good to eat change as the food becomes more familiar, as it is accepted by others around them or for no apparent reason at all.

3. *Is it packaged in a quantity that meets family needs?* Large cans and packages may represent a saving over small containers. If, how-

ever, the large container means leftovers that eventually are discarded, it is no bargain.

4. *Can it be properly stored at home until used?* Very large quantities can often be purchased at low-unit cost—a quarter of beef, a bushel of apples or a case of green beans. If such items can be properly stored to prevent spoilage and are not in such large quantities that the family will tire of them before they are used up, they represent a real saving.

5. *Does the homemaker have time and skill to prepare it?* Few homemakers are interested in preparing all foods from "scratch," even if it means money saved. To most, making bread at home, for example, is too time-consuming to be worth the pennies saved. The store offers more and more foods that are prepared or partially prepared for the homemaker's convenience. The cost of this preparation sometimes, but not always, adds to the price of the food item. The homemaker who knows how much more she pays for frozen French fried potatoes than for those she prepares at home is able to make a wise decision as to whether the time she saves is worth the extra amount paid.

6. *How does its cost compare with the cost of other foods of similar food value?* The moneywise shopper knows which kinds or groups of foods go together to make up a good diet and economizes by selecting best buys from each of these groups.[1]

DEMAND FOR FIBERS

The demand for fibers is closely related to population, incomes, style trends and methods of living. For example, the large increase in spare time, travel and recreation causes greater demand for casual and sports clothes but less demand for suits, hats and more formal attire. There are numerous other examples of style trends. Income effects are noticeable on the market for furs and unusual leather goods. The increasing proportion of elderly people in the U.S. population causes more demand for less-formal attire for the older-aged group and the decreasing proportion of farmers and farm people in the U.S. population means less demand for work clothes.

---

[1]Peterkin, Betty, *Your Money's Worth in Foods*, H & G Bul. No. 183, U.S. Dept. of Agriculture, Washington, D.C., June 1977.

COMPUTERS IN THE HOME

The advent of computers in household management is proceeding steadily. One of the first applications of computers was the banking and credit functions related to household finance. Other developing applications are projected to include preparing income tax reports, planning menus, compiling shopping lists, filing recipes and controlling thermostats.

CONSUMER PROBLEMS

Consumers are not without problems, even in an affluent society. Because they have discretionary income, consumers attract greater sales efforts in the form of fancier packages, advertising, frills and merchandising gimmicks. Accurate labeling and grading of consumer products are another problem.

Lack of Organization

Consumers, on the whole, are neither articulate nor organized. The producer can and does combine with others to further his interests, making his demands effective both through the price system and through legislation. Through organization, labor forces its wishes upon producers. As individuals, consumers may loudly protest against price or quality, but collectively they do very little.

The organization of local, state and national housewife and consumer councils appears to be a much needed step in providing consumers with a more active voice in economic affairs.

It is important also to realize that the consumer possesses no yardstick with which to measure his wants or the efficiency of his "plant." The home is too small a unit to operate with anything like the same efficiency as that of an industrial plant. In a factory, machines may operate 24 hours a day, while in the home, a piece of equipment—the vacuum cleaner or washing machine—may be used but a few minutes each day. Under such limitations the household cannot hope to have guides and measurements to assist in the study of consumption that a factory does.

Understanding Consumer Credit

Consumer credit is a service with a price that should be examined carefully. Many people do not know what they pay for credit. Rates vary considerably from dealer to dealer, depending upon the size of the purchase, the credit reputation of the buyer, the length of the loan period—even the laws of the particular state.

Instead of buying on an installment plan, it is often possible to borrow money from a credit union, from a bank or elsewhere at cheaper rates, pay cash for the purchase and repay the money faster than would be possible under the contract offered by the dealer.

An understanding of how to figure interest costs and rates can save many dollars over a period of years.

When buying on a monthly installment plan, the following formula may be used in figuring true annual interest:

$$ir = \frac{I}{\frac{1}{2}P} \times \frac{N}{Y} \times \frac{1}{(N+1)}$$

ir = true annual interest rate
I   = total finance charges or interest
P   = principal borrowed
N   = total number of payments made
Y   = number of years of loan

As an example, assume appliances are purchased for $1,000 with a down payment of $100 and $900 to be financed monthly over a two-year period for total interest charges of $160. The interest rate is calculated as follows:

$$ir = \frac{\$160}{(\frac{1}{2})(\$900)} \times \frac{24}{2} \times \frac{1}{25}$$

$$ir = \frac{\$160}{\$450} \times \frac{12}{1} \times \frac{1}{25} = \frac{\$1,920}{11,250}$$

$$ir = 17.07\%$$

Consumer Nutrition Education

It has been suggested that new nutrition education should be a broad-based long-term venture both diet and health oriented. It should be based on the most accurate and up-to-date scientific knowledge and specifically designed to meet the needs and expectations of consumers—motivating and equipping them to make informed choices. Consumer nutrition education should be distinguished from media advertising of a firm's products because such advertising is aimed mainly at sales promotion rather than to the education of consumers about the nutritive values of its products.

● ● ●

In the next chapter, the relationship of government to agribusiness is considered.

TOPICS FOR DISCUSSION

1. What is the final objective of all production?
2. Present a profile of the U.S. consuming population.
3. Discuss the trends in consumer expenditures.
4. Present a profile of food consumption.
5. Discuss some of the problems faced by consumers and how they may be remedied.

SELECTED REFERENCES

1. Armstrong, Jan, and J. N. Uhl, "Consumer Education Programs in the U.S.," *Journal of Home Economics,* Oct. and Nov. 1971.
2. George, P. S., and G. A. King, *Consumer Demand for Food Commodities in the United States with Projections for 1980,* University of California, Giannini Foundation Monograph 26, Berkeley, Mar. 1971.
3. Handy, C. R., and Martin Pfaff, *Consumer Satisfaction With Food Products and Marketing Services,* ERS, A. E. Rept. 281, U.S. Dept. of Agriculture, Washington, D.C., Mar. 1975.
4. Kass, B. L., *Understanding Truth in Lending,* SBA–SMA 139, Washington, D.C., Jul. 1977.
5. Kinsey, Jean, "Consumer Movement and Farm and Food Policy," *Minnesota Agricultural Economist,* Minn. Agr. Ext. Serv., St. Paul, Oct. 1977.
6. Lane, Sylvia, "Economics of Consumer Class Actions," *Journal of Consumer Affairs,* Summer 1973, p. 13.
7. Niss, J., *Consumer Economics,* Prentice-Hall, Inc., Englewood Cliffs, N.J., 1974.

8. Padberg, D. I., "Consumer Protection for a Modern Industrialized Food System," *American Journal of Agricultural Economics,* Dec. 1970, p. 821.
9. Peterkin, Betty, *Your Money's Worth in Foods,* ARS, H&G Bul. 183, U.S. Dept. of Agriculture, Washington, D.C., Jun. 1977.
10. Staff, *The Consumer Information Catalog,* General Services Adm., Washington, D.C., 1977.
11. Staff, *Directory of Federal Consumer Offices,* Office of Consumer Affairs, Dept. of HEW, Washington, D.C., Nov. 1977.
12. Staff, *Food Consumption, Prices and Expenditures,* ERS–138, U.S. Dept. of Agriculture, Washington, D.C., Jan. 1977.
13. Staff, *Guide to Federal Consumer Services,* Dept. of HEW, Washington, D.C., Jan. 1976.
14. Uhl, J. N., and others, *Survey and Evaluation of Consumer Education Programs in the USA,* Purdue Research Foundation, Lafayette, Ind., Mar. 1970.

10

Agribusiness and
Government

Among the many types of government activities that affect agribusiness, those of greatest importance are: (1) government purchase of
commodities and services, (2) provision of basic information and (3)
regulation of agribusiness. Government price supports and acreage
control legislation are not considered.

Agribusiness is subject to many laws and regulations. There are
about 103,000 governmental units in the United States.

A. Local and State Governmental Authority

Where local and intrastate trade takes place, the jurisdiction of
nonfederal governmental units is recognized. However, local and federal laws often supplement each other in the regulation of, or service
to, agribusiness.

ANTITRUST LAWS

In addition to the federal antitrust laws, almost all of the states
have some type of state antitrust legislation. These laws are, on the
whole, poorly enforced because of low appropriations, the difficulty of
controlling out-of-state firms and the fact that the federal government
already has a large amount of resources in this area.

State antitrust laws differ somewhat from the federal statutes, putting less emphasis on controlling monopoly and more emphasis on regulating sales below cost and preventing unfair, discriminatory practices within specific industries.

CONSUMER PROTECTION

Local and state governments often have a series of laws which aim to protect the consumer, including checks of scales to insure proper weights and measures; health checkups of food establishment workers; sanitation regulations over food processing and dispensing establishments; inspection of meats, milk and certain other foods for wholesomeness; stream and air pollution regulations over businesses such as paper mills, feed mills and fertilizer factories, among many others. Municipal inspection may include surveys and examinations of supply warehouses, retail stores, delivery trucks, refrigeration systems and restaurants, hotel dining rooms and other public eating places.

LABOR LAWS

State governments, in conjunction with federal law, impose taxes on business to fund unemployment compensation. There are also various state laws dealing with the welfare of workers and conditions of employment. Of course, wherever agribusinesses operate in interstate commerce, federal laws apply.

WORKMEN'S COMPENSATION LAWS

Workmen's compensation laws insure prompt medical care and cash benefits to a worker when he is injured in connection with his job or cash benefits to his dependents if he is killed.

In over half of the states, these laws are mandatory for all employers in the types of businesses covered by the law. In the remaining states, an employer may elect not to come under the system, but in such cases he is not permitted to use the defense against workers' claims that he would have been able to use under common law. Employers meet the cost of workmen's compensation by insurance and usually have two choices—to insure with a private insurance company or to self-insure.

In some states there is a third choice—that of insuring with the state. In a few states, all employers are required to insure with the state.

LICENSES, PERMITS AND REGISTRATIONS

Most types of agribusinesses are subject to various licenses, permits and registrations issued by local, county, state and, in some cases, federal agencies.

Persons who peddle or sell produce house-to-house usually must obtain a permit from the local government. Better business bureaus also actively supervise business practices.

State governments may register and license wholesale produce dealers, poultry and egg dealers, milk plants and meat packing plants. The state may also require performance bonds.

MARKETING INFORMATION AND ASSISTANCE

State departments of agriculture often conduct market news services for various agricultural products in conjunction with the federal market news service.

Financial assistance in erecting agricultural marketing facilities is often provided by state agriculture departments.

Promotion of farm products by various state commissions is also found.

Enactment of state grading standards and regulations, in conjunction with federal standards, is often found for fruits, vegetables, meats, poultry and eggs. Also applicable are weights and measures regulations.

REGULATIONS OVER FARM INPUTS

Most states have programs aimed at evaluating the registration and labeling of seeds, feeds, fertilizers and other types of farm inputs, thus protecting the agricultural producer in his buying activities.

Regarding herd health, most states have brucellosis, pullorum, hog cholera and other livestock and poultry disease control programs administered by appropriate state agencies.

Plant disease control, nursery product inspection and pest control programs of various kinds are also administered in most states. Regulation of the use of agricultural chemicals is also widespread.

REGULATORY COMMISSIONS

The principal state regulatory commissions consist of those regulating the sale of corporate securities; the operation of intrastate motor carriers; the distribution of utility services, such as water, natural gas, electricity and telephone; and the operation of warehousing facilities, which includes the requiring of bonding of the operators and the proper conduct of storage operations for commodities, including: grains, cotton, tobacco and others.

Prominent in some states are milk marketing and pricing regulations which may go so far as to regulate the price of milk to farmers, handlers and consumers.

TAXES

Agribusinesses must comply with some or all of the following revenue and tax laws and regulations: (1) state corporation income tax; (2) state, county and local property taxes; (3) state, county and local sales taxes; (4) business permits, licenses or fees; (5) domestic franchise tax; (6) tax on vehicles, movables, inventories, etc.; (7) inspection and regulatory fees and reports; (8) payroll taxes; (9) excise taxes; (10) annual corporation or license fee; (11) state unemployment insurance tax; (12) state gasoline and fuel taxes; (13) highway use tax; (14) health and sanitation permits; (15) workmen's compensation; (16) gross receipts tax; (17) capital stock and stock transfer tax; (18) stock dividends tax; (19) severance taxes; and (20) chain store taxes.

States differ in their requirements; therefore, it is imperative that appropriate state statutes and legal counsel be consulted regarding these and other laws and regulations.

ZONING LAWS

Many local governments have zoning laws which regulate certain uses of property. For example, feed mills, meat packing plants, poultry slaughter plants and fertilizer plants, among others, may be subject to zoning regulations. Because of zoning regulations, care should be exercised before locating an agribusiness plant.

B. Federal Government Authority

As agribusiness operations have grown larger and expanded across state lines, the role of the federal government has increased. Various laws and regulations, classified by their functions, are presented.

CONSUMER FOOD PROGRAMS

Food Stamp Act

This act authorizes a food stamp program under which low-income persons may receive a coupon allotment for the purchase of foods from retail food stores.

National School Lunch Act

Under Sections 4 and 11, the act provides for measures to aid schools in establishing nonprofit lunch programs, to aid some students in receiving free or reduced-cost lunches and to "safeguard the health and well-being of the Nation's children and encourage the domestic consumption of nutritious agricultural commodities and other food."

CONSUMER PROTECTION

The U.S. consumer is protected from adulterated and poor quality foods and fibers by a series of local, state and federal regulatory and inspection laws.

Meat Inspection Act

This law requires federal inspection for wholesomeness of all meat and meat products prepared in plants that are engaged in interstate or foreign trade.

Poultry Products Inspection Act

This act requires federal inspection for wholesomeness of all poultry and poultry products processed in plants engaged in interstate or foreign commerce and of all imported poultry and poultry products.

Textile Fiber Products Identification

The U.S. Congress has enacted legislation dealing with textiles and furs:

1. The Wool Products Labeling Act of 1939.
2. The Fur Products Labeling Act of 1951.
3. The Flammable Fabrics Act of 1953 and 1967.
4. The Textile Fiber Products Identification Act of 1960.

The Federal Trade Commission's Division of Textiles and Furs enforces these acts and has the responsibility to inspect, analyze and test textile products.

Food and Drug Administration (FDA)

The Food and Drug Act of 1906, plus other amended actions, constitutes the basic law that insures better, purer food for consumers by dealing with a wide range of problems, including filth, decomposition and adulteration. Provisions also protect consumers by forbidding misbranding, mislabeling and the use of misleading containers and by requiring that the weight, measure or count be specified and the ingredients listed. This legislation is supplemented by the Public Health Service, which establishes uniform sanitary codes, and by state and local officials, who enforce appropriate laws controlling products distributed within their respective areas.

Besides the Bureau of Food and Drugs in the FDA in the Department of Health, Education and Welfare (HEW), other FDA bureaus are the Bureau of Radiological Health, the Bureau of Veterinary Medicine, the Bureau of Biologies and the Bureau of Medical Devices and Diagnostic Products. The FDA also operates the National Center for Toxicological Research.

Food Container Standards

These standards, the first developed in 1963 by the U.S. Department of Agriculture, cut across commodity lines and are designed to give a statistically sound, practical basis for evaluating the exterior condition of filled food containers.

Other Consumer Legislation

Three important acts have been enacted to benefit consumers: (1) the Fair Packaging and Labeling Act of 1966, which prohibits unfair and deceptive methods of packaging and labeling consumer commodities in interstate commerce; (2) the Consumer Credit Protection Act of 1968 (Truth-in-Lending), which compels lenders to disclose all credit terms to borrowers; and (3) the Fair Credit Reporting Act of 1971, which gives consumers the right to review their credit file; requires credit grantors to tell rejected applicants why they were turned down; makes it illegal for creditors to discriminate on the basis of race, religion, color, national origin, sex, marital status or age; and provides procedures for settling billing disputes.

Occupational Safety and Health Act of 1970 (OSHA)

The purpose of OSHA is "to assure every working man and woman in the Nation safe and healthful working conditions and to preserve human resources."

The act applies to employers engaged in a business that affects interstate commerce. This includes farmers who employ one or more workers at any time during the year but excludes the farmers' immediate family members.

To assure compliance with the act, a national consensus of work safety and health standards has been developed and inspectors have been employed. Citations of noncompliance may be issued and penalities may be imposed. Recordkeeping and reporting are required.

Administration of the act is the responsibility of the U.S. Department of Labor.

Consumer Product Safety Commission (CPSC)

The CPSC is an independent regulatory agency, which is directed by five commissioners appointed by the president. CPSC's purpose is to protect the consumer against unreasonable risks associated with consumer products; assist consumers in evaluating the comparative safety of consumer products; develop uniform safety standards for consumer products to minimize conflicting state and local regulations; and promote research and investigations into product-related deaths, illnesses and injuries.

Environmental Protection Agency (EPA)

The EPA is an independent agency headed by an administrator appointed by the president. EPA has established program offices and research laboratories to abate and control pollution systematically by proper integration of a variety of enforcement activities related directly to the interests of consumers such as setting standards, monitoring and researching and include: (1) developing regulations for air pollution control; (2) identifying and regulating noise sources; (3) maintaining a national inspection program for measuring radiation levels in the environment; (4) performing technical assistance for development, management and operation of solid waste management activities; (5) developing regulations for water pollution control and water supply; and (6) regulating pesticides that occur in or on food to establish tolerance levels assuring human safety.

Perishable Agricultural Commodities Act

This act prohibits unfair and fraudulent practices in the marketing of fresh or frozen fruits and vegetables and requires that dealers, commission merchants, brokers, shippers and growers' agents handling these commodities in interstate or foreign commerce be licensed.

Pesticide Acts

The Insecticide Act of 1910 provided the public with federal protection against fraudulent, ineffective and unsafe chemicals used against crop, animal, household and human pests. Protection was broadened further as new chemicals came into use against a widening range of pests. The Federal Insecticide, Fungicide and Rodenticide Act now requires registration, testing and proper labeling of more than 50,000 interstate-shipped or imported products for household, institutional and structural as well as agricultural pest control.

COMPETITIVE TRADE LAWS AND REGULATIONS

Sherman Antitrust Act

The Sherman Antitrust Act is essentially an anti-monopoly law which was enacted in the era when trusts and combinations exercised power considered dangerous to the public welfare. The fundamental purpose of the act is the prevention of restraints to free competition which tend to limit production, raise prices or otherwise control the market. The law also seeks to secure equality of opportunity for businessmen and to protect purchasers of goods and services.

Clayton Act

The Clayton Act is designed to reach devices or practices which are discriminating and which, under certain circumstances, might lead to the formation of trusts and monopolies. It is intended to supplement the Sherman Antitrust Act.

The Clayton Act prohibits price discriminations, knowingly inducing or receiving a discrimination in price, exclusive dealing arrangements and tying contracts, certain mergers, interlocking directorates and intercorporate stockholding and various other practices having a certain degree of adverse effect on competition. Additionally, it prohibits discriminations in the payments for, and the furnishing of, services and facilities and makes certain types of brokerage payments illegal.

Federal Trade Commission (FTC)

The Federal Trade Commission, an independent administrative agency established in 1914, is made up of five commissioners appointed by the president. They are charged with FTC's basic responsibility to keep competition free and fair.

Overseeing the day-to-day work of the FTC is the executive director. Reporting to him are the agency's three major bureaus—the Bureau of Competition, the Bureau of Consumer Protection and the Bureau of Economics.

The Bureau of Competition deals with unfair trade practices, mergers that serve to restrict competition, interlocking directorates and other such activities. The Bureau of Consumer Protection offers consumer education materials and oversees advertising and marketing practices. The Bureau of Economics compiles economic evidence and statistics for the commissioners to base decisions when they are considering the investigation of a topic or industry.

FTC operates 12 regional offices in major cities around the country. Among its principal activities which relate to the food industry are: (1) preventing general trade restraints, including price fixing, boycotts and other such tactics; (2) preventing false or deceptive advertisements; (3) preventing practices leading to unfair competition, such as price discrimination, exclusive deals, mergers or joint ventures which may reduce competition "substantially"; and (4) regulating packaging and labeling of products which do not come under FDA jurisdiction.

Robinson-Patman Act

The Robinson-Patman Act, which became law on June 19, 1936, has as its purpose the prevention of discrimination in price and of other practices injuriously affecting free competitive enterprise. The act's purpose may be reduced to four basic provisions relating to interstate commerce:

1. Discriminatory prices that would injure competition may not be given to any buyer.
2. Commissions normally paid to brokers may not be received by any buyer.
3. Unfair discrimination between customers may not be made in regard to allowances or payments for advertising and promotion work.
4. Discrimination may not be made between customers in regard to special services, such as the extension of credit.

However, the act does permit a seller to discriminate in price between buyers if the purpose is to meet the legitimately lower price of a competitor.

Capper-Volstead Act

The Capper-Volstead Act enacted in 1922 clarified the status of farmer cooperatives under the Sherman and Clayton Acts. It makes legal an association of farmers for marketing purposes in interstate trade provided such an association:
1. Is operated for the mutual benefits of its members.
2. Conforms to one or both of the following:
   a. No member is allowed more than one vote.
   b. Dividends on capital stock or membership capital do not exceed 8 per cent per year.
3. Does not deal in products of nonmembers to an amount greater in value than the amount of the products it handles for its members.

Webb-Pomerene Act

The Webb-Pomerene Act of 1918 was passed for the purpose of allowing domestic firms to form export associations in order to compete more effectively in foreign trade.

The heart of the act is the provision that nothing in the Sherman Antitrust Act is to be construed as declaring illegal "an association entered into for the sole purpose of engaging in export trade and actually engaged solely in such export trade, or an agreement made or act done in the course of export trade by such association, provided such association, agreement or act is not in restraint of trade within the United States and is not in restraint of the export trade of any domestic competitor of such association."

REGULATION OF MARKETS AND MARKETING

Agricultural Marketing Agreements Act of 1937

This act authorizes establishment of marketing orders and agreements to regulate the handling of milk and the setting of minimum prices to farmers and also to regulate the quality or quantity of shipments and types of containers and packs of specified fruits, vegetables, tree nuts and certain other commodities. It requires regulation of imports into the United States of certain commodities whenever domestic shipments are subject to quality regulations under a marketing order.

Marketing orders regulate commodities at the handler level. The exact definition of "handler" depends upon the particular crop and area. Generally speaking, a handler is defined as anyone who performs a function such as acquiring, grading, processing, selling or transporting the commodity. All handlers, except hired carriers such as railroads and trucking firms, are responsible for seeing that their product meets the grade, size, quality or other requirements set up under a marketing order program.

Neither growers nor retailers can be regulated under marketing orders so long as they perform only as growers or retailers. If growers or retailers perform marketing functions, such as operating a packing shed, they are also handlers and become subject to regulation.

There are seven principal items regulated under marketing orders: (1) quality, (2) quantity, (3) standardization of packs and containers, (4) research and development projects, (5) unfair trade practices, (6) price posting and (7) market information.

Federal Seed Act

The Federal Seed Act requires truthful labeling of seed shipped in interstate commerce, outlaws false advertising and prohibits importation of low-quality seed and screenings.

Packers and Stockyards Act (P & S)

The Packers and Stockyards Act regulates practices in the livestock, poultry and meat industries. Specifically included are livestock markets (terminal or auction markets), livestock market agencies, livestock dealers, meat packers and processors and poultry dealers and processors. The law prohibits unfair, deceptive, discriminatory and monopolistic trade practices in regulated industries.   ·

The P & S Act seeks to maintain fair and open competition in the marketing of livestock, poultry and meat to assure that true market value is received. Livestock markets and others subject to the act must maintain accurate scales to weigh livestock, poultry and meats.

Market owners, agencies and dealers must keep complete and accurate records that disclose the true nature of all transactions. True written accounts of each transaction must be furnished to customers.

Stockyard owners and operators are required to provide reasonable services and facilities at reasonable and nondiscriminatory rates for the use of those selling livestock. Any change in rates must be approved by the P & S Administration.

The agency also offers several programs intended to provide a measure of financial protection for livestock producers. These include prompt payment, custodial account, solvency and bonding requirements and reparations.

U.S. Warehouse Act

This act authorizes licensing and bonding of public warehouses for storage of agricultural products and provides for periodic inspection of warehouses and goods to insure the safekeeping of the items stored.

Commodity Futures Trading Commission

This authority strives to assure correct registration of prices, protects the "hedging" services of the futures markets and assures fair practices in futures. Futures prices must be protected against unfair or manipulative trading, because they are used as guides in the buying and selling of "cash" wheat, corn, soybeans and other crops at country points and at terminal markets. Hedging, which is the nonspeculative buying or selling of futures to offset or diminish price risks in handling actual commodities, is commonly engaged in by merchants, processors, farmer cooperatives and some individual farmers. It is an operation which obviously depends for its effectiveness on fair trading practices.

Lanham Act

The Lanham Act (1947) provides that certain types of marks, including brand names, may be protected by law and makes provision for the registration of the names or trademarks. This law applies only to goods involved in interstate or foreign commerce. Registration simply gives public notice of a firm's intention to use a particular brand or trademark, serving as evidence that the name or trademark belongs to the party who registered it. The fact that a name is registered and used for five years, without being contested, essentially gives the owner the right to use it permanently for his product.

Not all possible trademarks or brand names can be registered. Some that cannot be registered and protected are:

1. A surname only.
2. A geographical name.
3. One so similar to others that deception or confusion is possible.
4. One that suggests a connection with an important person without proper permission.

Securities Act

The Securities Act is a federal law enacted in 1933 and administered by the Securities and Exchange Commission (SEC). The SEC is an independent regulatory agency comprised of five commissioners headed by a chairman, all of whom are appointed by the President for staggered five-year terms. SEC's purpose is to regulate the issuance and trading of securities (stocks and bonds). It protects the public in the investment and trading of securities by: (1) requiring disclosure of information by companies having publicly held securities, (2) overseeing the operations of the securities markets and (3) taking enforcement action through court actions or administrative proceedings or both.

Interstate Commerce Commission (ICC)

In 1887, the Congress passed the Interstate Commerce Act, which created the ICC. The law demanded that unreasonable rail rate discrimination cease, that rates be published and that fares be reasonable. In 1906, the ICC was given jurisdiction over pipelines; in 1935, over highway transport; and in 1940, over all interstate inland waterways.

The ICC is an independent regulatory agency that reports directly to Congress but whose 11 commissioners are appointed by the president, who designates one member as chairman. ICC regulates operating certification, rates, finance and control of interstate railroads, trucks, buses, barges, ships, oil pipelines, express delivery companies and freight forwarders.

MARKETING SERVICES

Agricultural Marketing Act

The Agricultural Marketing Act of 1946 provides the basic authority for a scientific approach to the marketing of farm products and the establishment of an integrated administration of all federal laws aimed at improving the distribution of farm products through research, marketing aids and services and regulatory activities. This act authorizes federal standards for farm products, grading and inspection services, market news services, cooperative agreements, transportation services, market expansion activities, consumer education work and various other functions.

U.S. Cotton Standards Act

This act provides for: (1) establishment, preparation, distribution and use of official standards for cotton and (2) a cotton classing service on a fee basis for shippers, spinners and the general public.

U.S. Grain Standards Act

This act authorizes official standards for grain; requires an inspection, based on these standards, of grain sold by grade in interstate or foreign commerce when shipped from or to a designated inspection point; and prohibits deceptive handling and inspection practices.

Tobacco Inspection Act

This legislation provides for establishing and promoting standards of classification for tobacco and for maintaining official tobacco inspection and market news services.

Wool Standards Act

This act authorizes the use of certain funds for wool standardization and grading work.

Market News

The U.S. Department of Agriculture maintains more than 170 year-round market news offices to furnish daily and weekly reports on prices, supplies and other market conditions of all of the major farm products. Many of the offices are operated cooperatively with the states. Market information is collected from all of the major trading centers and disseminated through the press associations, newspapers and radio and television stations.

LABOR-RELATED LEGISLATION AND PROGRAMS

Wagner Act

The Wagner Act of 1935, otherwise known as the National Labor Relations Act, provides that employers recognize worker unions if the majority of workers vote for union representation. It prohibits employers from interfering with attempts by unions to organize or with workers seeking unionization. It establishes a list of unfair management practices toward workers.

Taft-Hartley Act

This 1947 act seeks to redress the imbalance of bargaining power arising from the Wagner Act. It provides employers an opportunity to present their cases to workers in the process of unionizing and establishes a list of unfair labor practices toward management, among other provisions.

Labor Reform Act

This 1959 act spells out the rights of rank-and-file union members, provides for secret balloting and majority rule on major issues and regulates reporting of the financial status of labor unions and some of their financial transactions.

National Labor Relations Board (NLRB)

The National Labor Relations Board is a five-member independent agency created in 1935.

Its two principal functions are to prevent and remedy unfair labor practices by employers or by unions and to conduct secret ballot elections to determine whether employees wish to be represented by a union, and if so, which union.

Federal Mediation and Conciliation Service (FMCS)

While it has no law enforcement authority, the FMCS is able to bring considerable persuasive power to bear in carrying out its job of preventing or minimizing disruption of commerce because of strikes.

FMCS has seven regional offices and maintains subsidiary offices in 75 cities. It is headed by a national director.

The agency can become involved in a labor-management dispute in any industry affecting interstate commerce, either on its own initiative or at the request of one or more of the parties to the dispute.

Employers and unions are required to notify FMCS whenever a dispute affecting commerce is not settled within 30 days after notice of termination or modification of contract. FMCS will also assist in selecting an arbitrator for labor-management disputes.

Equal Employment Opportunity Commission (EEOC)

Preventing discrimination and encouraging voluntary programs against job bias are the twin mandates of the EEOC, established by the 1964 Civil Rights Act.

EEOC acts on the basis of written charges against employers or may initiate its own actions. If an agreement between EEOC and the company charged is not reached within 30 days, a suit may be filed in federal district court.

Social Security Administration (SSA)

The SSA provides monthly benefits to insured persons and their dependents in the event of retirement, disability or death and provides health insurance (Medicare) to persons 65 years of age and over (and to some under age 65 who are disabled). SSA administers a federal program of cash assistance payments to the needy, aged, blind and disabled. Both the employer and the employee contribute to the Social Security system.

Fair Labor Standards Act

The Fair Labor Standards Act (Federal Wage-Hour Law) of 1938 is the federal law of most general application concerning wages and hours of work. It applies to employees engaged in, or producing goods for, interstate commerce.

For employees within its coverage, the act sets minimum wages, maximum hours and overtime pay standards; restricts the employment of child labor; and prohibits wage discrimination on the basis of sex.

Unless specifically exempt, all covered employees must be paid at least the applicable minimum wage, regardless of whether they are paid by the hour, by salary, by piece work or by any other method. However, learners, apprentices, messengers, handicapped workers and full-time students employed in retail or service establishments outside of school hours, under certain circumstances, may be paid special lower minimum wage rates, provided that special certificates are first obtained.

Any farmer employing enough workers to have 500 man-days of hired work performed on his farm during any quarter of the preceding year must comply with the minimum wage law. The 500 man-day test includes any employee who performs work for one hour or more during any day.

Farm Labor Contractor Registration Act

The Farm Labor Contractor Registration Act, which became law January 1, 1965, requires registration of certain farm labor contractors with the U.S. Secretary of Labor. The aim of this legislation is to improve conditions for interstate migrant agricultural workers by requiring that farm labor contractors observe certain rules in their dealings with both workers and employers. Farm labor contractors covered by the law are required to apply for a certificate of registration annually at any local office of the State Employment Service. Those who meet the requirements of the law are issued a certificate of registration and must carry it on their person at all times.

Unemployment Insurance (UI)

The UI system collects taxes on the payrolls of covered employers while employees are working and pays benefits to eligible employees who become involuntarily unemployed. The system is administered cooperatively by federal and state agencies. Federal provisions set minimum basic coverage provisions, qualifying requirements and taxing procedures. The states' provisions must meet these minimum federal standards to obtain federal assistance and rebates on UI taxes; however, the states are free to exceed federal standards in determining their own particular eligibility requirements and dollar benefit amounts. Only former employees of covered employers can receive compensation from UI. Businesses are subject to the Federal Unemployment Tax Act (FUTA) if they either paid wages of $1,500 or more in any calendar quarter or had one or more employees for some portion of at least one day during each of 20 different calendar weeks, whether consecutive or not.

Federal legislation enacted during 1976 extended unemployment insurance coverage to some agricultural workers effective January 1, 1978. Coverage was extended to agricultural labor for employers who hire 10 or more workers in 20 weeks or who pay $20,000 or more in cash wages in any calendar quarter.

SOIL AND WATER CONSERVATION

The Soil Conservation Service (SCS) gives technical assistance to farmers, ranchers and city, county and state governments to help them reduce erosion and sedimentation and plan better land and water uses.

SCS provides help largely through 2,949 local conservation districts that are organized under state law by local people. In addition to direct help to landowners and operators, SCS has U.S. Department of

Agriculture leadership for the National Cooperative Soil Survey and provides technical and financial assistance to sponsoring groups in planning and installing small watershed protection projects authorized under Public Law 566. The service participates in various river basin surveys and investigations and provides flood hazard information for communities.

BUSINESS INSURANCE

Agribusinesses should be fully insured and have coverage for the following: fire and other hazards, legal liability, vehicle, workers' compensation, business interruption, crime, glass, rent, employee benefits, and key-man or owner-operator life and disability insurance.

FEDERAL TAXES

Agribusinesses, like other businesses, are subject to federal excise taxes on certain items such as fuel taxes, regulatory fees, payroll taxes, unemployment compensation taxes and federal income taxes, among others.

Federal income taxes on net income of corporations are computed at the rate of 17 per cent on the first $25,000 or less and up to 46 per cent on amounts above $100,000. In turn, the dividends paid to stockholders are taxed again on a personal income basis, subject to certain exclusions.

● ● ●

In the next chapter, the competitive aspects of agribusinesses are considered.

TOPICS FOR DISCUSSION

1. Discuss the various local and state laws and regulations affecting agribusiness.
2. Discuss the various federal food programs and consumer protection programs.
3. Discuss the various federal fair trade laws and regulations.

4. Discuss the various federal regulations over markets and marketing services.
5. Discuss the various labor-related legislation and programs.

SELECTED REFERENCES

1. Elterich, J. G., "Unemployment Insurance, Estimated Cost Rates, Benefits and Tax Burden by Type of Farm," *American Journal of Agricultural Economics,* Nov. 1977, p. 683.
2. Greene, Mark R., *Insurance Checklist for Small Business,* SBA–SMA 148, Washington, D.C., Oct. 1976.
3. Radics, S. P., Jr., *Steps in Meeting Tax Obligations,* SBA–SMA 142, Washington, D.C., Jan. 1975.
4. Staff, *Guide to Federal Consumers Services,* Office of Consumer Affairs, Dept. of HEW, Washington, D.C., Jan. 1976.
5. Staff, *Tax Guide for Small Business,* IRS–334, U.S. Treasury Dept., Washington, D.C., 1977.
6. Stickells, Austin, *Legal Control of Business,* The Lawyers Co-operative Publishing Co., Rochester, N. Y., 1965.
7. Thatch, D. W., and W. E. Adams, *Agricultural Operations That Have Voluntarily Elected Unemployment Insurance,* N. J. Agr. Exp. Sta. A. E. 370, New Brunswick, Mar. 1977.
8. Weyant, J. Thomas, and others, *An Introduction to Agricultural Business and Industry,* The Interstate Printers & Publishers, Inc., Danville, Ill., 1971.

11

Agribusiness and
Market Competition

Competition is the effort of two or more parties, acting independently, to secure the patronage of a third party by offering the most favorable terms. Competition is the chief power that causes firms to sell at reasonable prices, provide what consumers want, develop superior products and provide better services. Each member in an industry knows the force of his competition. Supermarkets located in a shopping center are an example, each store knowing that its business life will be short unless it can successfully compete for the consumers' business.

Generally, when one charges unreasonably high prices, he soon finds his volume of sales declining because a competitor is selling the same or a similar product at a lower price, thus taking away his business. If there is no immediate competitor, there probably soon will be one. The free enterprise system provides for legal "right of entry," which means that a new competitor is permitted to start a store or business. He will likely do so if the profit opportunity looks promising enough. As a result of such competition, the firm which has temporarily enjoyed high prices soon has too small a volume to make a maximum profit—no matter how high it sets the prices. In fact, if the firm raises its prices still higher, its sales and profits may decline even more.

Thus, competition, or the threat of competition, strongly tends to keep prices "reasonable."

Competition may be imposed by:

1. Existing firms.

2. Prospective firms that will enter provided the opportunity for profits is promising enough.
3. Products that may be substituted, including some yet to be developed or invented.
4. Imports from foreign countries.

CLASSIFICATION OF MARKET SITUATIONS

Agribusiness firms, when selling goods, usually function in one of the following types of market situations: (1) pure competition, (2) monopolistic competition, (3) oligopoly or (4) monopoly.

When buying goods, firms operate in market situations usually classified into: (1) pure competition, (2) monopolistic competition, (3) oligopsony or (4) monopsony. A simplified portrayal of these situations is shown in Table 11-1.

Table 11-1. The Nine Market Situations, According to the Number of Buyers and Sellers in Each

Buying side	Selling side		
	Many sellers	Few sellers	One seller
Many buyers	Pure competition	Oligopoly	Monopoly
Few buyers	Oligopsony	Bilateral oligopoly	Monopolistic oligopsony
One buyer	Monopsony	Monopsonistic oligopoly	Bilateral monopoly

Source: Nicholls, W. H., *Imperfect Competition Within Agricultural Industries*, Iowa State College (now University) Press, Ames, Ia., 1941, p. 14.

Pure Competition

Under pure competition, entrepreneurial groups are so numerous that no one firm has any effect in the marketplace relative to controlling supply, fixing prices, advertising or differentiating its product. Each is a price-taker rather than a price-maker. For pure competition to exist, it is necessary that new firms be free to enter the business and that present firms be free to discontinue business.

Farming is one example of a perfectly competitive market. Millions of farmers compete with one another in selling their products to middlemen, who in turn compete with one another in selling them to consumers. This contrasts with the situation in many manufacturing and service industries in which competition may have less effect upon changes in price.

Of course, even agricultural markets are not really perfectly competitive. Farmers have modified the structure of markets somewhat by setting up co-op associations. Also, big processors and distributors have come into the picture. Even more important, the government has taken an active hand in agricultural markets through such mechanisms as support prices and marketing orders. Competition is still the dominant force in agricultural markets, however.

Monopolistic Competition

As the term signifies, this type of market situation contains elements of both monopoly and pure competition. The number of firms is large, each representing a fairly small share of the total and exerting only a limited amount of control over market price. However, the products or services provided by these firms are not homogeneous but differentiated in some way, such as by brand names, advertising, packaging or other means employed to create a difference, real or fictional, in the minds of the users of the products and/or services.

This emphasis on differentiation is important, because users may be inclined to pay a differentiating firm more for its products or services than they are competing firms for their unadvertised products. In conjunction, a differentiating firm will tend to sustain its sales efforts more in the nonprice area of competition, such as by extending credit, delivering packages, giving trading stamps and decorating the store, among a host of other techniques. Also, since each firm in monopolistic competition considers itself relatively insignificant, some price-cutting is practiced and fear of retaliation by its competitors is small. Firms engaged in retailing often compete in terms of monopolistic competition.

Oligopoly-Oligopsony

This type of market situation is one in which a few firms dominate a certain line of business and rival firms observe one another closely relative to prices and pricing policies. When this market situation occurs on the selling side, we refer to it as *oligopoly,* and on the buying side, as *oligopsony.*

There are also two subtypes of oligopoly-oligopsony: perfect and differentiated. Perfect oligopoly-oligopsony refers to situations in which the products or services are not differentiated or set apart. Perfect oligopoly is found, for example, in steelmaking, whereas differentiated oligopoly is characteristic of automobile and truck manufacturing.

The main characteristics of oligopoly-oligopsony are fewness and interdependence of firms, which, along with large investment requirements, make it difficult for new firms to enter the business.

Oligopolists are also more interested in nonprice than price competition. They recognize that if one of their number reduces price, the others will more than likely have to do the same. On the other hand, by keeping prices steady, rivals can resort to competition in more subtle ways. Cigarette companies, for example, relish nonprice competition through branding and advertising programs.

While we usually think of oligopoly-oligopsony as being the creature of a few large firms, it may also characterize local markets where numbers of firms may be large but where each firm recognizes its rivals in setting price policies. Retail gasoline stations are a case in point, periodic gasoline price wars being indicative of a temporary breakdown in this oligopoly structure.

Monopoly-Monopsony

In monopoly-monopsony, one firm controls all the supply or demand and sets prices to suit itself limited only by imports, by the availability of substitutes for its product or by public regulation as in the case of utility companies. When the federal government intervenes in a market situation, controls supply or acreage and sets prices, it is acting as a monopolist also. The difference between a private monopolist and a public monopolist, such as the federal government, is that the latter is granted this privilege by elected representatives of the people. Private monopolies are illegal unless franchised or regulated by government. Utility companies are one type of monopoly which is sanctioned because it is more efficient to have only one firm supplying utility needs rather than several.

SELECTED ASPECTS OF COMPETITION

The subject matter of market competition is vast. In this section, only a few selected aspects of competition as they pertain to agribusiness are discussed.

Local Versus National Markets

Contrary to popular belief, local markets are often less competitive than national markets. It has been customary in economics to focus attention on competition in national markets, such as for auto and steel manufacturing. Unfortunately, the status of market competition in local markets is often overlooked or ignored. Before the automobile and the truck arrived on the American scene, the one locally owned general merchandise store was quite monopolistic, having no real competitors and charging almost any price it desired. In addition, by extending credit it was able to keep its customers in debt for long periods of time, especially when the store supplied both farm and home consumption goods. It was only when motor vehicles and good roads arrived that the monopoly power of the general storekeeper was broken. In early America, there were other instances of local monopoly-monopsony power, such as the single railroad, cotton gin, livestock buyer, produce buyer or grain buyer. Presently, local monopoly-monopsony power is rare because the availability of substitute stores, plants, products and transportation, and the increasing business skill of the American people tend to prevent the formation of a monopoly-monopsony situation.

On a national basis, also, monopoly-monopsony power has been weakened, not only by technology but also by enlightened legislation such as the Sherman and Clayton Acts and by various government regulating authorities.

Differentiation

Differentiation is an important factor in competition, for by differentiating in one form or another, a firm hopes to set itself apart from its competitors in some noticeable way. Differentiation arises through location, branding, advertising, styles, designs and packaging.

Figure 11-1. Differentiating products by brands and labels is a favorite competitive device to isolate one's product from excessive price competition. (Courtesy, Cooperative League of USA, Chicago, Ill.)

Differentiation is the result of a calculated and deliberate effort by firms to reduce the rigors of price competition. In many cases it allows the seller to obtain a higher price than he could obtain in a purely competitive market.

On the whole, as an economy gets more affluent, differentiation increases because affluent consumers are less affected by price considerations and, consequently, are more impressed by differentiation such as by advertising.

Market Segmentation

Market segmentation means that the market for a product can be divided so that sales and prices in one market segment are not disturbed by sales and prices in another. One example involves milk and dairy products. Fluid whole milk has a market all of its own. People do not vary their purchases of fluid whole milk a great deal, and prices remain fairly stable. On the other hand, raw milk has other, less profitable alternative uses, such as for cheese and butter. Therefore, milk marketers try to move just enough of the product as fluid whole milk in the so-called premium-price market and convert the remainder to butter and cheese for sale in secondary-price markets. By so doing, milk processors maximize profits, because once milk is converted into butter or cheese, it cannot come back as fluid whole milk. Therefore, the latter market is protected from diversion.

Price Leadership

In markets which are oligopolistic or where firms recognize their interdependence, price leadership is often dominant. In certain industries supplying agribusiness inputs, price leadership is common, the largest firm in the group being confident that its smaller competitors will follow in its footsteps on price changes, either up or down. If they do not, the largest firm may inflict certain punishments on its smaller rivals; therefore, all the firms tend to act in unison. This unity of action is not always thorough or long-standing, however.

Market Entry

The entry of new firms into a market is most fundamental to a free enterprise economy. Barriers to entry are numerous, some being erected purposely by firms already in the market and others resulting from technology, government, etc. In any case, market entry should be made easier and restrictions held to a minimum.

Among the factors which could lead to easier market entry are these: (1) preventing issuance of patents to firms which have discovered technology with government funds, (2) expanding sources of capital for new businesses, (3) preventing monopoly over raw-material supplies, (4) discouraging excessive advertising and product differentiation and (5) reducing political activity associated with the awarding of government franchises, licenses and permits.

Promotion Expenses

Promotion expenses are selling costs incurred to stimulate sales in two general ways: first, by informing potential buyers of the availability, characteristics and prices of the products and, second, by persuading potential customers to buy. Thus, promotions are both informational and persuasive. Costs devoted to informational purposes are functionally justified and are essential to the effective working of a market system. Promotional activities with a persuasive orientation, however, are not usually justified from the standpoint of public welfare, since they reflect a diversion to sales promotion of productive resources which could otherwise be devoted to producing and distributing a larger volume of useful goods and services at lower costs.

While promotion expenses devoted to providing information are to be encouraged, persuasion expenses should not be.

EVALUATING THE MARKETS

The mere classification of a market does not provide sufficient appraisal of the performance of the firms in that market.

Bain, for example, suggests that markets be evaluated in terms of how they are *organized,* how the firms *conduct* themselves and what are the end results or *market performance.*[1]

Obviously, *market performance* is the most important criterion because no matter how markets are organized or conducted the end re-

---

[1]Bain, Joe S., *Industrial Organization*, John Wiley & Sons, Inc., New York, N.Y., 1968.

sults are what count. Bain offers five questions which need to be asked in ascertaining market performance:

1. How are prices charged related to the average production cost, and how large are the profits?
2. How do the size and efficiency of firms relate to the most efficient firm, and what is the extent of excess capacity?
3. What is the extent of sales promotion costs relative to production costs?
4. What about the character of the products, including design, quality and variety?
5. What is the rate of technological progress in the industry?

PERFORMANCE OF SELECTED AGRIBUSINESSES

Farm Supply Inputs

Agribusinesses manufacturing farm supply inputs, such as feed, fertilizer and machinery, are relatively few in number, although there is a large number of firms *retailing* these supplies to farmers. Therefore, farmer-purchasers are more likely to be impressed by competitive conditions at the local retail level than by those at the manufacturing level. In this discussion, however, we refer primarily to the manufacturing level.

Positive market performance is evident in the manufacturing of farm supplies relative to product development and adoption of new technology. Also, profit levels do not appear excessive.

Poor market performance is evidenced by some unused plant capacity, or overcapacity; many plants that are too small, with resulting high costs; and excessive advertising and product differentiation, which are many times fictional.

However, on the whole, it appears that market performance in farm supply manufacturing industries is improving when compared with performance in the past several years. The fertilizer industry, in particular, has recently undergone many changes geared to the interest of farmers (the production of bulk and high-analysis fertilizer, for example). In feed milling, local mills geared to the farmers' feeding needs have been started with far less emphasis on brand names. In farm machinery, mergers and consolidations have produced fewer firms but, on the whole, the surviving firms are more vigorous in their competition than before. Imported products have also helped competition.

Handling and Processing Farm Products

The processing of farm products is not so concentrated as the manufacturing of farm supplies. Each farm commodity usually has several outlets or methods of disposition. Buyers and processors of farm products are quite numerous and range from local to national and international in the scope of their operations.

In *meat packing*, many smaller firms have entered the business at local levels, tending to lessen the market power formerly held by major packers.

In *poultry and egg marketing*, the advent of vertical and horizontal integration has reduced the number but expanded the size of firms, resulting in greater efficiency and increased price competition.

In *fluid milk marketing*, the number of firms has decreased and plant size has increased. The growth of major firms has been stymied in recent years by government action. On the other hand, price stability for raw milk has been achieved by state-federal marketing orders and agreements. Prices charged consumers have become the object of control by many state boards, however.

In *vegetable and fruit processing*, many small plants have been discontinued and larger, year-round operations have developed. The practice of packing vegetables for food stores under the retailers' labels has increased. Processors also contract with farmers for most of their supplies, which has brought stability to that end of the business.

In *grain handling and processing*, the influence of government price support, storage and export programs has distorted the true competitive aspects of this business. Grain prices to farmers have been stabilized by government action, however. Overcapacity in grain handling is evident in older producing areas, and lack of capacity is seen in newer grain areas.

Wholesaling

With the decline of many independent food wholesalers and the rise of co-op and voluntary wholesalers, the overall market performance of wholesaling has improved. Costs have been reduced, new techniques have been adopted and the relationship of wholesaling to retailing has become closer and more integrated.

Retailing

The advent of co-op and voluntary food stores affiliated with their respective wholesalers has lessened the dominance of chain stores in food retailing. However, in many areas stores have been overbuilt both in number and in size. It will take some time before population growth matches this overcapacity. Also, some excessive promotional expenses, such as in trading stamps and merchandise games, may have shifted competition from price to nonprice factors. The development of food discount stores and generic foods has added a competitive dimension which appears advisable, however.

CREATING MORE MARKET COMPETITION

If a free enterprise economy is to survive, more rather than less competition must exist among competing firms. This is essential if new ideas, products and techniques are to be developed and used. Prices should not be any higher than necessary for the judicious conduct of business, an adequate financial reward to investors and risk-takers and the sustenance of a firm over the long run. Also important is the relationship between prices: if one industry is very competitive pricewise and others are not, then the competitive one suffers as a result. A distortion is created in the command and utilization of resources. Labor, capital and management will be attracted to the industry with higher-than-normal prices and profits. Therefore, it is in the general interest of all to maintain a price competitive economy.

The following are a few suggestions for achieving a more price competitive economy:

1. Market entry should be encouraged and barriers to entry eliminated or reduced.

2. Excessive mergers and consolidations should be discouraged, especially where their end result is market power rather than cost-saving.

3. Credit to new businesses and to small businesses should be maintained and encouraged.
4. Improvement of management in smaller firms should be encouraged.
5. Excessive power in labor and/or management should be curtailed.
6. Federal and state antitrust policy should be more vigorously pursued and enforced in the public interest.
7. Where excessive market power is found in the domestic economy, tariffs should be lowered and imports used as a restraint on this power.
8. Excessive promotion expenses devoted to persuasion rather than to information should be reduced.

● ● ●

In the next chapter, agribusiness organization is discussed.

TOPICS FOR DISCUSSION

1. Discuss each of the four types of market situations: pure competition, monopolistic competition, oligopoly-oligopsony and monopoly-monopsony.
2. Discuss differentiation as a competitive factor.
3. What is market segmentation?
4. Discuss price leadership.
5. Discuss market entry and promotion expenses.
6. Discuss the performance of selected agribusiness markets.
7. How can greater market competition be created?

SELECTED REFERENCES

1. Anthony, R. N., "The Trouble With Profit Maximization," *Harvard Business Review,* Nov. and Dec. 1960, pp. 126-134.
2. Bain, Joe, *Industrial Organization,* John Wiley & Sons, Inc., New York, 1968.
3. Dahl, Dale C. (ed.), *The Law and the Market,* Minn. Agr. Exp. Sta. Misc. Rept. 75, St. Paul, Sept. 1966.
4. Handy, C. R., and D. I. Padberg, "A Model of Competitive Behavior in

Food Industries," *American Journal of Agricultural Economics*, May 1971, p. 182.

5. Marion, Bruce W., and C. R. Handy, *Market Performance: Concepts and Measures*, ERS, A. E. Rept. 244, U.S. Dept. of Agriculture, Washington, D.C., Sept. 1973.

6. Scofield, William H., "Analyzing the Structure of Agribusiness Relations," *Journal of Farm Economics*, Dec. 1966, p. 1379.

7. Sosnick, Stephen, "A Critique of Concepts of Workable Competition," *Quarterly Journal of Economics*, Vol. 72, Aug. 1958.

8. Sosnick, Stephen, "A Theoretical Scaffolding for Analysis of Market Structures," *Journal of Farm Economics*, Vol. 43, No. 5, Dec. 1961.

9. Staff, *Farmers in the Market Economy*, Iowa State University Press, Ames, 1964.

10. Walsh, R. G., and J. R. Moore, *Market Structure of the Agricultural Industries*, Iowa State University Press, Ames, 1966.

12

Agribusiness Organization

In organizing agribusiness, there are several steps to be followed: (1) recognizing an economic need, (2) conducting a survey to quantify and appraise this need, (3) selecting a proper type of business organization, (4) adopting articles of incorporation such as bylaws and/or other legal instruments and (5) starting the business.

RECOGNIZING ECONOMIC NEED

A business always succeeds best when it fills a critical need in the economy. Agribusiness offers many instances of such needs.

For example, soybeans represent an important new crop in many areas as well as an expanding one in many older producing areas. Besides the creation of a need for supplying seed, fertilizers, chemicals and machinery for the crop, marketing opportunities also arise. Elevators and storage facilities, including drying facilities, are required. Transporting beans to terminal outlets becomes essential, and brokers and sales agents are needed. The exporting of beans is important as well as the crushing and processing of them. In turn, sales of oil and meal come into the picture. Finally, the synthesis of beans into fabricated protein meats is being rapidly developed. All these business opportunities accrue to just one agribusiness product—soybeans. There are many other examples.

MAKING A FEASIBILITY SURVEY

Before an agribusiness is organized, an appropriate survey is needed to determine the feasibility of the enterprise. Most economic surveys involve an estimate of the volume of business to be expected, the facility required for various amounts of production, the amount of capital required and the availability of management and employee skills to operate the business successfully.

In every endeavor there are both wrong ways and right ways to go about attempting to achieve the desired goal. Starting a new business is no exception. Launching an enterprise without having considered the problems involved and the resources available is definitely wrong. There is seldom, of course, just one right way—usually several possibilities will work. However, running through most successful new-business starts is a common thread of steps which should be taken before operations begin. According to the Small Business Administration, businessmen who have started firms successfully suggest eight key factors: First, make sure that objectives and plans are reduced to writing and double-checked for clarity, completeness and soundness. Second, study the market which the prospective venture will seek to attract. Third, insist on the most efficient production facilities. Fourth, review

Figure 12-1. A feasibility study for establishing an agribusiness is a necessary and vital step. (Courtesy, Farm Credit Administration, Washington, D.C.)

trade experience and technical know-how available and make sure that both are adequate. Fifth, bring capable associates into the organization. Sixth, obtain, at an early stage, firm commitments for the capital needed to launch the venture. Seventh, provide for keeping adequate records of operations. And eighth, consider carefully whether the necessary personal qualifications are present for managing a business.

Specific Feasibility Factors

Agribusiness plant location is usually dependent upon such basic factors as availability of raw materials (for processing businesses) or customers (for retail businesses); power, fuel and water supplies; labor supply and wage scales; transportation rates and facilities; access to markets; location of competitors; plant location inducements; and level

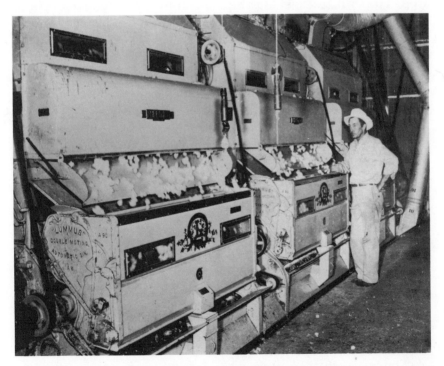

Figure 12-2. Cotton gins, like other types of agribusiness, require considerable amounts of capital. (Courtesy, Houston Bank for Farmer Cooperatives, Houston, Tex.)

of property tax, among other factors. A fuller discussion of plant location factors is reserved for a later chapter.

Buying an Existing Business

Sometimes an agribusiness already in operation may be for sale. The same feasibility procedure for establishing a new agribusiness should be followed when buying an older business. Usually, there will be some evidence of its profitability over time, and the prospective owner(s) should be permitted to examine such records. An appraisal by a disinterested but knowledgeable person is highly recommended.

KINDS OF BUSINESS ORGANIZATIONS

The principal types of legal structure for businesses are (1) sole proprietorship; (2) partnership, including limited partnership; (3) corporation; and (4) cooperative.

Legal craftsmanship can often tailor one of these to the needs of the individual enterprise. Thus, prudent selection of a business form involves choosing not just from among the standard forms in their typical patterns but from the forms as they can be fashioned by skillful planning and drafting.

Sole Proprietorship

This is the simplest form in which a business can be conducted. The owner simply goes into business with the assets in his own name. State laws do not prescribe organization procedures, nor is a sole proprietorship required, as corporations are, to register or to qualify before doing business in other states.

Partnership

REGULAR PARTNERSHIP.—In a partnership the business is conducted by a number of persons who usually have equal status and authority as owners or principals. Setting up a partnership ordinarily involves contribution by the partners of property, money, credit, skill or labor that will make up the capital or foundation of the business.

A written agreement (articles of partnership) spelling out the rights and duties of the partners is highly desirable; but no contract, either written or oral, is required. A partnership can be created simply by several persons conducting a business for profit as co-owners. When a written agreement is drawn up, it is a private document and need not be filed with a public agency.

Businessmen often think of a partnership as a business unit distinct from the partners as persons for accounting purposes. American law, however, generally does not regard the partnership as an entity but as a group of individuals.

Like the sole proprietorship, the partnership ordinarily may do business across state lines without registering or qualifying in any way.

LIMITED PARTNERSHIP.—The limited partnership is a variation of the partnership form of business. It permits persons contributing capital to the enterprise to avoid unlimited liability by becoming special, or "limited," partners.

This form of organization is somewhat more difficult to set up. Procedures prescribed by law must be carefully followed.

Corporation

A corporation is recognized by law as having an existence apart from that of the owners (shareholders). In the adjustment of rights, duties and other legal relations arising out of the enterprise, the corporation is treated as a distinct entity.

Incorporation papers setting forth certain basic information must be prepared and filed with designated public officials. The corporation's financial structure and management pattern must conform to standards in the corporation statute.

Cooperative

A cooperative is a business voluntarily organized, operating at cost, owned, controlled and financed by member patrons sharing risks and benefits proportional to their participation.

● ● ●

Table 12-1. Four Methods of Doing Business Under the Free Enterprise System

Key point	Single proprietorship	Partnership	Profit-type corporation	Cooperative
1. Why is the firm operated?	To buy, sell or produce goods and services.	To buy, sell or produce goods and services.	To buy, sell or produce goods and services.	To buy, sell or produce goods and services.
2. To whom are the goods sold and the services rendered?	The public or nonowner customers.	The public or nonowner customers.	The public, incidentally to stockholders.	Chiefly its own members.
3. How is the firm started?	Decision of individual.	Agreement between associates who become partners.	Organization by associates who become stockholder-investors.	Organization by associates who become owner-members.
4. How does the firm become legal?	By the owner's attaining legal age and controlling the business.	By contract between two or more individuals, preferably written and recorded.	Usually in incorporating under general laws which give corporations great freedom in their operations.	Usually by incorporating under special laws which require operation according to co-op principles.
5. Where is the business chartered?	No charter is required.	No charter is required. Partnership contract may be recorded.	Charter required. Only states can charter; no federal charter.	Charter required. States charter most cooperatives; a few are federally chartered.
6. How does one get into the firm?	By starting business himself or buying it.	By consent of the partners and a new agreement.	By buying stock.	By meeting the qualifications for membership, obtaining approval of the board and doing business with the association.
7. Who controls the firm, selects the manager and makes policy decisions?	The individual.	The partners by agreement.	The board of directors elected by the stockholder-investors.	The board of directors elected by the member-patrons.

(Continued)

Table 12-1 (Continued)

Key point	Single proprietorship	Partnership	Profit-type corporation	Cooperative
8. How is voting done?	None necessary.	Informal agreement; sometimes by vote of partners.	One vote for each share of common stock; preferred stock is sometimes voted too.	Usually one member, one vote; sometimes by patronage.
9. Who owns the business?	The individual.	Two or more individuals.	The stockholders.	The member-patrons.
10. What is put into the business by the owner(s)?	The individual puts in personal effort and capital.	Each partner may put in capital or personal effort, or both.	Capital is supplied by investors seeking profits.	The members do business through the cooperative and put in funds or leave net patronage returns.
11. What returns can be received on the money invested?	Unlimited.	Unlimited.	Unlimited.	Usually limited to a maximum of 8 per cent or as prescribed by state law.
12. How may net earnings be used?	As desired by individual.	As agreed upon by partners.	As dividends to stockholders or as reserves, or both.	Prorated to patrons on patronage basis.
13. What is the owner's(s') liability?	All property of individual, excepting legal exemptions.	All property of all partners, excepting legal exemptions unless a limited partnership.	Assets of the corporation.	Assets of the cooperative.
14. How may business be ended?	Death, disability, bankruptcy or retirement of owner.	Death of any partner, bankruptcy or decision to dissolve.	Bankruptcy or legal dissolution of company.	Bankruptcy or legal dissolution of cooperative.
15. How are net earnings taxed?	As an individual.	As an individual.	At regular corporate tax rates.	As a partnership, with certain stipulations.

Source: Roy, Ewell P., Cooperatives: Development, Principles and Management. The Interstate Printers & Publishers, Inc., Danville, Ill. 1976. Chapter 1.

The four main types of organization (proprietorship, partnership, corporation and cooperative) are compared on several key points in Table 12-1.

A COMPARISON OF CORPORATIONS AND COOPERATIVES

The main points of difference between corporations and cooperatives are grouped for discussion as follows: (1) recipients of goods and services, (2) joining the business, (3) control of the business, (4) ownership of the business, (5) return on investment, (6) disposition of net earnings and (7) taxation of net earnings. For comparison of single proprietorships and partnerships on these seven points, consult Table 12-1.

Recipients of Goods and Services

Profit-type corporations sell goods and services to, and trade them with, the general public and may, incidentally, trade with their owners. On the other hand, co-op corporations trade primarily with their own members or stockholders, not with the general public. Cooperatives may, incidentally, trade with nonmembers within limits prescribed by law.

Joining the Business

In a profit-type corporation, one joins by buying one or more shares of stock on an exchange, through a broker or through private purchase. There are no other requirements.

In a co-op corporation, one must first meet the qualifications specified for membership; second, be approved by the board of directors; and, third, be active in the affairs of the association, besides purchasing at least one share of voting stock or equity for membership.

Control of the Business

In the profit-type corporation, the investor-stockholders elect a board of directors, which, in turn, elects officers and appoints top management. Voting is done according to shares of stock—one share, one vote. Proxy voting is permitted, and the sale or transfer of stock is easily accomplished.

In a co-op corporation, member-patrons elect a board of directors, which selects officers and top management. Voting is usually done according to persons—one man, one vote. Proxy voting is usually prohibited, as is sale or transfer of stock unless approved by the board of directors. Co-op stock is redeemable at par value, while regular corporate stock is usually traded at current market value.

Ownership of the Business

In a profit-type corporation, the stock itself is entrepreneurial or acquisitive for profit. The firm seeks to acquire profit from anyone and by any transaction. Its capital is impersonal and may trade freely.

In a cooperative, the capital subscribed is neither entrepreneurial nor acquisitive. It is a loan from a member and/or patron to his cooperative with either a stipulated, fixed interest rate or a specified maximum. The cooperative seeks profits, not for itself, but for its member-patron entrepreneurs. Its capital is personal and does not trade freely or openly.

Return on Investment

There are no limits to the return on investment made in a profit-type corporation. In a cooperative, dividends or, more correctly, interest paid on capital invested is usually limited to a maximum of 8 per cent or as prescribed by applicable state law. However, in a cooperative, there are no limits on the returns or earnings which may be refunded to patrons based on the volume of business they have done with the cooperative.

Disposition of Net Earnings

In a profit-type corporation, net earnings after income taxes are distributed to investor-stockholders as dividends on the basis of stock shares, are kept as retained reserves in the corporation or are divided between these two methods of disposition.

In a cooperative, all the net earnings are prorated to the patrons or users on a patronage basis according to the volume of business done by each patron in relation to the total volume of business done by all patrons. If the cooperative fails to follow this procedure in total or in part, then the portion of net earnings not so prorated is subject to federal and state income taxes as if the business were a profit-type corporation.

Advantages and disadvantages of the several types of businesses are shown in Table 12-2.

Table 12-2. Advantages and Disadvantages of Certain Forms of Business Organization

A. SINGLE PROPRIETORSHIP

Advantages:

1. Low start-up costs.
2. Freedom from regulation.
3. Owner in direct control.
4. Minimal working capital requirements.
5. Tax advantages to small owner.
6. All profits to owner.

Disadvantages:

1. Unlimited liability.
2. Lack of continuity.
3. Difficult to raise capital.

B. PARTNERSHIP

Advantages:

1. Ease of formation.
2. Low start-up costs.
3. Availability of additional sources of risk capital.
4. Broader management base.
5. Possible tax advantages.
6. Limited outside regulation.

Disadvantages:

1. Unlimited liability, unless a limited partnership.
2. Lack of continuity.
3. Divided authority.
4. Hard to find suitable partners.
5. Difficulty in raising large amounts of capital.

C. PROFIT-TYPE CORPORATION

Advantages:

1. Limited liability.
2. Specialized management.
3. Ownership is transferable.
4. Continuous existence.
5. Legal entity.
6. Possible tax advantages.
7. Easier to raise capital.

Disadvantages:

1. Closely regulated.
2. More expensive to organize.

(Continued)

Table 12-2 (Continued)

---

3. Charter restrictions.
4. Double taxation.
5. Management more complicated.

D. COOPERATIVE CORPORATION

Advantages:

1. Limited liability.
2. Specialized management.
3. Continuous existence.
4. Legal entity.
5. Substantial tax advantages.
6. Easier to raise capital.
7. Enjoys certain antitrust and regulatory exemptions.

Disadvantages:

1. Incorporation statutes quite restrictive.
2. Cooperation among members difficult to achieve.
3. Slow in organizing and getting started.
4. Members fail to recognize their ownership responsibilities.
5. Business community resentment against co-ops.

Source: *Choosing a Form of Business Organization*, Small Business Administration, Washington, D.C., 1965.

Taxation of Net Earnings

A profit-type corporation pays 17 per cent tax on the first $25,000 or less of net income and up to 46 per cent on amounts above $100,000. In turn, the dividends on stock shares paid to stockholders are taxed again on a personal income basis but subject to an exclusion privilege applying only to the first $100 in stock dividends received by a taxpayer. Corporate net earnings retained and not paid out are taxed only once at the corporate level.

A cooperative, on the other hand, is obligated to pay at least 20 per cent of its net earnings in cash to its patrons based on their patronage of the cooperative. In addition, for the cooperative lawfully to exclude the remaining 80 per cent from its taxable income, its patrons must have given prior consent for including all the co-op's distributions, cash and noncash, in their income tax returns. This consent may be given in writing, as part of a bylaw amendment or by a patron's endorsing a qualified check. In any case, either the cooperative or the patron must pay the tax on net earnings of the cooperative.

ADOPTING LEGAL INSTRUMENTS

Laws governing the procedure for obtaining a corporate charter vary with the individual state. Detailed information about the requirements of any state can be obtained from the Secretary of State or other state official who supervises issuance of corporate charters.

Articles of Incorporation

Generally, the first step in the required procedure for setting up a corporation is preparation, by the incorporators, of "articles of incorporation." Most states require that this document be prepared by three or more legally qualified persons in a manner prescribed by law. Frequently, the articles must designate the names and addresses of the persons who are to serve as the directors until the first annual meeting of the corporation.

If the designated state official determines that the name of the proposed corporation is satisfactory, that the articles contain the necessary information and have been properly executed and that there is nothing in the corporation's proposed activities that violates state law or public policy, he will issue the charter.

Thereafter, the stockholders must meet to complete the incorporation process. This meeting is extremely important and usually is conducted by an attorney or someone familiar with corporate organizational procedure.

Many states have standardized articles of incorporation forms which may be used by agribusinesses. Copies of these may be obtained from the official who issues charters in a particular state.

Bylaws

At the first general meeting, the corporate bylaws are adopted and a board of directors is elected. This board, in turn, elects officers, who have charge of the corporation.

The bylaws of the corporation may repeat some of the provisions of the charter and state statute but usually cover items such as:
1. Location of the principal office of the corporation.
2. Date and place of stockholders' meetings and provisions for calling and conducting meetings.
3. Necessary quorum for stockholders' meetings.
4. Voting privileges of stockholders.

5. Number of directors and method of electing them and of creating or filling vacancies.
6. Time and place of directors' meetings.
7. Requirements for a quorum at directors' meetings.
8. Method of selecting officers and determining their duties, terms of office and salaries.
9. Stock certificates, their transfer and control.
10. Power and ways to amend bylaws.

STARTING THE BUSINESS

Among the things that should be acted upon by the board of directors at its first meeting are the following:
1. Election of officers as specified in the bylaws.
2. Instructions to the president and the secretary to obtain and to issue stock certificates.
3. Authorization of the president and the secretary to have copies of the articles of incorporation and the bylaws printed and distributed to stockholders.
4. Adoption of the form of any marketing agreement or contract to be used.
5. Acceptance of all the subscription agreements for capital stock and the authorization of officers to obtain additional subscriptions and additional signatures to the marketing agreement if one is used.
6. Selection of a depository bank.
7. Designation of officers or employees who are authorized to handle funds and issue checks.
8. Arrangements for the bonding of officers and employees in accordance with the bylaws.
9. Arrangements for bookkeeping and auditing.
10. Instructions to the secretary to obtain the corporate seal in the form provided by the bylaws.
11. Decisions regarding credit, pricing, purchasing, marketing, servicing and other policies.
12. Transaction of any other business relating to matters such as insurance and bonds and the hiring of the manager and other employees.

• • •

In the next chapter, agribusiness financing is discussed.

TOPICS FOR DISCUSSION

1. What is "economic need"?
2. Discuss the importance of a feasibility study.
3. Discuss and compare the four main kinds of business organization.
4. How do the articles of incorporation differ from the bylaws?
5. What are some of the necessary steps once the business is chartered?

SELECTED REFERENCES

1. Kelley, P. C., *How to Organize and Operate a Small Business*, Prentice-Hall, Inc., Englewood Cliffs, N. J., 1961.
2. Olmi, A. M., *Selecting the Legal Structure for Your Firm*, SBA–MA 231, Washington, D.C., Nov. 1977.
3. Rohrlich, Chester, *Organizing Corporate and Other Businesses*, Matthew Bender & Co., Inc., Albany, N. Y., 1958.
4. Roy, Ewell P., *Cooperatives: Development, Principles and Management*, The Interstate Printers & Publishers, Inc., Danville, Ill., 1976.
5. Staff, *Business Plan for Small Manufacturers*, SBA–MA 218, Washington, D.C., Jul. 1973.
6. Staff, *Business Plan for Small Retailers*, SBA–MA 150, Washington, D.C., Nov. 1977.
7. Staff, *Business Plan for Small Service Firms*, SBA–SMA 153, Washington, D.C., Oct. 1973.
8. Staff, *Checklist for Going Into Business*, SBA–SMA 71, Washington, D.C., Sept. 1977.
9. Staff, *Choosing a Form of Business Organization*, SBA Topic 11, Washington, D.C., 1965.
10. Staff, *Cooperatives in Agribusiness*, FCS Educ. Cir. 33, U.S. Dept. of Agriculture, Washington, D.C., Mar. 1968.
11. Staff, *Incorporating a Small Business*, SBA–MA 223, Washington, D.C., Jan. 1976.
12. Vorzimer, L. H., *Using Census Data to Select a Store Site*, SBA–SMA 154, Washington, D.C., Apr. 1974.

13

Agribusiness Financing

Financing agribusiness is one of the main problems in today's business world. A firm must be properly capitalized if it is to succeed, and sometime during the life of the business, capital will likely have to be borrowed. For those agribusinesses engaged in selling products to others on credit, the wise extension of credit is a necessity.[1]

SIZE OF AGRIBUSINESS INVESTMENTS

The three types of capital commonly referred to in business are fixed, operating and organizational capital.

Fixed capital refers to funds invested in land, buildings, equipment and vehicles.

Operating capital refers to funds needed for inventories, wage and salary payments, credit outstanding, utility bills and sales expenses, among other items.

Organizational capital is required in legally starting a business.

WHAT IS EQUITY CAPITAL?

Equity capital is that part of the capitalization of a business which is ownership interest. In most agribusinesses, equity capital or the owner's(s') share of the business is held privately by the proprietor, partners, family members of close associates: a situation called *inside*

---

[1]Financing agricultural production is excluded from the discussion in this chapter.

equity capital. On the other hand, when the business goes beyond the family or very close associates, we have a situation of *outside* equity capital.

PROBLEMS IN SPREADING EQUITY CAPITAL

As long as an agribusiness remains as a single proprietorship, or under one-man ownership, it may suffer capitalwise. The owner can get more equity in his business only by: (1) plowing back a share or all of his net income, (2) using money from another family business or enterprise and/or (3) borrowing money (debt capital), such as from a bank, which will then allow him to expand and perhaps enhance his prospects for greater net income. At this point he may pay back the bank loan and plow back some of the resulting increased net income into his business.

The owner's liability in a single proprietorship is great. He does have all the control, however.

If a single proprietor shifts his business to a partnership consisting of two or more persons, he will be able to get more equity capital. However, he loses some of his control over the business because control and direction with a partner or partners must be shared. His liability remains as large as ever. Sometimes partners will bring into the business not only money, but also talent, in which case the business might be strengthened. Great care should be exercised in choosing business partners.

If a single proprietor decides to form a corporation instead, he may get equity capital by selling common stock (voting stock) and/or preferred stock (nonvoting stock, usually). As long as he controls over 50 per cent of the common or voting stock, control stays with him.

ADVANTAGES AND DISADVANTAGES
OF OUTSIDE EQUITY CAPITAL

The advantages of outside equity capital, coupled with the corporation method of doing business, are as follows:

1. It permits more rapid growth of the company than would otherwise be possible.
2. It expands the credit base of the business—more equity, more

Figure 13-1. Fertilizer manufacturing plants are an integral part of the farm supply phase of agribusiness. (Courtesy, Southern States Cooperative, Richmond, Va.)

Figure 13-2. Rice mills, like other agribusinesses, require large capital investments. (Courtesy, Blue Ribbon Rice Mills, Inc., Houston, Tex.)

borrowing power; it lowers interest rates; it provides longer terms and fewer loan restrictions.

3. It reduces the risks by dividing the ownership.
4. It permits continuity of the business in case an owner dies.
5. It provides a better framework for management counsel and talents.

The following are disadvantages of outside equity capital:

1. The proprietor's control is reduced or diluted, as is his participation in any profits of the business.
2. Flexibility of operation and decision making possessed by the sole owner is lost when outside equity capital is used.
3. The sale of a portion of the equity may entail increased expense.
4. The "timing" in obtaining outside equity capital is very critical. If an attempt is made too late to secure such capital (as when a

business is declining), investors become reluctant. If this capital is obtained too early, the proprietor could be sacrificing both control and profits.

Sometimes it may be wiser to obtain debt capital or borrowings rather than go to equity capital financing.

SOURCES OF EQUITY CAPITAL

Among the sources of equity capital are: (1) individuals in high income-tax brackets interested in capital gains; (2) employees, customers or suppliers of the business; (3) friends of the owner who know him and have confidence in his abilities; (4) private or professional investors acting either alone or in groups such as syndicates or capital pools; and (5) other corporations in a related line of business or an outside line wishing to diversify through holding of minority interests.

RAISING EQUITY CAPITAL

The two principal instruments for raising equity capital in stock corporations are common stock and preferred stock. For nonstock, nonprofit corporations, the two principal instruments are membership fees and capital certificates.

Common Stock

Every corporation will use common shares in its capitalization. Often this type of stock is the only kind of capitalization with which small corporations start in business.

Normally, common stock represents the residual ownership of the company, which is the first to suffer in case of a reorganization due to unsuccessful operation. On the other hand, holders of common stock ordinarily benefit most from the success of the company. Common stockholders control the company, elect directors and do such other things as shareholders are permitted and required to do, voting on the basis of stock shares.

Preferred Stock

Preferred stock generally entitles its holders to receive a stated preferential dividend payment, limited in amount, before anything may be paid on shares that are junior to this stock, including the common stock. It usually has no additional claim on earnings. Likewise, such stock generally has a preference in liquidation over any junior shares. If, for any reason, the company should liquidate, voluntarily or involuntarily, the claim of the preferred stockholders must be satisfied before any payment may be made to junior shareholders.

Retained Earnings

Net earnings not distributed to stockholders or patrons, as the case applies, are an internal source of equity capital. The extent to which retained earnings can be used as a source of capital will depend upon the type of business organization used, the competitive position of the firm and the industry earnings. Co-op corporations rely heavily upon retained earnings for growth, for example.

Retained earnings involve no reduction in the proportionate position of any stockholder and may be an important source of increased equity. However, current tax laws, the vicissitudes of business and the normally slow growth of a new venture often limit the amount of earnings which may be added to the equity of a small business.

Other Types of Equity Capital

In nonstock corporations, such as cooperatives, membership fees are used as the equivalent of common stock while capital certificates are treated as the equivalent of preferred stock.

When associations are organized on a nonstock basis, the members are given certificates of membership upon payment of membership fees. The sale of these certificates may supply all the capital which is needed or may fall short of doing so. The latter is usually the case, for in many associations the collection of membership fees is considered merely an incidental means of financing. Since no interest is paid on membership fees, this manner of financing is insignificant from the cost standpoint.

As has been mentioned, capital certificates are used in nonstock cooperatives and are equivalent to preferred stock certificates. They may be sold in denominations of $25, $50, $100 or $500, may bear interest and may have due dates but usually do not. They ordinarily have no voting rights.

These certificates provide an efficient way of raising money in that they may be allocated to a member's account along with his membership fee and patronage credits. Nonmembers may also purchase capital certificates which have no voting power.

SOURCES OF BORROWED CAPITAL

Agribusinesses needing capital and having to borrow have several alternative sources, including public funds through various government agencies as well as private sources of borrowed capital. Some of these are discussed subsequently.

Commercial Banks

The principal types of bank loans are straight-commercial, installment, character, term, accounts receivable, warehouse receipt, equipment and collateral loans.

STRAIGHT-COMMERCIAL LOANS.—These loans are usually made for a period ranging from 30 to 90 days and often are single-name paper without endorsement and based upon financial statements. They are self-liquidating in expectation that they will be repaid from the proceeds of the transactions which gave rise to them. This type of loan is used particularly for seasonal financing and for building up inventories.

INSTALLMENT LOANS.—A loan of this type is commonly made by a larger bank for almost any productive purpose and may be extended for almost any period that the bank sees fit to offer. Repayments are usually made on a monthly basis, but as the obligation is reduced, it may be possible to obtain refinancing at more advantageous rates. Installment loans may be tailored to the seasonal requirements of the business, with heavier repayments in peak months and smaller repayments during off-season periods.

CHARACTER LOANS.—Such loans are usually of the consumer credit variety, although they are sometimes used for business purposes.

TERM LOANS.—Such loans have maturities of from 1 to 10 years and may be either secured or unsecured. Loan repayments may be made on almost any agreed basis—monthly, quarterly, semiannually or annually. Early repayments are often relatively small, with a large final repayment. A term loan is usually covered by a comprehensive agreement calculated to protect the lender against drastic changes in the value of collateral security or in business income available for repayment of principal and payment of interest. Because of the extended maturities of such loans, a borrower will find it necessary to submit periodic statements during the life of his loan.

ACCOUNTS RECEIVABLE LOANS.—Accounts and notes receivable may be used as a basis for bank borrowing, the bank taking over these items on a notification or a non-notification plan. If the former is used, the bank notifies the debtor that the receivables have been assigned to it and that it will collect them as they fall due. The bank credits collections to the account of the borrower after deducting its service charges. Under the non-notification plan, the borrower collects his accounts as usual and then pays off his indebtedness at the bank.

WAREHOUSE RECEIPT LOANS.—Under this form of financing, goods are stored in warehouses and the warehouse receipts given to the bank as security for a loan to pay off the supplier. As fast as the purchaser is able to sell the merchandise he has on hand or to use materials in manufacturing operations, he buys back a portion of the warehouse inventory. This type of borrowing enables him to get along with a smaller investment in working capital but applies only to nonperishable items that are readily marketable.

EQUIPMENT LOANS.—Loans are made to finance the purchase of machinery and equipment under one of two plans, depending upon the applicable state law. In either case, the buyer has possession and use of the equipment while he is paying for it.

Using one approach, the equipment involved is sold under a "conditional sales agreement," with the bank (or other financing institution) retaining title until installment payments have been completed. In a number of states, however, advances on machinery and equipment are made under an arrangement by which the bank takes a chattel mortgage as security for payment.

COLLATERAL LOANS.—Business borrowers may be able to obtain bank loans on the basis of collateral such as chattel mortgages on personal property, real estate mortgages, life insurance up to the cash surrender value of the policy or stocks and bonds.

Commercial Finance Companies

Traditionally, consumer-oriented commercial finance companies are the major source of minority, small business funding. These companies are in business to make high-risk loans. Commercial finance companies can make most types of personal and business loans.

Most finance companies extend seasonal or short-term business credit. The majority of loans must be repaid within 90 days to one year. The loan's purpose affects its maturity. For example, if a company loans a retailer funds to build up pre-Christmas inventory, the loan would normally be repaid in January. However, if the company loans a manufacturer funds to purchase production equipment, the loan term could run as long as five years.

Life Insurance Companies

Life insurance companies represent perhaps the largest national source of commercial financing. These companies extend credit for: (1) long-term capital; (2) land acquisition; (3) fixture, furniture, machinery and equipment purchases; and/or (4) physical facility purchases, construction, renovation and expansion.

Life insurance companies extend long-term credit in the form of mortgages. The mortgage loan's purpose affects its maturity. Typically, fixture, furniture, machinery and equipment mortgages have a 7- to 15-year payback, and physical facility mortgages have a 15- to 25-year payback. Insurance companies do not extend financing unsecured by saleable physical assets. They do not finance more than 75 to 80 per cent of the asset's appraised value. They prefer not to finance propositions of projects less than $50,000. These companies charge interest rates close to the prime rate.

Economic Development Administration (EDA)

EDA loans are available to agribusinesses located in EDA-designated areas for job-generating enterprises. The maximum amount loaned by the EDA is 65 per cent of the cost of the land and facilities for a maximum term of 25 years at relatively low interest. EDA loans may not be made for use as working capital or as assistance in industrial relocation.

Small Business Administration (SBA)

The business loan program of the Small Business Administration is expressly designed to assist small enterprises which are independently owned and operated and not dominant in their fields. The SBA's business loans enable small concerns to finance construction, conversion or expansion; to purchase equipment, facilities, machinery, supplies or materials; and to acquire working capital.

Generally, the SBA loan program is designed for small businesses that are unable to obtain from private sources the intermediate- and long-term credit required for general purposes and normal growth. In addition to the fundamental requirements for government loans, an applicant for an SBA loan must also meet these other requisites:

1. Must be of good character.
2. Must show evidence of ability to operate his business successfully.
3. Must have enough capital in the business so that with the SBA loan it will be possible to operate on a sound financial basis.
4. Must show for a term loan, one which is repayable in installments over a period of several years, sufficient probable future income to provide reasonable assurance of repayment, which may be determined from his past records and future prospects. It is necessary that the loan be adequately secured by real estate, chattel mortgages or other suitable collateral.

The SBA makes several different types of loans: (1) bank participation loans, (2) direct loans, (3) disaster loans (to farmers also), (4) state and local development company loans, (5) displaced business loans, (6) minority enterprise loans, (7) guaranteed loans made by other financial agencies and (8) lease guarantee insurance policies.

Agribusinesses may avail themselves of the SBA guaranteed bank loan program if their sales are under $10 million per annum. SBA loans may be made for a maximum of $500,000 with terms of up to 15 years in case of real property loans. SBA will guarantee 90 per cent of the loan while the applicant must put up 10 per cent equity. Banks are the usual lender with the SBA guarantee.

SBA also provides various types of management and technical assistance to small businesses. These may include training for small business owners, management counseling, publications and engineering and economic surveys for assisting the development of small businesses.

Details on SBA loans are available from district field offices and from the SBA, 1441 "L" Street, N.W., Washington, D.C. 20416.

Small Business Investment Companies (SBIC)

Under the Small Business Investment Act of 1958, the Small Business Administration licenses and regulates privately owned small business investment companies and may, on occasion, provide them with financial assistance. These companies, in turn, make equity-type and long-term financing available to small business concerns. Often SBICs also provide management assistance to the companies they finance. These are their only functions. They cannot, for instance, sell insurance, trade in property or become holding companies for groups of operating businesses.

New SBICs derive their initial capital from private investors and may obtain matching funds from the government. An SBIC finances small firms in two general ways—by straight loans and by equity-type investments—which give the SBIC actual or potential ownership of a portion of a small business's stock. All financings must be for at least five years, except that a borrower may elect to have a prepayment clause included in the financing agreement. SBICs invest in practically all types of manufacturing and service industries and in a wide variety of other types of businesses, including construction, retailing and wholesaling. Many seek out small businesses offering new products or services because they believe these firms have unusual growth potential.

State Development Companies (SDC)

A state development company is a corporation organized under or pursuant to a special state legislative act and has for its purpose the furtherance of economic development of industry throughout its respective state. There are many such organizations, promoting and assisting the growth and development of small business concerns in the areas of their operations by supplying financial and managerial assistance. The SBA makes loans (known as Sec. 501 loans) to these companies, which in turn provide funds to small businesses.

Local Development Companies (LDC)

Under Sec. 502, the SBA can make, participate in on an immediate or deferred basis or guarantee loans to a Local Development Company for small business concerns. An LDC can be either a profit-making or a nonprofit corporation. It must be founded by public-spirited citizens. It must have 25 members. It must be incorporated under the laws of the state in which it does business. The LDC's charter and articles of incorporation must authorize it to promote and assist small business growth and development in the community where it operates. And, it must be at least 75 per cent owned and controlled by persons living in or doing business in that community.

An LDC can assist identifiable small business concerns to finance plant or commercial space construction, conversion or expansion including land acquisition and/or machinery and equipment acquisition and installation.

To borrow SBA funds and pass them through to a small business, the LDC must contribute a reasonable portion of the total project cost. The LDC raises its contribution by selling equity shares or debt securities. It also can contribute a cash equivalent such as land. SBA expects the LDC to sell its equity and debt obligations to private sources.

Banks for Farmer Cooperatives (BFC)

The 12 regional banks for farmer cooperatives plus one central bank provide funds to farmers' purchasing, marketing and service associations mainly. Fishery and rural electric co-ops may be funded also.

The banks for cooperatives extend three types of loans:

1. *Physical facility*—These loans are made for the purpose of financing or refinancing the acquisition of land, buildings and plant equipment. The security generally consists of a first mortgage on the facilities, but it could be other collateral.

2. *Operating Loans*—These loans are short- and medium-term loans. Short-term loans are repayable during an operating season and may be secured or unsecured depending upon the circumstances. Medium-term loans generally carry a three-year maturity and are usually secured. The amount loaned depends on the cooperative's financial condition, management and ability to repay.

3. *Commodity loans*—These loans are for a very short term. They are made on the security of staple commodities (cotton, sugar, rice, grain, etc.) usually over the normal marketing season. Each loan is secured by a first lien on commodities and cannot exceed 75 per cent of the net value of unhedged commodities or 90 per cent of the net value of hedged ones.

To be eligible to borrow from a bank for cooperatives, a cooperative must be an association in which farmers or fishermen act together in doing one or more of the following:

1. Processing, preparing for market, handling or marketing farm or fishery products.
2. Purchasing, testing, grading, processing, distributing or furnishing farm supplies.
3. Furnishing farm business services.

It is also necessary that an association be operated for the mutual benefit of its members and not do more business with nonmembers than with members. In an association eligible to borrow, no member may have more than one vote, or else dividends on the cooperative's stock or membership capital must not exceed 8 per cent a year. A further requirement is that at least 80 per cent of the voting rights of a cooperative must be held either by farmer-members or by associations owned and controlled by farmers.

In summary, the banks for cooperatives consider these factors in granting a co-op loan:

1. Evidence of the economic need for a cooperative.
2. Existence of sufficient volume to assure successful operation.
3. Quality of membership (stability, leadership, cohesion, etc.).
4. Market outlets or sources of supply.
5. Facilities needed, if any, and cost.
6. Capital requirements and source of capital, including amount contributed by members.

7. Determination that the cooperative is legal, its organization papers permitting the operation on a sound, cooperative basis.
8. Management capability.
9. Collateral offered as security for the loan.
10. Availability of supplementary sources of finance.

Commercial Paper

Commercial paper is another important source of short-term credit for the larger and well-established firm. Technically, commercial paper is a short-term, negotiable, unsecured promissory note sold by corporations to investors, other corporations and banks that have excess capital. Such notes are generally sold on a discount basis, but occasionally at the request of the buyer, they are sold at par, with interest due at maturity. Commercial paper is sold in the "money market" by placing it directly with either the investor or a dealer. Investors may obtain the paper directly, or through a dealer, or they may authorize a major bank to act as their agent.

Unfortunately, the smaller firms and investors are shut out of the commercial paper market. The smallest and most usual denomination amount traded in the secondary commercial paper market is $100,000. Trades of smaller denominations are rarely traded in the secondary market and must be handled by a dealer, who often places them directly.

Other Sources of Borrowed Capital

In many states, marketing and processing loans to agribusinesses are available from certain *state agencies*.

Various types of *bonds* are also used by agribusinesses. Secured bonds are of three types: real estate mortgages, chattel mortgages and collateral trust bonds, or those secured by a pledge of stocks or other negotiable instruments. Unsecured or debenture bonds are not protected by any specific property.

Oftentimes *individuals* make loans to agribusinesses through the medium of notes.

In other cases, *equipment companies* manufacturing and selling various types of equipment used in agribusiness will offer financing. While their interest rates may be slightly higher than those of the banks, their repayment terms may be more lenient.

In 1972, Congress passed the *Rural Development Act,* which authorized the Farmers Home Administration (FmHA) to make loans to agribusinesses for the purpose of establishing certain rural-based industries and services to provide greater employment in rural areas, to reduce the emigration of rural people to cities and to balance agriculture with industry. FmHA's Business and Industrial Loan program is quite liberal, guaranteeing 90 per cent of the loan, usually made by banks, for up to 30 years on real property and shorter terms on more liquid assets. Interest rates are set by the lender.

Use of Debt Versus Equity Capital

Although any business has to have some equity capital before it can obtain debt capital, a comparison of features of debt and equity instruments is shown in Table 13-1.

Table 13-1. Major Features of Basic Securities With Respect to Risk and Other Factors Affecting Quality[1]

Features	Term loans, bonds, and other debt instruments	Preferred stock	Common stock or residual equity
Due date	Yes	No	No
Claims on earnings	First	Second	Third
Claims on assets	First	Second	Third
Tax-deductible claim on earnings	Yes	No	No
Voting status	None	Limited	Yes
Returns variability	Fixed	Relatively fixed	Variable
Risk level:			
Supplier	Low	Intermediate	High
Firm	High	Intermediate	Low
Risk modifications:			
Favoring supplier	Pledge of assets; agreed on debt limits; amortization or sinking fund plans; dividend restrictions	Sinking funds; voting rights under specified conditions	Preemptive rights which protect against possible dilution of existing stock by new issue
firm	Repayment linked to earnings; accelerated maturity	Voluntary retirement	Residual claim on income and assets
Cost to firm	Low	Medium	High

[1]Adapted from: Haseley, Arnold, and Leon Garoian, "Financing Long-Term Capital Needs," *Management News for Agricultural Business,* Oregon State University, Corvallis, Mar. 1962.

METHODS OF CONSERVING CAPITAL

There are numerous business techniques for conserving capital or otherwise minimizing capital outlays, which may lessen the need for borrowing. Some of these are discussed subsequently.

Leasing

One of the foremost methods of conserving capital is by leasing needed facilities, equipment and vehicles.

The advantages and disadvantages of leasing are shown in Table 13-2.

Table 13-2. Leasing: Pros and Cons

Advantages	Disadvantages
1. Gives tax advantages in some cases—lease payments often exceed depreciation plus interest.	1. May be more expensive than other financing.
2. Releases capital which when used elsewhere may give greater returns.	2. May result in tax deductions less attractive than under ownership.
3. Acts as a hedge against equipment becoming obsolete.	3. Often binds firm to use equipment until lease expires.
4. Often offers more liberal terms than other credit sources.	4. May bring tax complications unless all angles are studied closely.
5. Increases sources of credit—preserves lines of credit from bank.	5. Eliminates the chance to experience pride of ownership.
6. Can be as flexible as the lessee's reputation allows.	6. May result in obligations that will affect borrowing power elsewhere.

Source: *Implement and Tractor*, Kansas City, Mo.

Factoring

Factoring refers to a business technique whereby a firm sells its accounts receivables to a finance company or other factor at a fee or discount. The factor assumes the accounts or debts, while the firm selling the receivables obtains cash for the credit paper. This procedure relieves a firm of carrying accounts and provides it with more liquidity. The factor profits from the discount, or the difference between what is paid and what is ultimately collected.

Through this service, the business credit organization administers and finances transactions between one business (the factoring client) and another (the client's customer). Clients include manufacturers, wholesalers, jobbers and distributors who maintain accounts for their business customers.

In factoring, clients usually sell their business receivables outright to the business credit organization. Accounts are purchased without recourse; if an account is uncollectible, the business credit company—not the client—incurs the loss.

The total service, including credit checking, assumption of credit risk, bookkeeping and collection, is known as maturity factoring. For this service, the business credit organization usually charges a fee of about 1 per cent of total annual factored sales.

Payment to the client is made monthly, usually on the average due date of the client's invoices. The factor pays his client whether or not the customer has paid his bill.

Discount factoring is an additional business credit service available to clients. Through this form, the client receives from the business credit organization cash in advance of the date receivables are due for payment. There is a modest interest charge on the funds advanced in addition to the factoring fee. Because it is a cash advance and not a loan, the transaction is not noted as a liability on the client's balance sheet.

Because factoring usually is identified with the textile and apparel industries, some businessmen feel that it is available exclusively to, or suitable only for, those industries. This, too, is incorrect. Although some 75 per cent of the companies now using factoring are in textiles or apparel, any concern that generates receivables of 30 to 90 days can benefit. Other industries in which factoring can be desirable include: hardware, lumber and wood products, leather products, furniture and fixtures and paper and allied products.[2]

Consignments

Consignments consist of merchandise left by the supplier to be paid for as sold, with remaining stocks returned after a certain period of time. Retail-type agribusinesses often use the consignment technique as a way of conserving capital funds. Consigned goods may cost more than if they had been purchased outright.

---

[2]Goldman, Roger O., "Factoring," *Case and Comment,* Nov.-Dec. 1975, p. 27.

Trade Credit and Discounts

Manufacturers, wholesalers and other types of suppliers usually extend large amounts of trade credit for various time periods and terms. The use of trade credit, when carefully managed, is a sound method of financial operation. However, it may be quite costly if the discounts allowed are not utilized properly.

These discounts are expressed as a percentage reduction or a series of percentage reductions, such as 20, 10 and 5 per cent from the list price. A special type of trade discount is the *quantity discount* used by sellers to encourage customers to buy in larger quantities. There is also the *cash discount,* which is a premium given to buyers for settlement of accounts before they are due. The discounts normally offered by sellers are higher than the current rate of interest. Consequently, it is usually advantageous to pay an invoice even if funds have to be borrowed within the discount period to do so.

An example of several cash discounts and their equivalent rates of interest are:

$^1/_{10}$, net 30	18% per year
$^2/_{10}$, net 60	14% per year
$^2/_{10}$, net 30	36% per year
$^3/_{10}$, net 30	54% per year
$^3/_{30}$, net 60	36% per year
$^2/_{30}$, net 60	24% per year
$^2/_{15}$, net 30	48% per year
$^2/_{20}$, net 30	72% per year
$^2/_{20}$, net 60	18% per year

Assume that an invoice for $1,000 is dated April 2. It carries terms of 2/10, net 30, one of the common discounts in use today. If the invoice is paid by April 12, deduct 2 per cent from the invoice and remit $980. If the invoice is not paid during the discount period, the full amount, $1,000, must be paid.

In effect, therefore, 2 per cent (or $20) can be saved by paying 20 days before the due date.

Industrial Inducement Programs

In many states and their subdivisions, industrial inducement programs make possible the local financing and ownership of industrial lands and plants. The laws under which the plans operate provide that any political subdivision may own and lease to businesses land and buildings for manufacturing. The state subdivision may finance such projects by issuing full-faith and credit bonds in an amount not to exceed 20 per cent (usually) of the assessed valuation of all property within its corporate limits.

Agribusinesses using industrial inducement programs pay rentals, which are encumbered for retiring bonds thus issued.

The advantages of industrial development bond financing include lower interest costs on these bonds, 100 per cent financing, longer repayment terms, exemption from local property taxes and stronger community support for the industrial plant project.

Disadvantages may include delays in placement of these bonds on the market and voter approval of the bond issues.

Capital Consumption Allowances

How does depreciation, which is a deterioration of assets, provide business with any funds? The answer is that the process of depreciation does not provide funds. But when goods are sold, the accountant divides the proceeds into several categories. One includes the costs of labor, materials, etc., involved in producing the goods, and since these expenses are paid in cash, the funds in this category are not available for financial purposes. Another part of the proceeds from sales is regarded as a reimbursement for the loss of value in depreciation. This part is available for meeting the firm's financial needs and is usually listed among the sources of funds simply as "depreciation."

Employees' Stock Ownerhip Plans (ESOP)

An ESOP is neither a "scheme" nor a "cure-all." But for many corporations, it can be an innovative method of securing capital funds while providing deferred compensation benefits that need not increase corporate expense. This is possible when ongoing deferred compensation plans are modified or converted to ESOPs so that contributions can be used to buy employer stock as a private placement. For example, when a corporation contributes $100,000 to a profit-sharing plan, these "hard" dollars leave the corporation forever and are invested by a trustee in securities that qualify under the so-called "prudent man rule." If the profit-sharing plan is converted to an ESOP and the same $100,000 is contributed to the ESOP (thus no increase in corporate expense), then the ESOP Trust can use the entire $100,000 to purchase authorized but unissued corporate stock, and those same "hard" dollars are returned for use by the corporation. The effect of such a transaction is simply a private placement.

ESOPs have a variety of beneficial uses for corporations, shareholders and employees. An ESOP can: (1) provide low-cost capital through conversion or modification of deferred compensation plans, (2) provide for a smooth change of ownership in closely held corporations or in public companies where large blocks of stock are held by a few individuals, (3) refinance debt with pre-tax dollars, (4) create an in-house market for closely held stock and create an additional market for public corporations, (5) provide maximum employee motivation for greater productivity and (6) lessen management-employee polarization.[3]

GUIDELINES FOR AGRIBUSINESS
CREDIT EXTENSION

Agribusinesses which sell feed, farm supplies and machinery to farmers and other retailers are becoming increasingly involved in credit extension.

While it may be competitively sound to extend credit, agribusiness managers, nevertheless, recognize that there are costs and pitfalls in granting credit.

There are many research reports analyzing the cost of extending farm supply credit. One study shows the cost at from 3.8 to 5.4 per cent of credit sales, which produces an interest rate of from 14 to 20 per cent on the money involved.

In any case, the cost items in extending credit are these: (1) interest on the money borrowed or used in carrying accounts; (2) discounts lost on purchases when a firm is short of capital; (3) cost of

---

[3]Crichton, J. H., "A Quiet Revolution in Corporate Finance," *Atlanta Economic Review*, Atlanta, Ga., Nov.-Dec. 1977, p. 33.

time, materials, application forms and other items related to the initiation of credit accounts; (4) bookkeeping costs in connection with credit accounts (salaries, materials, etc.); (5) costs of collecting accounts, such as for wages, salaries, postage, materials, legal fees, travel, phone, collectors' fees and recording fees; and (6) bad debt losses.

Credit sales may involve a great deal of cost other than just the interest on funds needed to finance the receivables. Even if no other costs are involved, interest costs alone can slash away a substantial portion of any net margin realized on a credit sale.

To illustrate, let us assume that a $3 net margin (after $1 depreciation) is realized on a $100 credit sale. Assume the interest rate on funds to carry the receivables is 6 per cent. The following schedule shows the amount of the $3 net margin which is left when the account is collected in full after different periods of time:

One month	$2.70
Two months	2.40
Three months	2.10
Six months	1.20
Nine months	.40
Twelve months	−.45

Are all these costs of extending credit less than, equal to or more than revenues received for having made these credit sales? One economist has expressed this test of costs versus revenues as follows:

> In order to determine how much credit he should extend, each storeowner needs to estimate both the dollar benefits and the dollar costs of his credit sales. He can profitably extend credit so long as the total dollar benefits exceed the total dollar costs. But he cannot afford to extend credit to the point where the added costs are greater than the added benefits.[4]

Credit Policy

Assuming that the agribusiness storeowner has determined or estimated his costs of extending credit, he should next have a sound credit policy. Following are some essentials of a good policy:

---

[4]Phillips, R., *Farm Store Merchandising*, Minneapolis, Minn., 1961 reprint.

1. Establish a realistic credit policy.
   a. Adopt a formal, written credit policy.
   b. Obtain approval of the policy from the board of directors of the store (if this applies).
   c. Minimize exceptions to the policy.
   d. Hold the store manager responsible for enforcement rather than formulation of credit policy if the manager is not the owner.
   e. Delegate the tasks of extending credit to a person who can become a specialist in this area.
   f. Discuss the policy and its specific terms for mutual understanding between the management and employees.
2. Adopt specific procedures for extending credit.
   a. Select credit applicants carefully, using a written application. A little time devoted to screening applicants will save a large amount of time later in trying to collect bad accounts.
   b. Maintain a list of patrons who are not eligible for credit and those whose credit is limited.
   c. Have employees sell the credit policy along with the commodities. Employees should explain all the terms carefully when making a credit sale.
   d. Age all accounts receivables for monthly review.
   e. Prohibit any employee or director from buying on credit at the store. This is to prevent conflicts of interest.
   f. Check on the credit reliability of a customer by using the services of a credit bureau, a bank, a salesman, other stores, other merchants and court house records.
   g. Limit the amount of credit extended to any one individual.
   h. Issue credit cards to patrons who have demonstrated their credit reliability to facilitate transactions.
   i. Drop at once patrons who do not demonstrate their credit reliability; do not carry their accounts endlessly.
3. Establish sound collection practices.
   a. Send monthly statements to patrons with accounts.
   b. Be firm with account holders in enforcing credit policy. Make special efforts to obtain payment on the due date.
   c. Use notes on slow accounts.
   d. Use collection agencies as a last resort.

4. Recognize and allocate the costs of credit.
   a. Consider credit as a service, and set a price on it.
   b. Either allow a cash discount or make a charge for credit, but inform all patrons of the policy and treat all patrons alike.

Interest Charged

Storeowners are divided about charging interest on regular accounts and/or on overdue accounts. On a 30-day account it is doubtful if interest should be charged. On an account between 31 and 60 days old, perhaps one-half per cent per month on the unpaid balance should be charged (the equivalent of 6 per cent per year). On an account that is over 60 days old, possibly 1 per cent per month on the unpaid balance should be charged (the equivalent of 12 per cent per year).

Shifting Credit Burdens to Other Agencies

In an increasing number of cases, agribusinesses have been successful in shifting credit extension to finance agencies. Commercial banks, production credit associations, credit unions, agricultural and agribusiness credit corporations and factoring companies, among others, have taken over the role of credit supplier from agribusiness retailers.

● ● ●

In the next chapter, the roles of stockholders, directors, managers and employees in agribusiness management are considered.

TOPICS FOR DISCUSSION

1. Select one type of agribusiness and determine its fixed and operating capital requirements.
2. Name and discuss some sources of equity capital.
3. Name and discuss some sources of borrowed capital.
4. Name and discuss methods of conserving capital.
5. Present guidelines for effective extension of credit by agribusinesses.

SELECTED REFERENCES

1. Barry, P. J., and J. R. Brake, *Financial Strategies and Economic Decisions of the Firm,* Mich. Agr. Exp. Sta. Rept. 185, East Lansing, Feb. 1971.
2. Blake, W. H., *Retail Credit and Collections,* SBA Bibliography 31, Washington, D.C., Jul. 1977.
3. Johnson, R. B., and S. J. Miller, *Farm Lending Practices of Commercial Banks in Louisiana,* La. Agr. Exp. Sta. DAE 520, Baton Rouge, Jun. 1977.
4. Kelley, Paul K., "New Financing Techniques on Wall Street," *Financial Executive,* Nov. 1974, pp. 30-42.
5. Robinson, R. I., *Financing the Dynamic Small Firm,* Wadsworth Publishing Co. Inc., Belmont, Calif., 1966.
6. Roy, Ewell P., *Cooperatives: Development, Principles and Management,* The Interstate Printers & Publishers, Inc., Danville, Ill., 1976.
7. Schermerhorn, R. W., and R. E. Page, *Financial Statement Analysis for Agribusiness Firms,* Okla. Agr. Ext. Serv. Cir. E-812, Stillwater, Feb. 1970.
8. Staff, *The ABC's of Borrowing,* SBA–MA 170, Washington, D.C., Apr. 1977.
9. Van Horne, J. C., *Fundamentals of Financial Management,* Prentice-Hall, Inc., Englewood Cliffs, N.J., 1974.
10. Zwick, Jack, *A Handbook of Small Business Finance,* SBA Aid No. 15, Washington, D.C., 1965.

14

Agribusiness Management:

Stockholders, Directors, Managers and Employees

For a single proprietorship or partnership, the roles of stockholder, director, manager and employee quite often are combined. For a corporation or cooperative, these roles usually are separate and distinguishable and are the primary concern in this chapter.

STOCKHOLDERS[1]

Stockholders or members of a corporation have specific *powers* under the law as enumerated in the chartering documents. They also have *responsibilities,* some moral and others legal, with regards to these powers.

Powers of stockholders usually include the right to:

1. Adopt the articles of incorporation and bylaws as well as to amend them.
2. Elect and recall directors.
3. Vote upon appropriations of money for various purposes, increase or decrease the capitalization and decide upon pooling practices and contractual arrangements.

---

[1]In profit-type corporations, the owners are the stockholders; in co-op corporations, the owners are known either as stockholders (in stock co-ops) or as members (in nonstock co-ops).

4. Require both directors and officers, as well as their agents and employees, to run the business according to the articles, bylaws and contracts.
5. Hold directors and officers liable for any damage injurious to the stockholders/members.
6. Elect a competent committee to examine the records and audit the books periodically.
7. Examine the reports at the annual meeting or at other times.
8. Dissolve or merge the corporation.

Regardless of the type of corporation, those holding voting rights have approximately the same set of *responsibilities*, whether they are classed as stockholders or members.

These responsibilities are:

1. Providing the necessary capital.
2. Controlling the business through the board of directors as their elected representatives.
3. Patronizing the business to the fullest extent possible, if it is a cooperative (not entirely applicable if it is a profit-type corporation).
4. Assuming the business risks.
5. Paying the costs of operation.
6. Keeping informed about the corporation.
7. Maintaining the corporation.

Qualifications for Stockholders in Profit-Type Corporations

In general, there are no particular qualifications for being a stockholder in a profit-type corporation except for having the capital to invest in stock. In a sense, stockholding may be qualified, such as in a closed or family corporation where stock is unavailable to outsiders.

Qualifications for Membership in Cooperatives

Membership in a cooperative is not automatic but is applied for, reviewed by the board (or a committee of the board) and accepted or rejected by a majority vote of the board. Some cooperatives err by permitting memberships which are too open, assuming that a member's patronage is the only valid concern and forgetting that, in a cooperative, the member is both patron and owner. If membership in a cooperative is restricted and its qualifications are high, prospective members will place a higher premium on the worth of the cooperative. A cooperative with loose membership qualifications is not apt to be respected or trusted.

Another aspect of co-op membership is that all members should be thoroughly educated in co-op principles and practices before being admitted to membership. While this is a slow process, over the long run both the members and the cooperative will be better off. The educational program can consist of a series of weekly meetings featuring lectures and discussion groups. Upon the termination of the study sessions, the cooperative can then be organized or the members admitted.

Since a cooperative is controlled by the membership, there must be machinery for the members to exercise control. The annual meeting is a part of this machinery, giving the members an opportunity to elect the board of directors, to set policies for the board and to hear and evaluate a report of the year's operations.

BOARD OF DIRECTORS

Within the broad policies laid down by the stockholders/members, the board of directors is the governing body in the corporation. Acting as a group, the directors employ the manager, establish specific operating policies and supervise the management of the corporation. The directors are the elected representatives of the stockholders/members.

Generally, directors have these *powers:*

1. To function collectively as a board in a duly called meeting. No authority resides in the directors as individuals.
2. To prescribe the form and maintenance of stockholder/ membership records.
3. To prescribe the form, extent and nature of financial reports.
4. To make changes in the bylaws (when the power to do so is vested in the directors).
5. To adopt, use and alter the corporate seal.
6. To borrow money and issue such evidence of indebtedness as required.

7. To render services, furnish supplies and market products in accordance with the purposes of the corporation as enumerated in the organization documents.
8. To commingle funds of the corporation from all sources and to decide on the investments in other businesses and/or other enterprises.
9. To employ the general manager; determine his responsibilities, duties and compensation; and dismiss him if necessary.
10. To determine which employees are to be bonded, fix the amounts of their bonds and provide for adequate insurance protection for all facilities, equipment and personnel.
11. To call special meetings of the board.
12. To elect officers of the board, remove them for cause and fill vacancies.
13. To provide for the installation of an accounting system.
14. To employ an auditor.
15. To establish rules and regulations regarding the transfer of stock or memberships and other evidences of equity in the corporation.
16. To issue and sell stock or other evidences of equity capital.
17. To determine the manner, form and amount of patronage refunds (if in a co-op corporation).
18. To declare dividends on stock or equity capital.
19. To enter into contracts and to sue and be sued.
20. To formulate and evaluate external and internal operating policies, both for the short run and for the long run.

Generally, directors have these *responsibilities:*
1. To serve the best interests of the stockholders/members whom they represent rather than their own individual interests.
2. To hire the best trained and most efficient manager that they can employ and to create the best possible working conditions for him that are compatible with the interest of the members and the success of the corporation.
3. To determine operating policies and, not interfering in the day-to-day operation of the business, check to see that these policies are followed.
4. To know and understand the financial operation of the corpo-

ration and satisfy themselves that the records kept are accurate in every detail.

5. To keep the stockholders/members informed about the corporation and insure that the entire organization is permeated with spirit of service to, and respect for, the stockholders/members.
6. To maintain the corporation as an efficient business institution worthy of the good will of the community and area it serves.
7. To keep records of all meetings of the board.
8. To further their knowledge of, and training in, management and to familiarize themselves with corporate law, the articles of incorporation and the bylaws of their corporation.

Officers of the Board

The officers of the board are usually elected from the board members, not the stockholders/members. The duties of the president are to preside at all meetings, carry out the will of the stockholders/members and watch over all affairs of the corporation. The vice-president takes over the responsibilities of the president in the latter's absence. The secretary serves at the meetings of both the directors and the general membership. His duties are to keep the minutes and records, to attend to correspondence and to act as the official custodian of the seal and the stock book and/or the membership records. The secretary is sometimes also the treasurer. The treasurer supervises the bookkeeping and accounts and takes such steps as are necessary to assure himself that the accounts are being kept accurately and that the funds are being handled properly. He makes periodic reports to the board and to the stockholders/members.

The officers and other board members usually meet once monthly to review the financial statements, receive the manager's report and decide on policy matters. The president issues the call and agenda for these meetings, while the secretary transmits them to each board member. It is important that a detailed agenda be distributed to each board member before every meeting.

Board Policies

Some of the policies which a board of directors is obliged to define upon taking office are these:

1. *Finance policy,* which includes determinations of equity and creditor capital, revolving funds, rates of expansion or contraction, operating budgets, construction programs, etc.
2. *Service policy,* which includes the type and scope of services to be offered to or provided for members or patrons.
3. *Pricing policy,* which includes markup practices, quantity discounts, etc.
4. *Credit extension policy,* which includes the type and terms of credit extended, credit application procedures, collection methods, etc.
5. *Membership relations policy,* which includes the preparation and distribution of newsletters, the handling of stockholder/member grievances, etc.
6. *Public relations policy,* which includes joining trade groups or business councils, working with youth groups, releasing information, etc.
7. *Employee relations policy,* which includes salary and wage scales, incentive and training programs, promotions, fringe benefits, collective bargaining, etc.
8. *Internal operations policy,* which includes the organization of the business, the keeping of operating and technical records, etc.
9. *Management development policy,* which includes a program of seminars, courses, workshops, etc., for the managerial staff and directors.
10. *Long-range planning policy,* which includes long-term investments, budgets and operational strategies.

BUSINESS MANAGER

In most businesses, success or failure hinges on management competence, the manager commonly being thought of as the spearhead. He must: (1) solve the technical business problems, which include sales promotion, preparation of products for market, purchasing and many problems that relate to the physical distribution and pricing of commodities and services and (2) manage the accounting, financing, personnel and other internal operations. Furthermore, the board of directors must be a constant challenge to the manager, if he is to work effectively with it. The manager is selected by the board and is accountable to it.

The *powers* of a corporate manager are:

1. To hire and fire his subordinates according to a general policy adopted by the board.
2. To plan, organize, direct, coordinate and control all the administrative and financial operations of the corporation.
3. To train or have trained employees of the corporation.
4. To supervise, conduct and direct all jobs and activities delegated to him by the board of directors.
5. To represent the corporation to the public as the board may outline.

The board may outline the manager's *responsibilities* as follows:

1. The manager shall supervise the detailed operations of the corporation in accord with the policies agreed upon by the board of directors.
2. The manager shall maintain an adequate bookkeeping and accounting system, provide for its regular examination by competent outside auditors selected by the board of directors and present to the stockholders/members at the regular annual meeting a statement of the financial condition of the corporation.
3. The manager shall attend all board meetings and make available to the board a business report and pertinent financial statements.
4. The manager shall make periodic reports to the board of directors, together with recommendations concerning corporate operations.
5. The manager shall devote full time to the affairs of the corporation.
6. The manager shall develop budgets of anticipated income and expected operating costs and present them to the board as it may require.
7. The manager shall bring to the board's attention all matters requiring board consideration and action.
8. The manager shall confer with the board of directors on the development of new policies and help appraise the effectiveness of policies already adopted.

The making of all operating decisions, the employment and supervision of personnel, the implementation of policies and the conduct of day-to-day activities are clearly a part of the manager's duties. He alone is charged with these responsibilities.

The manager shares some responsibilities jointly with the board, such as long-range planning, the area in which teamwork is most productive. Long-range planning is the most important function of the board of directors, and a primary duty of the manager is to assist the board in this endeavor. The purpose, future direction, broad basic policies, aims and objectives of the corporation are decided upon by this mutual process. Note that the board members make the policy decisions and that the manager must be careful to confine his activities to assisting in these decisions.

Qualifications of a Manager

A good corporate manager should possess all or most of these qualifications:

1. *Intellectual ability,* to think correctly and possess technical and administrative competence.
2. *Creative ability,* to be imaginative.
3. *Visionary ability,* to look ahead at the trends in his business.
4. *Leadership ability,* to have others want to follow him.
5. *Work ability,* to carry forward the details in operating the business.
6. *Decision-making ability,* to make correct decisions rapidly.
7. *Moral ability,* to distinguish right from wrong and to hold high standards of conduct.
8. *Judgment ability,* to be flexible enough so that variations in people are recognized.
9. *Public relations ability,* to write and speak effectively in behalf of the corporation.
10. *Coordinating ability,* to bring together different viewpoints, analyze them and compromise them in an effective manner.

Very few persons can have perfect scores in all 10 abilities. Some of these abilities are native to the person; others can be developed through study and experience. Persons with high scores in all abilities must be paid adequately since they are so rare.

Selecting the Manager

When a small business is ready to locate a manager, its board of directors should: (1) specify the nature of the job, qualifications sought and method of compensation; (2) advertise the vacancy in the local and area press; (3) prepare and distribute application blanks for prospective candidates; and (4) interview the most likely prospects at a special board meeting. After the hiring is completed, a short but intensive training period should take place, depending on the person's qualifications. Other management assistance may be available from colleges, trade councils and trade associations.

In a large business, selection of a manager is more formal. Assistant managers and department heads in both the business and other corporations are likely candidates. Very often, junior executives in other businesses, who have no room to move to the top, are a good source of personnel. Management staffs should never be too inbred. Businesses should periodically hire management from other related businesses, from other areas and, sometimes, from nonrelated businesses.

There are no exact criteria for selecting a good manager. Perhaps the best overall criterion is that the board know precisely what kind of a manager it is looking for and then attempt to fill this position in the best manner possible.

Compensating the Manager

A business must pay salaries high enough to attract and retain management sufficiently capable to attain the goals and objectives of the stockholders/members expressed through the board of directors.

Various compensation methods may be used, such as: (1) straight salary; (2) salary plus some type of commission based on sales, profits, volume, etc.; (3) salary plus a percentage of net earnings; (4) salary plus various fringe benefits (life insurance, health insurance, retirement plan); (5) salary plus bonus on net sales; (6) salary plus bonus based on percentage of annual salary; (7) straight commission; and (8) combinations of the aforementioned. Each has advantages and disadvantages. It is likely that a straight salary plus a bonus of some type and fringe benefits will yield the best results. Fringe benefits may include paid vacations, sick leave, sabbatical leave, life insurance, hospital and medical insurance, discounts on merchandise and retirement plans. One or more of these have become firmly established in almost all personnel compensation plans.

Stock or debenture options are another possibility for compensating managers and managerial personnel. Opportunity for employees to buy into the company is very common in profit-type businesses, primarily through stock options. Corporations might consider paying half of the bonus in cash and half in stock or debenture bonds up to a certain amount. Voting control, however, must always remain with the stockholders/members.

EMPLOYEES

Although the manager must be competent, he must realize that he is not an expert in all fields. Because of this, he selects and trains capable employees and is knowledgeable of the art of delegating responsibility. The manager realizes that training does not cost money; what costs is paying for the mistakes of untrained people. He creates conditions that encourage employees to maintain high productivity on their own accord. Advancements are made on the basis of merit, performance and planned standards.

Job Evaluation

Job evaluation involves two main steps: job description and job pricing.

Job description, depending on the work to be done, can be either involved or simple. It is a written record of the duties, responsibilities and requirements of a particular job. A description includes a summary of the significant facts pertaining to a job. These facts give the owner-manager and the employee a general understanding of what the job is (what responsibilities are involved), how it is to be done (what skills are required) and why the worker does it. They also indicate how the job is related to other jobs in the plant.

Job pricing is the last phase of the evaluation, the procedure by which dollar rates of compensation are adopted for the jobs which previously have been analyzed.

Selecting Employees

In the process of the selection and orientation of employees, the manager should:

1. Have each applicant complete an application for employment.
2. Require a physical examination and, if possible, see that some type of aptitude test is given.
3. Give the newly hired employee a probationary appointment.
4. Give the employee a copy of the job manual and his job description and quiz him on these some time later.
5. Make it clear at the beginning of the employment what the employee is supposed to do and how much of it he is expected to do during an hour, day or other time unit.
6. Give proper training.
7. Observe and inspect the employee's work at regular intervals to make certain that it is done right.
8. Tell each subordinate how he is doing, what the weaknesses in his job are and how to overcome them. The manager should help him if necessary.
9. Create work happiness, giving the subordinate a sense of self-satisfaction on the job and the feeling that he is doing worthwhile, useful work. The employee must be made to understand his role in the overall organization and his possibilities for advancement.

Compensating Employees

Various types of compensation are used, depending on the nature of the jobs involved. Obviously, the warehouse boy will necessitate a compensation plan different from those plans for salesmen. Straight salary, salary plus incentives, hourly wage, piece-rate pay, commissions, bonuses, shift premiums, stock options and purchases and profit sharing are ordinary methods of compensation.

In any case, wages or salaries plus incentive-type payments are recommended whenever applicable. The competition for employees in an area, minimum wage laws, union wage scales, skills required, cost of living indexes and other factors must be considered in compensating employees.

Fringe benefits are important. Vacation with pay, sick leave, life and disability insurance, hospital and surgical insurance, credit union, savings plans, training programs, discounts on merchandise, funeral and jury duty leave pay, retirement plans and educational courses, among others, are involved.

An effective employee benefit plan should give the worker some protection against at least four major financial hazards:

1. Loss of future income for the family because of the worker's premature death.
2. Loss of current and future earnings due to disability.
3. Excessive medical expenses arising from illness or accident.
4. Insufficient income following retirement from productive employment.

Effective coverage can be given in each of these areas through an employer's voluntary benefits plan working in conjunction with the governmental plans required by law, such as social security.

Employee Morale

The strongest incentives management can use to develop employee morale include:

1. Recognition of individual abilities through merit-pay plans.
2. Opportunity to make optimum utilization of abilities and interests.
3. Creation of pride in a job well done.
4. Rewards based on performance.

The attitude of employees towards the executives and supervisors of the business for which they work is about the most important factor in determining their morale, which in turn plays a large role in promoting their efficiency.

Employee Training

The organization and operation of an employee training program constitute a basic necessity in the successful functioning of a business. Trained employees are so vital to any business that it is not necessary to elaborate on their importance.

Training programs seem to bring best results when the emphasis is on self-development, with the scope and progress geared to individual ability and interest. Self-development comes from within—it is personal growth. Major areas in which self-development can be effected are: (1) improvement in technical skills, (2) expansion of management skills, (3) broadening of knowledge of company philosophy and objectives, (4) improvement of initiative and self-direction, (5) achievement of emotional maturity and stability, (6) improvement in management of one's time and energy and (7) improvement of thinking habits.

Labor Unions

Increasingly, agribusiness management is confronted with collective bargaining by its employees. A collective bargaining agreement is a contract between the employer and his employees. In general, the contract contains one or more clauses covering union recognition and security, wages, hours, fringe benefits, discipline, grievances, working conditions and terms, scope and length of the agreement.

THE FUNCTIONS OF MANAGEMENT

Management is both the science and the art of combining ideas, facilities, processes, materials and people to produce and market a worthy product or render a service profitably. The prime essential of good management is that the manager manage himself—organize his own work and thoughts, decide on a course of action, execute decisions and impartially analyze the results. He must also be his own best critic—not wait to hear criticism from others. Until he manages himself effectively, no amount of ability, skill, experience or knowledge will make him an effective executive.

The board of directors and the manager and his employee team are charged with the responsibility of planning (P), organizing (O), directing (D), coordinating (C) and controlling (C) the business. These steps are often referred to as the PODCC of management.

Planning

Planning is the thoughtful determination and systematic arrangement of all the factors required to achieve the goals and objectives of the business.

It is getting ready to do the work, not actually performing the job.

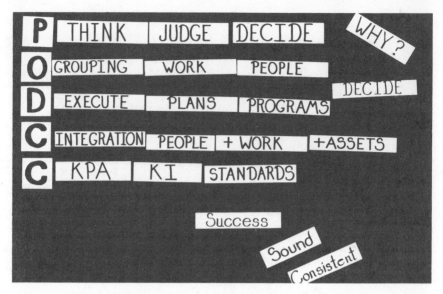

Figure 14-1. The five management functions are: (1) planning, (2) organizing, (3) directing, (4) coordinating and (5) controlling. (Courtesy, N.C. Agr. Ext. Serv., Raleigh)

Planning is the *thinking, judging* and *deciding* aspect of the manager's job, the mental process that should be carried on before any action is taken. It starts with the formation of the ideals and objectives of the business and predetermines what shall be done, why it shall be done and how and by whom it shall be done in order to attain these desired goals and objectives. It completes its course by providing controls that will tell management how well it is doing and where it needs to replan. Unless definite procedures are established for reaching a certain goal, we have an idea—not a plan.

Organizing

Organizing is the grouping of activities and the fitting together of people in the best possible relationships to get the work done effectively and economically and to help achieve the objectives and goals of the enterprise.

After plans are established, the factors necessary to put these plans into operation must be arranged and placed in their proper relationship. Personnel must be procured, developed and motivated. Relationships between superiors and subordinates and between various executives must be established and outlined. Procedures, methods and systems must be installed and made ready for operation, and needed tools, equipment and supplies must be provided.

The cardinal points in organization are as follows:

1. Specifically, there are four accepted types of organization today: (a) line, (b) line and staff, (c) functional and (d) committee. In the *line* type, authority and responsibility are direct from head to assistant to worker. In the *line and staff* type, the line command is dominant, but there are certain staff personnel who furnish specialized advice to the line managers. Larger and more complex enterprises use this technique. In the *functional* type, assignments are made according to the job to be done; for example, the transportation chief is in charge of transportation, the warehouse superviser is in charge of warehousing functions, etc. The last type, or *committee,* consists of two or more persons acting jointly in their authority and responsibility. This is used less as a dominant type than others, although it may be used widely as a supplementary management tool.

2. There should be a definite hierarchy with clean lines of authority running from the top to the bottom of the organization, and it should be understood by everyone.

3. A subordinate should not have to receive orders from more than one superior.

4. Unity of command functions should be grouped together.

5. Responsibility should be coupled with commensurate authority.

6. Authority should be delegated as far down the line as possible.

7. Administrative efficiency increases with an increase in specialization.

8. Continuous in-service training is essential for staff members to be competent in performing their assignments.

9. Committees can be a useful adjunct to the organization, but they should be limited in number and have specific duties.

10. No administrator should be required personally to supervise and account for more than 10 persons and should be in charge of fewer if the administration is complex.

Directing

Directing is getting the day-to-day execution of plans and projects, including the activities performed by others for which the incumbent is responsible and also those which he performs personally. The manager, in his directing role, is involved with job delegations, specific assignments, instructions, communications, human relations, motivation, approvals, decisions, recommendations, conduct of and attendance at conferences, review or preparation of reports, interviews and negotiations.

One of the most important factors in directing a business is the delegation of work and authority to subordinates. Too often a manager does not delegate authority. Since the manager is responsible for the whole business and its operations, he often tries to do all of the directing and winds up actually performing the jobs of employees himself. Such a situation does not leave time for the manager to perform the actual functions of managment—mainly, decision making on the basis of a careful analysis of the best information available.

The essence of direction is the ability to command the work of others. In directing, management should recognize ability in others. Authority goes hand in hand with responsibility; thus, responsibility must be delegated along with authority. It is of prime importance that a manager know what and when to delegate. A few simple rules are listed.

The manager should:

1. Delegate anything anyone else can do as well or better and use specialists to do the jobs which they can handle and for which they were hired to handle.
2. Delegate jobs which he might do poorly because of a lack of time.
3. Delegate when a subordinate can do the job well enough for the cost or time involved. Often a subordinate cannot do the job so well as the manager; but if the manager did the job, it would interfere with more important jobs. It may take the manager less time to coach a subordinate than it would take to do the job himself.
4. Delegate when it costs too much for him to do the job.
5. Delegate the job as a means of developing subordinates, if costs

and time permit and the job does not involve too much risk.

6. Always delegate when he has something more important to do.
7. Delegate the work or develop someone to whom this work can be delegated if he finds he is spending too much time on operations and not enough time on management.
8. Not delegate when he has the time and know-how to do the job.

Coordinating

Coordination is the function of management which results in the synchronization of the activities of people, of the use of facilities and materials and of the handling of the assets of an enterprise to accomplish a unified approach to a predetermined goal or objective. Coordination involves the integration of relationships between various departments and applies specifically to activities for which the incumbent is responsible but involving other personnel sharing, checking, reviewing, appraising or controlling activities. It includes working-team relationships with the board of directors.

There are basically four major areas of coordination:

1. Coordination in planning.
2. Coordination of individual assignments.
3. Coordination of the activities of the various departments or units, particularly necessary when the success of one department depends on another for services, materials, etc.
4. Coordination of internal activities of the business with the political, social and economic activities outside the business.

Controlling

Controlling is the function which involves seeing that the plan of action is followed according to specifications and taking remedial action to prevent unsatisfactory results. This includes the responsibility of the incumbent to keep informed of progress within his organization; to interpret trends and results; and to know when, where and how to initiate timely remedial action. Some preventive or facilitative controls may be exercised over the work of others who do not report to the incumbent. Some necessary preventive controls are personal signatures, inspections and approvals. Facilitative controls, such as budgets, are very important. Controlling is not a restrictive measure but rather an informative one. It is likened to the gauges on the dashboard of an automobile, indicating how the various parts are performing.

MANAGEMENT BY OBJECTIVES (MBO)

The minimum requirements for an MBO program are:
1. Each manager's job includes 5 to 10 goals expressed in specific, measurable terms.
2. Each manager proposes goals in writing.
3. Each goal consists of the statement of the goal, how it will be measured and the work steps necessary to complete it.
4. Results are systematically determined at regular intervals (at least quarterly) and compared with the goals.
5. When progress towards goals is not in accordance with plans, problems are identified and corrective action is taken.
6. Goals at each level of management are related to the level above and the level below.

● ● ●

In the next chapter, the economic tools used in agribusiness management are discussed.

TOPICS FOR DISCUSSION

1. Discuss the powers and responsibilities of stockholders.
2. Discuss the role of the board of directors in a corporation.
3. Discuss the powers and responsibilities of the business manager.
4. Discuss the role of employees in business.
5. List and discuss the five functions of management.
6. What is MBO?

SELECTED REFERENCES

1. Becker, B. M., and Fred Tillman, *Management Checklist for a Family Business*, SBA–MA 225, Washington, D.C., Apr. 1976.
2. Cahill, T. E., *Setting Pay for Management Jobs*, SBA–MA 195, Washington, D.C., Jul. 1977.

3. Craig, R. L., and C. J. Evers, *Training for Small Business*, SBA Bibliography 86, Washington, D.C., Apr. 1976.
4. Cruger, F. M., *Preparing an Employee Handbook*, SBA–MA 197, Washington, D.C., Sept. 1977.
5. Duft, Ken, *Management by Objective*, Wash. Agr. Ext. Serv., Pullman, Oct. 1971.
6. Duft, Ken, *Matrix Management*, Wash. Agr. Ext. Serv., Pullman, Aug. 1970.
7. Goodpasture, Bruce, *Danger Signals in a Small Store*, SBA–SMA 141, Washington, D.C., Jan. 1978.
8. Jacobson, Barbara, *Personnel Management*, SBA Bibliography 72, Washington, D.C., Jun. 1976.
9. Matts, Rex, *How to Write a Job Description*, SBA–MA 171, Washington, D.C., Sept. 1976.
10. Morton, R. C., "Compensation: A Critical Facet of Managing," *Feedstuffs*, Minneapolis, Minn., Jan. 21, 1974, p. 23.
11. Pelissier, R. F., *Planning and Goal Setting for Small Business*, SBA–MA 233, Washington, D.C., Jan. 1978.
12. Roy, Ewell P., *Cooperatives: Development, Principles and Management*, The Interstate Printers & Publishers, Inc., Danville, Ill., 1976.
13. Roy, Ewell P., *Locating, Selecting, Training and Evaluating Business Managers*, Tri-State Co-op Committee, Baton Rouge, La., 1975.
14. Smith, L. J., *Checklist for Developing a Training Program*, SBA–MA 186, Washington, D.C., Jun. 1977.
15. Staff, *Recruiting, Training and Developing Workers for Farmer Cooperatives*, FCS Info. 77, U.S. Dept. of Agriculture, Washington, D.C., Oct. 1971.

15

Agribusiness Management:

Economic Tools for Decision Making

Management of agribusiness is a complex operation involving many principles of economics as well as those of other disciplines. Knowledge of business management is obtainable through experience, observation, supervised study and self-study, travel, discussions and various other means. But management principles are not sufficient in themselves; correct application of principles is most citical.

In this chapter only a few of the many economic principles applicable to agribusiness management are considered. For a more thorough discussion of economic principles the reader is referred to standard texts on this subject.

LAW OF COMPARATIVE ADVANTAGE

The selection of a certain type of agribusiness in which to engage is subject to the law of comparative advantage. That is, to maximize profits, one should engage in a line of business—considering output, costs and returns—in which the percentage return on equity capital is greatest. However, this does not necessarily mean that one should engage only in a line of business that is most profitable. One must look at those enterprises which are most profitable relative to all available production choices and trade possibilities. Thus, one may engage in a line of business with the greatest comparative advantage or the least absolute disadvantage.[1]

LAW OF DIMINISHING RETURNS

The law of diminishing returns states: *When successive equal units of a variable resource are added to a given quantity of a fixed resource, there will come a point where the addition to total output will decline.* This is illustrated in Table 15-1 and Figure 15-1.

Table 15-1. Hypothetical Example of the Law of Diminishing Returns

Units of input	Total units of output[1]	Added output[2]	Average output[3]
1	1	1	1.0
2	3	2	1.5
3	6	3	2.0
4	10	4	2.5
5	15	5	3.0
6	20	5	3.3
7	24	4	3.4
8	27	3	3.4
9	29	2	3.2
10	30	1	3.0
11	28	−2	2.5
12	24	−4	2.0

[1]Total physical product.
[2]Marginal physical product.
[3]Average physical product.

At first, we note increasing returns per unit of input. That is, each successive unit of input from 1 to 5 yielded more units to output. Then, at 6 units of input, a plateau or point of *constant* returns per unit was reached, followed by *decreasing* or *diminishing* returns per unit from 7 to 10. From 11 to 12 units of input, an actual decline in total output occurred. But, physical data alone do not decide the profitable point to produce. We must combine economic and physical data to find this point, considered next.

PROFIT MAXIMIZATION

Profits are maximized when the income or revenue from the sale of the last unit of output equals the cost needed to produce it. At this

[1]Roy, Ewell P., and others, *Economics: Applications to Agriculture and Agribusiness,* The Interstate Printers & Publishers, Inc., Danville, Ill., 1980.

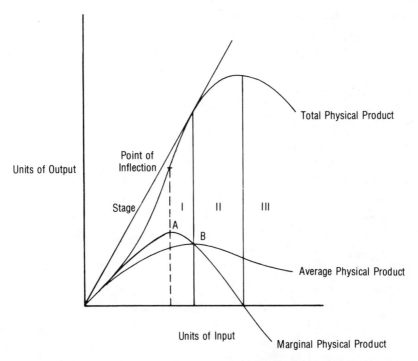

Figure 15-1. The total physical product function with average and marginal physical product relationships defining stages of production.

point, marginal costs equal marginal revenue, and total net profit is greatest (Table 15-2).

In the table, the point of maximum profit production is at 10 input and 30 output units, resulting in a maximum net profit of $100, the point where marginal cost is equal to marginal revenue. It is noted that the point of maximum net profit is not necessarily at the point of lowest average variable cost, which is, instead, at 7 input and 24 output units.

INPUT SUBSTITUTION ANALYSIS

Important to agribusinessmen is the principle of input substitution to produce a given output. For example, a business manager might consider using clerks exclusively for all clerical jobs or perhaps using a certain combination of clerks and computers. The exact combination selected will depend upon the productivity and wage cost of the clerks

Table 15-2. Hypothetical Illustration of the Profit Maximization Principle

Input units	Total output units	Marginal product	Marginal cost[1]	Marginal revenue[2]	Total variable cost[3]	Total revenue[4]	Net profit[5]	Average variable cost
	(No.)	(No.)	($)	($)	($)	($)	($)	($)
1	1	1	5	5	5	5	0	5.00
2	3	2	5	10	10	15	5	3.33
3	6	3	5	15	15	30	15	2.50
4	10	4	5	20	20	50	30	2.00
5	15	5	5	25	25	75	50	1.67
6	20	5	5	25	30	100	70	1.50
7	24	4	5	20	35	120	85	1.46
8	27	3	5	15	40	135	95	1.48
9	29	2	5	10	45	145	100	1.55
10	30	1	5	5	50	150	100	1.67
11	28	-2	5	-10	55	140	85	1.96
12	24	-4	5	-20	60	120	60	2.50

[1]Marginal cost per unit of additional input.
[2]Marginal product times $5.
[3]Input units times $5.
[4]Total output units times $5.
[5]Before fixed costs.

compared with the productivity and cost of a computer. If the clerks' output declines and/or their hourly wages rise, the use of a computer becomes more feasible. Conversely, if the computer's output declines and/or its rental cost goes up, the use of clerks becomes more feasible. It is likely that one certain combination of clerks and computers will produce the least clerical cost. While it is quite likely that clerks might be used exclusively, it is not likely that computers would be used exclusively. Thus, there is a limit to the substitution process.

There are at least two tools available to assist business managers in attaining a least-cost combination of inputs: budgeting and linear programming. Both allow selection of the most profitable combination of enterprises where alternative uses for limited resources are to be considered or selection of the least-cost combination of inputs where many alternative inputs are to be combined to meet numerous specifications for the end product. Linear programming allows very complicated budgeting problems to be solved by electronic computers.

FIXED AND VARIABLE COSTS

Separation of fixed and variable costs allows better planning where prices of inputs and products are variable. Fixed costs are the annual overhead costs associated with the capacity to produce and do not depend on the actual level of production; some examples are taxes, insurance, depreciation and interest on investment. Variable costs are out-of-pocket costs varying with production; some examples are labor, materials, supplies, repairs and fuel. In short-range planning, which is not concerned with changes in facilities such as buildings and machinery, production is profitable if the price of the product is greater than the variable cost per unit. In long-range planning, which is concerned with changes in facilities, production is profitable only if the price is equal to or greater than the average total cost per unit.

Business managers recognize the importance of fixed and variable costs. Revenues which fail to cover costs spell eventual bankruptcy to a firm. But revenues which fail to cover fixed as well as variable costs are not so disastrous in the short run, because the firm can postpone meeting some or all of the fixed costs. Furthermore, any revenue above variable costs applies to fixed costs, which is better than no contribution at all.

BREAK-EVEN POINT

In many agribusinesses, the use of marginal cost equals marginal revenue analysis to determine the point of most profitable output is complex and difficult to achieve. Instead, *break-even* analysis is used.

The break-even point is the point of sales volume at which sales income will equal costs and neither a profit nor a loss will be realized. To find the break-even point, the manager needs only the totals for fixed and variable costs at any given sales volume. The following formula can then be used:

$$\text{Break-even Point (Sales Dollars)} = \frac{\text{Total Fixed Costs}}{1(100\%) - \dfrac{\text{Total Variable Costs}}{\text{Dollar Sales}}}$$

For example, suppose a manufacturer has fixed costs of $400,000. When sales total $1,200,000, his variable costs are $720,000. His break-even sales point, then, is:

$$\frac{\$400,000}{1.00 - \dfrac{\$720,000}{\$1,200,000}} \text{ or } \$1,000,000$$

To determine *break-even volume*, the formula is:

$$\text{Break-even Volume} = \frac{\text{Total Fixed Costs}}{\text{Selling Price} - \text{Variable Cost per Unit}}$$

For example, Ajax Plastics has determined its fixed costs to be $100,000 and its variable costs to be $50 per unit. If the selling price per unit is $100, then Ajax's break-even volume is:

$$\text{Break-even Volume} = \frac{\$100,000}{\$100 - \$50} = 2,000 \text{ units}$$

The advantage of figuring the break-even point by means of a formula is simplicity. The break-even chart, however, gives a broader, "moving" picture of business activity. It shows not only the specific break-even point but also the amount of profit or loss at any point of volume.

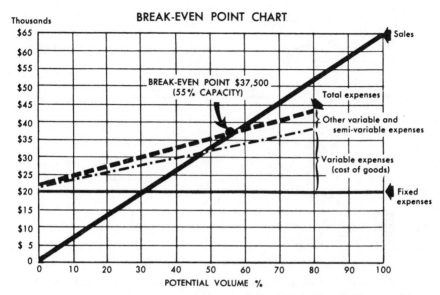

Figure 15-2. The break-even point is a useful managerial tool for budgetary control, sales and price analysis and expansion decisions. (Courtesy, Small Business Administration, Washington, D.C.)

In a break-even chart, some measure of volume (for example, units of production, per cent of plant capacity or sales value) is put on the horizontal axis of a graph, and dollars of sales income and costs are put on the vertical axis. Total costs and sales income are then plotted (Figure 15-2).

The point where the two lines cross represents the break-even point; the area between the two lines the loss or profit, depending on whether it precedes or follows the break-even point.

There are a number of variations of the break-even chart, but all start with the basic chart shown. A single break-even chart, of course, can present information only under a single set of assumed conditions as to market, costs, management decisions, product mix, etc. Any change in these circumstances will change the break-even pattern.

DISTINCTION BETWEEN DEMAND AND
PRICE ELASTICITY

Demand has to do with the various quantitites of a product which will be purchased at a given time, in a given place and at certain prices.

Price elasticity of demand refers to a ratio of quantities purchased to prices. It is the numerical value of the relative change in quantity which is purchased, divided by the corresponding relative change in price.

PRICE ELASTICITY OF DEMAND

Agribusiness managers, when selling machinery, feed, supplies and raw and/or processed farm products at wholesale or retail, face the problem of price elasticity—that is, if the price is lowered, how much more of a product will be sold? Or, if the price is raised, how much less will be sold? For example, it is known that products such as eggs have less price elasticity than broiler chickens, eggs having no perfect substitutes but broiler chickens having many. This gives a hint as to what might happen if egg prices were to go up. Only a slight drop in sales would be anticipated, but with broiler chickens, a much larger drop in sales for a given increase in price would be expected. Consumers would substitute other meats for broilers.

In Table 15-3 are shown the three kinds of price elasticity. Coefficients larger than 1.00 are elastic; 1.00 indicates unitary elasticity; coefficients less than 1.00 are inelastic. The *minus* sign indicates an inverse relationship between price and volume changes. A *plus* sign indicates a positive relationship between price and volume changes.

The price elasticity formula, whether for demand or supply, is:

$$e = \frac{\dfrac{Q_1 - Q_2}{Q_1 + Q_2}}{\dfrac{P_1 - P_2}{P_1 + P_2}}$$

Using data in Table 15-3 such as when $Q_1 = 8$; $P_1 = \$5.50$; $Q_2 = 10$; $P_2 = \$5.00$:

$$e = \frac{\dfrac{8 - 10}{18}}{\dfrac{5.50 - 5.00}{10.50}} = \frac{\dfrac{-1}{9}}{\dfrac{1}{21}} = \frac{-.111}{.048} = -2.31 \text{ (elastic)}$$

Table 15-3. Hypothetical Illustration of Price Elasticity

Price per unit	Units sold	Total sales	Coefficient of elasticity
($)	(No.)	($)	(No.)
7.00	2	14	
6.50	4	26	−8.91
6.00	6	36	−5.00
5.50	8	44	−3.29
5.00	10	50	−2.31
4.50	12	54	−1.73
4.00	14	56	−1.31
3.50	16	56	−1.00
3.00	18	54	− .76
2.50	20	50	− .58
2.00	22	44	− .43
1.50	24	36	− .30
1.00	26	26	− .20

Application of Price Elasticity

Often local feed merchants and sellers of other types of supplies cut prices to increase volume. However, it takes much more increased volume to justify a price cut than one might realize.

The Pennsylvania Millers & Feed Dealers Association cites the figures shown in Table 15-4, showing how much more business a store owner must do to justify a price cut.

A store owner may certainly gain sales by cutting price, but much depends upon the retaliation pricewise of his competitors. If they all cut price to the same extent, no one gains. Also, the increased sales made as a result of price-cutting add to the costs of handling these

Table 15-4. How Much More Business Must One Do to Justify a Price Cut?

Regular profit on selling prices	Price cut	Increase in dollar sales needed to maintain dollar profits
(%)	(%)	(%)
15	5	50
15	10	200
15	12½	500
20	5	33
20	10	100
20	12½	167
20	15	300
20	16⅔	488

Source: *Feed and Farm Supplier*, Mount Morris, Ill., Sept. 1964, p. 13.

extra sales. More importantly, not only are the added sales made at lower prices but also all sales made are likewise affected. Much depends on the point of departure for cutting price. Note in Table 15-4 that the 5 per cent price cut on a 20 per cent regular profit margin does not require as much added sales as the 5 per cent cut on a 15 per cent profit margin.

CROSS ELASTICITY OF DEMAND

Cross elasticity of demand refers to the effect a change in price of one commodity has on the sale or consumption of another commodity. If two products are close substitutes, the coefficient of cross elasticity will be much larger than if the two products are not.

The formula for calculating cross elasticity, where Q is the quantity of one product and P is the price of another product, is:

$$\frac{\dfrac{Q_2 - Q_1}{Q_2 + Q_1}}{\dfrac{P_2 - P_1}{P_2 + P_1}}$$

The following are estimated ratios of cross elasticity between retail broiler prices and per capita consumption of other meats (a *positive* ratio indicates that broiler prices affect consumption of other meats; a *negative* ratio indicates that broiler prices do not hurt consumption of other meats):

Other poultry meats (except turkey)	= +1.72
Veal	= +1.70
Lamb and mutton	= + .77
Pork	= + .40
Fish	= − .20
Beef	= − .84
Turkey	= −1.92

These ratios indicate that broilers are very substitutable for other poultry meat (except turkey), veal, lamb, mutton and pork but have less substitution power over fish, beef and turkey meat.

INCOME ELASTICITY

Income elasticity refers to the change in consumption of an item relative to a change in income. If clothing expenditures increase 3 per cent while income increases 3 per cent, the income elasticity for clothing is +1.00. Agribusiness managers consider the income elasticities of their products in arriving at pricing, advertising and merchandising policies. As incomes go up, the sales of many products do not necessarily rise in direct proportion, and the sales of some may even decline.

Supply Elasticity

Supply elasticity parallels demand elasticity and is a measure of the responsiveness of quantity offered to a corresponding change in price. When the percentage change in supply or quantity offered relative to the change in price is greater than 1.00, an *elastic* response is indicated. When the response coefficient is 1.00, a *unitary* condition exists. A response coefficient of less than 1.00 denotes an *inelastic* condition.

The broiler chicken business, for example, has an elastic supply response. If the price of chickens goes up a little, supply response is large and immediate. On the other hand, for larger animals with longer life cycles, the supply response is much less elastic; it takes time for supply to respond or to adjust to price changes.

The formula for calculating *supply* elasticity is similar to the one for *demand.*

PRICING METHODS

Most basic to good pricing practices is to recognize that there is more to pricing than internal costs. Two factors are important in developing prices: (1) to recognize that it is the market, not costs, that determines the price at which products will sell and (2) to be aware that costs and desired profits only establish a "price floor" below which one cannot sell and make a profit.

The area between the "price ceiling," established by the market, and the "price floor," determined by costs and desired profits, is the "relevant price range." Only if one can produce at a cost which will permit recovery of costs and the desired margin at the price the market determines can one expect to conduct business profitably.

Full-Cost Pricing

Many businessmen take the view that the price on each product must cover all the costs of that product. This approach, called full-cost pricing, means that the price will cover labor, materials and overhead costs, plus a predetermined percentage for profit.

However, few small businesses adhere rigidly to a full-cost pricing policy. Many managers express a preference for such an approach, but when it actually comes to establishing prices, their decisions are influenced by demand and other factors.

Flexible Markups

A common practice is to use full costs, not as an inflexible point at which the price is to be set, but as a floor below which the price will not be allowed to fall—a reference point to which flexible markups are added. Two kinds of flexibility are found in actual pricing: (1) adjustments over the course of time to changes in demand or in competition and (2) variations among different products at the same time, due to differences in the market for individual products.

Gross-Margin Pricing

Another widely used pattern of pricing is that of adding a markup to the cost (amount paid by the wholesaler to the manufacturer or processor or amount paid by the retailer to the wholesaler). This method, gross-margin pricing, is customary in both retailing and wholesaling. Some firms compute the markup as a percentage of cost while others compute it as a percentage of selling price.

As in full-cost pricing, firms using the gross-margin method usually do not apply the same markup on all items or at all times. It is more profitable to take into account the effect of different prices on sales volume and then decide which products will bear high markups and which will carry low ones.

Suggested and "Going Rate" Prices

Another approach to pricing is to follow an external guide. Some managers prefer not to make their own pricing decisions but to rely on prices suggested by manufacturers or wholesalers. Still other managers simply follow the prices set by similar firms.

Profit-Margin Formula

The profit-margin (p-m) formula of pricing takes into account cost, volume and profit relationships. This formula distinguishes between variable and fixed costs. It uses only the *variable* element as the starting point in setting prices; the *fixed* element is accounted for separately as a part of general plant overhead. The profit margin is the difference between net sales revenue and the total variable costs of the products sold. The first pricing objective is to cover all the variable costs charged directly to the item. The second objective is to produce, in addition, the largest possible number of profit-margin dollars that can be applied to overall fixed costs (Table 15-5).

The profit-margin formula is a highly practical measuring tool be-

Table 15-5. Forecasting Profit Margins at Various Selling Prices (Hypothetical)

Item	Per cent of unit selling price	Operating profit forecast at various selling prices[1]			
Unit selling prices under consideration		$ 18.00	$ 16.00	$ 15.00	$ 14.00
Direct variable selling costs:					
Sales commission	3.5				
Cash discount	2.0				
Provision for bad debts	0.5				
Total	6.0	1.08	.96	.90	.84
Freight and delivery		.50	.50	.50	.50
Direct product variable replacement cost of standard		7.00	7.00	7.00	7.00
Total direct variable costs		8.58	8.46	8.40	8.34
Profit margin per unit		9.42	7.54	6.60	5.66
Estimated sales volume (units)		400	600	800	900
Total P-M dollars		$3,768.00	4,524.00	5,280.00	5,094.00
Fixed costs and expenses at 100% capacity (1,000 units)		3,000.00	3,000.00	3,000.00	3,000.00
Operating profit		$ 768.00	$1,524.00	$2,280.00	$2,094.00

[1]These estimates lead to the conclusion that $15 is the optimum selling price. Other considerations, such as a need for particular price lines, might call for a decision to set a price yielding less profit. However, correct pricing arithmetic is essential in reaching a sound conclusion.

Source: Anderson, Jules, and E. C. Gassenheimer, *Pricing Arithmetic for Small Business Managers*, SBA Aid 100, Washington, D.C., Feb. 1959.

cause it gives the basis for sound management decisions. It helps, for instance, in deciding whether to make or to buy a part, to purchase additional machinery or to replace old equipment, to expand or contract capacity and to increase or decrease advertising outlays.

Here is a simple example. A businessman considers putting on new salesmen at a total monthly cost of $2,000. He also plans an increase in advertising of $5,000 per month. Based on recent experience, he estimates that these moves will increase his sales by at least 10 per cent and, possibly, as much as 50 per cent. Currently, 5,000 units are being sold at a per-unit margin of $11.06. Thus, he anticipates a dollar gain ranging between $5,530 (with a 500-unit increase) and $27,650 (with a 2,500-unit increase). All he needs to cover his gamble of $7,000 monthly is a sales increase of 12.66 per cent (633 units × $11.06 = $7,000, approximately).[2]

Differential or Discount Pricing

There are at least five types of legitimate pricing differentials: (1) *quantity* or *volume* discounts, given according to size of purchases in terms of either physical quantities or dollar volume; (2) *spatial* or *transportation* discounts or charges, according to whether the product is picked up or delivered; (3) *temporal* or *time-of-payment* discounts or charges, according to whether the customer buys with cash or on time and/or whether early order bookings are made; (4) *form of product* discounts or charges, according to the form in which the product exists at the time of sale (such as bulk versus bagged feeds and fertilizers); and (5) *combinations* of the preceding.

The ideal situation is to provide pricing differentials based on legitimate cost differences to avoid price discrimination. Illegitimate pricing differentials, on the other hand, are created when firms charge different prices to various buyers although the conditions surrounding the sales are substantially similar. Thus, a legitimate pricing differential becomes illegitimate when not documented or supported by true differences in the cost of making or selling the product. The Robinson-Patman Act prohibits illegitimate pricing differentials.

---

[2]Lennon, V. A., *What Is the Best Selling Price?*, SBA-MA 193, Washington, D.C., May 1977.

Agribusiness managers may maximize profits by following differential pricing. That is, if certain customers purchase multiple numbers of one item (large-scale buying), it usually costs less per unit to process and deliver the orders. Thus, a lower price per unit is charged for such sales. The increased sales revenue obtained by selling more units decreases fixed costs per unit and contributes to greater overall firm profit. Of course, differential pricing may reduce net profits if price reductions on large-volume sales exceed the reduced cost of handling the sales.

FINANCIAL STATEMENTS

The two types of financial statements most commonly used in business are the *operating statement* and the *balance sheet*.

The *operating statement* includes revenue from sales, cost of goods sold, gross profit on sales, operating expenses, net operating income and other income and expenses.

The *balance sheet* includes the assets, classified as current, fixed and prepaid; liabilities, classified as current and fixed; and net worth, the difference between total assets and total liabilities. Examples of these two financial statements are presented in subsequent sections.

RATIO ANALYSIS

Ratio analysis may be classified into three groups: balance sheet ratios, operating statement ratios and combinations of the two. Ratios illustrated here are applicable to *farm supply stores*.

The data used for calculating the ratios are shown in Table 15-6.

Balance Sheet Ratios

These ratios are calculated from balance sheets of assets, liabilities and net worth (for profit-type businesses) or patrons' equity (for co-op type businesses) (Table 15-7). Of the 17 ratios shown, 9 are "Very good," 4 are "Good" and 4 are "Weak" or "Very weak." The latter four ratios are: (1) acid-test, (2) inventory to net working capital, (3) long-term debt to net working capital and (4) current debt to net working capital. The Central Farm Supply Store (CFSS) is not liquid enough to

Table 15-6. Central Farm Supply Store

I. Year-End Balance Sheet		II. Annual Income Statement	
Current assets		Sales	$569,993
Cash	$ 23,800	Cost of goods sold	436,386
Marketable securities	650	Gross margin	$133,607
Accounts receivables	13,000		
Merchandise inventories	137,013	Operating	
Other current assets	2,235	expenses	$112,437
Total current assets	$176,698		
Investment in other firms	$254,976	Net operating margin	
		before tax	$ 21,170
Fixed assets (net)	146,316		
Total assets	$577,990	Net operating margin	
		after tax	$ 16,513
Current liabilities	$ 93,672		
Fixed liabilities		III. Other Data	
Long-term debt	100,100	Net working capital	
Net worth (owner's equity)	384,218	(current assets less	
Total liabilities and net worth	$577,990	current liabilities)	$ 83,026
		No. of employees	10
		Annual labor cost	$ 72,000
		Interest paid on	
		long-term debt	$ 9,000
		Net credit sales	$156,000
		No. of sales days	300

Source: Adapted and modified from: Smith, Frank J., and Ken Cooper, *The Financial Management of Agribusiness Firms*, Minn. Agr. Ext. Serv. Spec. Rept. 26, St. Paul, Sept. 1967, Chapter 7, p. 183.

Table 15-7. Balance Sheet Ratios: Suggested Ratios Versus Ratios for Central Farm Supply Store (CFSS)

Type of ratio		Suggested ratio	CFSS ratio	Comment
*1. Current =	$\frac{\text{Current Assets}}{\text{Current Liabilities}} = \frac{2}{1}$	2.00	1.89	Good
*2. Acid-test =	$\frac{\text{Cash + Accounts Receivables}}{\text{Current Liabilities}} = \frac{1.5}{1}$	1.50	.39	Very weak
*3. Equity to = total assets	$\frac{\text{Owners' Equity}}{\text{Total Assets}} = \frac{1}{2}$	.50	.66	Good
*4. Equity to = fixed assets	$\frac{\text{Owners' Equity}}{\text{Net Fixed Assets}} = \frac{2.5}{1}$	2.50	2.63	Good
*5. Fixed ratio =	$\frac{\text{Net Fixed Assets}}{\text{Fixed Liabilities}} = \frac{1.5}{1}$	1.50	1.46	Good
*6. Owners' equity to = net working capital (Current Assets Less Current Liabilities)	$\frac{\text{Owners' Equity}}{\text{Net Working Capital}} = \frac{1}{1}$	1.00	4.63	Very good
*7. Inventory to = receivables	$\frac{\text{Average Inventory}}{\text{Average Receivables}} = \frac{2}{1}$	2.00	10.54	Very good (too good)

(Continued)

Table 15-7 (Continued)

Type of ratio				Suggested ratio	CFSS ratio	Comment
*8. Debt to assets =	Total Liabilities / Total Assets	=	1/2	.50	.34	Very good
*9. Debt to equity =	Total Liabilities / Owners' Equity	=	1/1.5	.67	.50	Very good
**10. Inventory to net = working capital	Average Inventory / Average Net Working Capital					
	=	1/1.5		.67	1.65	Very weak
**11. Solvency =	Fixed Liabilities / Owners' Equity	=	1/2	.50	.26	Very good
**12. Current debt to = net working capital	Current Liabilities / Net Working Capital	=	1/1	1.00	1.13	Weak
**13. Fixed debt to = net working capital	Fixed Liabilities / Net Working Capital	=	1/2	.50	1.21	Very weak
**14. Current debt = to equity	Current Liabilities / Owners' Equity	=	1/2.5	.40	.24	Very good
**15. Receivables to = current assets	Net Accounts Receivables / Total Current Assets	=	1/2.5	.40	.07	Very good
**16. Assets to equity =	Total Assets / Owners' Equity	=	2/1	2.00	1.50	Very good
**17. Current debt = to inventory	Current Liabilities / Inventory	=	1/1	1.00	.68	Very good

*If ratios are greater than those shown, store is doing better than average.
**If ratios are less than those shown, store is doing better than average.

meet current liabilities and suffers from too heavy an inventory in relation to working capital. Its fixed and current liabilities are large for the net working capital. Overall, however, CFSS is very strong in its balance sheet ratios where it had 13 of 17 ratios equal to or better than the suggested ratios. This indicates that the store had had good years in the past but now may be relying too much on its past strength for the future, as shown next.

Profit-Loss Ratios

These ratios are shown in Table 15-8. Here we find one ratio "Good," one "Fair" and four "Weak," or high labor cost (too many employees), a higher operating expense ratio than average, low sales per employee and subpar net margins (before income tax). The one ratio

Table 15-8. Profit/Loss Statement Ratios: Suggested Ratios Versus Central Farm Supply Store (CFSS) Ratios

Type of ratio	Suggested ratio	CFSS ratio	Comment
*1. Gross earnings = Gross Margins (Sales− Cost of Goods Sold) = $\frac{1}{5}$ / Net Total Sales	.20	.23	Good
*2. Net margins before tax to sales = Net Margins (BT)[1] / Net Sales = $\frac{1}{20}$	.05	.037	Weak
*3. Net margins after tax to sales = Net Margins (AT)[2] / Net Sales = $\frac{1}{33}$	.030	.029	Fair
*4. Sales per employee = Annual Sales / No. of Employees = $\frac{\$75,000}{1}$	$75,000	$57,000	Weak
**5. Labor cost = Labor Cost / Net Sales = $\frac{1}{12}$ (will vary by type of supply items)	.083	.126	Weak
**6. Operating expenses = Total Operating Expense / Total Net Sales = $\frac{1}{6}$	.167	.197	Weak

*If ratios are greater than shown, store is doing better than average.
**If ratios are less than shown, store is doing better than average.
[1]BT – before income tax.
[2]AT – after income tax.

rated "Good" consists of "Gross Margins." On the whole, the P/L ratios are much weaker than the previously shown "Balance Sheet" ratios.

Mixed Ratios

These ratios are calculated from both the balance sheet and the P/L statement and are shown in Table 15-9. Note that of all 14 ratios, 2 are "Very good," 3 are "Good" and 9 are "Weak" to "Very weak." What are the problems? It appears that sales volume is too small in relation to inventory, or inventory is too large in relation to sales. If inventory is held constant, sales must increase, or if sales are held constant, inventory must decrease. Net margins on assets are poor, which indicates that net margins are too low, expenses are too high or assets are too many, some of which might be liquidated.

Owner's equity is not being rewarded too well. Not enough sales are being generated. Inventory turnover is very low. It appears also that accounts receivables may be too low; that is, not enough credit sales are being made which would allow more sales to be generated. Credit policy appears to be too tight, thus, the collection period on all

Table 15-9. Mixed Ratios (Balance Sheet and P/L Statement): Suggested Ratios Versus Ratios for Central Farm Supply Store (CFSS)

Type of ratio		Suggested ratio	CFSS ratio	Comment
*1. Sales to net working capital	$\dfrac{\text{Net Sales}}{\text{Average Net Working Capital}} = \dfrac{7}{1}$	7.0	6.9	Good
*2. Sales to total assets	$\dfrac{\text{Net Sales}}{\text{Total Assets}} = \dfrac{3}{1}$	3.0	1.0	Weak
*3. Sales to fixed assets	$\dfrac{\text{Net Sales}}{\text{Net Fixed Assets}} = \dfrac{10}{1}$	10.0	3.9	Very weak
*4. Returns on total assets	$\dfrac{\text{Net Margins (BT)}[1]}{\text{Total Assets}} = \dfrac{1}{10}$	.100	.037	Very weak
*5. Return on fixed assets	$\dfrac{\text{Net Margins (BT)}}{\text{Net Fixed Assets}} = \dfrac{1}{5}$	.200	.145	Weak
*6. Returns on owners' equity	$\dfrac{\text{Net Margins (AT)}[2]}{\text{Owners' Equity}} = \dfrac{1}{10}$	.100	.043	Very weak
*7. Equity turnover	$\dfrac{\text{Net Sales}}{\text{Owners' Equity}} = \dfrac{4}{1}$	4.0	1.5	Very weak
*8. Sales to inventory (will vary by products)	$\dfrac{\text{Net Sales}}{\text{Average Inventory}} = \dfrac{10}{1}$	10.0	4.2	Very weak
*9. Sales to receivables	$\dfrac{\text{Net Sales}}{\text{Average Accounts Receivable}} = \dfrac{12}{1}$	12.0	43.8[3]	Very good (too good)
*10. Inventory turnover	$\dfrac{\text{Cost of Goods Sold}}{\text{Average Inventory (at cost)}} = $ (will vary by product)	8.0	3.2[3]	Very weak
*11. Net margins to net working capital	$\dfrac{\text{Net Margins (AT)}}{\text{Net Working Capital}} = \dfrac{1}{6}$	.167	.199	Good
**12. Average collection period = $\dfrac{\text{Net Sales}}{\text{No. of Sales Days}} = $ Average Sales per Day $\dfrac{\text{Ending Accounts and Notes Receivables}}{\text{Average Sales per Day}} = $ Days		30.0	6.8	Very good (too good)
**13. $\dfrac{\text{Net Credit Sales}}{\text{No. of Sales Days}} = $ Average Daily Credit Sales $\dfrac{\text{Accounts and Notes Receivable}}{\text{Average Daily Credit Sales}} = $ Days		30.0	25.0	Good (too good)
**14. Fixed investments to net margins	$\dfrac{\text{Fixed Investments}}{\text{Net Margins (BT)}} = \dfrac{3}{1}$	3.0	19.0	Very weak

*If ratios are greater than shown, store is doing better than average.
**If ratios are less than shown, store is doing better than average.
[1]Before income tax.
[2]After income tax. CFSS estimated 22% tax liability (federal and state income taxes).
[3]Ending instead of average.

sales is too good. A somewhat more liberal but sound credit policy could generate more sales, increase inventory turnover, generate more net earnings and improve return on equity.

Overall, CFSS currently shows a strong *balance sheet* but this may become eroded over the next few years if the *P/L statement* does not improve. It appears that the store management is overly conservative at this time and willing to ride on its past strong laurels. However, this store can be more profitable than it is if management will carefully analyze its problems and attempt to solve them.

CASH FLOWS

Cash flow refers to the incoming and outgoing amounts of liquid assets, such as cash, that a business experiences over a given period of time. A firm may be quite solvent and prosperous yet suffer a deficiency of cash to meet its current bills or obligations. Thus, cash flow analysis helps a firm to predict when and how much it may be short of or long on cash (Table 15-10).

Table 15-10. Estimated Cash Budget

	Jan.	Feb.	Mar.
(1) Cash in Bank (Start of Month)	____	____	____
(2) Petty Cash (Start of Month)	____	____	____
(3) Total Cash (add 1 and 2)	____	____	____
(4) Expected Cash Sales	____	____	____
(5) Expected Collections on Accounts	____	____	____
(6) Other Money Expected	____	____	____
(7) Total Receipts (add 4, 5 and 6)	____	____	____
(8) Total Cash and Receipts (add 3 and 7)	____	____	____
(9) All Disbursements (for month)	____	____	____
*(10) Cash Balance at End of Month (subtract (9) from (8))	____	____	____
(11) Desired Cash Balance	____	____	____
(12) Surplus (+) or Deficit (−) in cash (subtract (11) from (10))	____	____	____

*This balance is the starting cash balance for the next month.

FUNDS FLOW STATEMENTS[3]

These statements consist of two elements: sources and uses of funds.

---

[3]Williams, R. J., and J. C. Snyder, *Using Funds Flow Statements as a Management Tool,* Ind. Agr. Ext. Serv. EC-304, Lafayette, Dec. 1965, p. 7.

Sources of Funds

Funds generated from operations are not the only source of funds. Additional funds may also be generated by borrowing, thus increasing debt; by selling more stock, thus increasing the capital account; or by selling fixed assets, thus decreasing fixed assets. *To generalize, one can say sources of funds are indicated by increases in equities, increases in liabilities and decreases in assets.*

Uses of Funds

If there is a system that makes funds available, the next most likely question is what to do with them. The prudent business manager has several alternatives open—he may add new fixed assets, add to working capital, retire debt, pay dividends to stockholders or repay capital to stockholders. *Uses of funds are indicated by increases in assets plus decreases in liabilities and equities.* The *sources* of funds must balance with the *uses* of funds as shown in Table 15-11.

COST OF CAPITAL[4]

However imperfect the means, a manager can and should arrive at some estimate of the costs of various types of capital to his firm. When he has done so, calculating the overall cost of capital (the cutoff rate used in the investment-decision process) becomes a matter of arithmetic. It is simply the weighted average of the cost of the several sources employed. The process is illustrated here:

Item	Amount used ($)	Proportion (%)		After tax cost (%)		Weighted cost (%)
Long-term debt	300,000	30	×	3	=	0.9
Preferred stock	100,000	10	×	8	=	0.8
Common stock	100,000	10	×	14	=	1.4
Retained earnings	500,000	50	×	7	=	3.5
	1,000,000					6.6

[4]Smith, Frank J., Jr., "Cost of Capital in Agribusiness Firms," *Minnesota Farm Business,* Minn. Agr. Ext. Serv., St. Paul, Jun. 1968, p. 3.

Table 15-11. Sources and Uses of Funds Flow Statement: An Example

Sources of funds from:[1]	Change between balance sheets		% of total
	($)		
Accounts payable	(+)	13,450	56.2
Net margins	(+)	5,800	24.2
Common stock	(+)	4,390	18.3
Accounts receivable	(−)	300	1.3
	Total	23,940	Total 100.0
Uses of funds for:[2]			
Notes payable	(−)	2,370	9.9
Cash on hand	(+)	300	1.3
Cash in bank	(+)	16,340	68.2
Inventory	(+)	4,650	19.4
Equipment	(+)	280	1.2
	Total	23,940	Total 100.0

[1](+) in equities and liabilities added to (−) in assets.
[2](+) in assets added to (−) in equities and liabilities.

The weighted average overall cost of capital in the example is 6.6 per cent. It reflects the proportion and cost of each type of capital used. In this case, investment projects promising a return of less than 6.6 per cent would be rejected. This figure is the screening rate for the firm. Of course, the proportions and costs of capital used in the example are purely illustrative and should by no means be considered standards.

ANALYZING CAPITAL INVESTMENTS

Agribusiness managers often are confronted with decisions involving the pay-out or profitability of an investment, such as for a new building or equipment.

According to Brewer,[5] three methods of computation are commonly used: (1) payback period, (2) average return on investment and (3) discounted cash flow.

Payback Period

This computation tells how much time it will take for expected

[5]Brewer, T. A., *Analyzing Investment Proposals*, Wash. Agr. Ext. Serv. Rept. 3491, Pullman, Aug. 1971.

earnings from a proposal to pay back the initial capital outlay. This period can then be compared with a standard payback period to determine whether the project is acceptable. Payback period is computed by the following formula:

$$\text{Payback Period (Years)} = \frac{\text{Investment Outlay}}{\text{Average Cash Earnings per Year}}$$

For example, if the installed cost of a new piece of equipment is $60,000 and the equipment will produce cash operating savings of $10,000 a year, it has a payback period of six years:

$$\frac{\$60,000}{\$10,000} = 6 \text{ Years}$$

Payback can serve as (1) a rough screen to pick out desirable high-profit projects and to reject those which show poor promise, (2) a measure of relative risks involved in projects and (3) a useful procedure when a shortage of funds forces accepting only proposals promising a payback period after taxes of two or three years.

Average Return on Investment

The following formula is used in computing the average return on investment:

$$\% = \frac{\text{Average Annual Cash Earnings} - \text{Annual Depreciation}}{\text{Average Lifetime Investment}}$$

Average lifetime investment may be computed by averaging the beginning and ending investment figures, no matter what method is used for depreciation. Using again the equipment example cited under "Payback Period," average investment is $30,000, assuming no salvage value. If the life span is considered to be 10 years, average annual depreciation is $6,000, and the average return on investment is 13.3 per cent.

$$\frac{\text{Average Net Earnings}}{\text{Average Investment}} = \frac{\$10,000 - \$6,000}{\$30,000} = 13.3\%$$

Discounted Cash Flow

The basis for this procedure consists of finding the interest rate that discounts future earnings of a project to a present value equal to its cost. This is the discounted rate of return on that investment. Briefly, the procedures involved are to:

1. Estimate total investment cost, including installation, etc.
2. Estimate gross annual earnings before depreciation.
3. Find, from a table of present values, the interest rate which equates the present value of the future earnings to the present cost of the investment: the discounted rate of return.
4. Compare this discounted rate of return with the minimum acceptable to the company. If the discounted rate of return is less than the desired cut-off point, the project should be rejected.

The underlying principle is that through an investment outlay, a company is actually buying a series of future annual incomes by making a current investment. This is illustrated in Table 15-12.

Comparing returns from a $60,000 investment with a uniform stream of earnings computed by both the average return on investment and the discounted cash flow methods, the average return on investment approach showed a 13.3 per cent return, compared to an 11 per cent return ($60,649) computed by the discounted cash flow approach. If the company had a cut-off point at 12 per cent, it would have accepted the project by the average return method but would have failed to recover its full discounted investment by −$1,762.

The discounted cash flow is a useful method for evaluating the desirability of investment outlays for these reasons:

1. It is economically realistic in confining the analysis to cash flows, disregarding arbitrary bookkeeping allocations.

Table 15-12. Discounted Cash Flow Rate of Return With Uniform Streams of Earnings

Item	Per cent return on initial outlay of $60,000			
	10	11	12	13
Annual gross earnings	$10,000	$10,000	$10,000	$10,000
Earnings discount factor, 10 years	6.3213	6.0649	5.8238	5.5958
Present value, 10 years	$63,213	$60,649	$58,238	$55,958
Net present value	$ 3,213	$ 649	−$ 1,762	−$ 4,042

Source: Garoian, Leon, and A. Haseley, *Planning Capital Investments*, Ore. Agr. Ext. Serv., Corvallis, Dec. 1962.

2. It focuses on the whole life of the project and on its lifetime earnings.
3. It reflects the real difference in the values of near and distant cash flows.
4. It gives results comparable to cost-of-capital ratios so that decisions can be made safely on the basis of the relationship between the indicated rate of return and the value of money to the company.
5. Earnings are stated as gross cash receipts (not figuring depreciation). Therefore, it is not necessary to allocate the cost of a machine over its life before computing return. Depreciation is allowed for because the interest rate discounting the sum of present values to zero is the rate of return on investment after annual provisions for repaying the principal.

COMPUTERS AND AGRIBUSINESS MANAGEMENT

Computers (electronic data processing) are being used increasingly in agribusiness management for accounting functions, least-cost solutions, maximum profit combinations, price analysis and forecasting, management decision games, transportation problems and many other purposes.[6, 7]

Each firm may choose from three options in approaching automated data processing: (1) purchasing or leasing its own "in-house" computer, (2) sharing the time of one large-scale central computer with many other users ("time-sharing") and (3) employing a computer service bureau which will perform the data processing. Service bureaus and time-sharing arrangements are both good ways to avoid the major expenses and transitional headaches of in-house computing.[8]

● ● ●

[6]Roy, Ewell P., "Computers in Agribusiness," *Feedstuffs*, Minneapolis, Minn., Feb. 26, 1966, p. 7.

[7]Thompson, Stanley R., and Leon Garoian, *Types of Computers and Their Use by Agricultural Cooperatives*, Ore. Agr. Ext. Serv. Spec. Rept. 329, Corvallis, May 1971.

[8]Caley, J. D., *Computers for Small Business*, SBA–SMA 149, Washington, D.C., Feb. 1977.

In the next chapter, the role of agribusinesses in local communities is considered.

TOPICS FOR DISCUSSION

1. Discuss the law of comparative advantage.
2. What is the law of diminishing returns?
3. Discuss profit maximization.
4. Contrast fixed and variable costs.
5. Describe break-even point analysis.
6. Discuss price and cross elasticity of demand.
7. Discuss the various pricing methods.
8. Discuss the use of financial ratios in business management.
9. Discuss the three methods of analyzing capital investments.
10. List several uses of computers in agribusiness management.

SELECTED REFERENCES

1. Berry, R. L., "Break-Even Analysis," *American Journal of Agricultural Economics,* Feb. 1972, p. 121.
2. Brewer, T. A., *Analyzing Investment Proposals,* Wash. Agr. Ext. Serv. Rept. 3491, Pullman, Aug. 1971.
3. Cooper, I. M., *Accounting Services for Small Service Firms,* SBA–SMA 126, Washington, D.C., Mar. 1977.
4. Duft, Ken D., "Management Strategies Through Break-Even Analysis," *Agribusiness Management,* Wash. Agr. Ext. Serv., Pullman, Jan. 1977.
5. Elliot, J. Walter, *Economic Analysis for Management Decisions,* Richard D. Irwin, Inc., Homewood, Ill., 1973.
6. Lennon, V. A., *What Is the Best Selling Price?*, SBA–MA 193, Washington, D.C., May 1977.
7. Litt, D. S., *Cash Flow in a Small Plant,* SBA–MA 229, Washington, D.C., Jun. 1976.
8. Mohn, N. C., and L. C. Sartorius, *Sales Forecasting Models,* Georgia State University, Atlanta, 1976.
9. Murphy, J. F., *Sound Cash Management and Borrowing,* SBA–SMA 147, Washington, D.C., Dec. 1977.
10. Olshan, N. H., *Recordkeeping Systems,* SBA Bibliography 15, Washington, D.C., May 1977.
11. Ramsgard, W. C., *Data Processing for Small Business,* SBA–SBB 80, Washington, D.C., May 1977.
12. Roy, Ewell P., and others, *Cost Control and Budgeting,* Tri-State Co-op Committee, New Orleans, La., Sept. 1974.
13. Schermerhorn, R. W., and R. E. Page, *Financial Statement Analysis for*

Agribusiness Firms, Okla. Agr. Ext. Serv. Cir. E-812, Stillwater, Feb. 1970.

14. Simon, J. L., *Applied Managerial Economics*, Prentice-Hall, Inc., New York, N.Y., 1976.

15. Vincent, Warren H., *Methods and Models in Managerial Economics: A Bibliography*, Mich. Agr. Exp. Sta. Rept. 108, East Lansing, Jul. 1968.

16. Walker, Bruce J., *A Pricing Checklist for Small Retailers*, SBA–SMA 158, Washington, D.C., Jun. 1976.

17. Wilsted, W. D., *Pricing for Small Manufacturers*, SBA–MA 226, Washington, D.C., May 1976.

18. Woelfel, C. J., *Basic Budgets for Profit Planning*, SBA–MA 220, Washington, D.C., Nov. 1973.

16

Agribusiness and the Local Community

Much of rural and urban America is closely linked with the fortunes of agribusinesses, including agricultural production itself. Grain elevators, cotton gins, farm supply stores, auction barns and farm equipment dealerships, to name a few, serve as cornerstones of many rural and small town areas in the United States and in other nations.

Any program aimed at improving the lot of agribusinessmen is bound to benefit the whole community, not just farmers and the owners of agribusinesses. Townspeople look to agribusinesses for employment, sales and property tax revenues and community leadership.

The benefits of any new manufacturing plant to a community depend on the size of the installation, number of people employed, type of work involved and kind of products used.

The success of a new enterprise hinges on many things, including the management, organization and financing of the firm. Success also frequently depends on the availability of one or more of the inputs used in the manufacturing process, such as labor, raw material, fuel and water. A potential market for the output of the firm is essential.[1]

COMPARATIVE ADVANTAGE

For a community to develop and to maintain a strong agribusiness

---

[1]Gunther, W. D., "Mathematical Models in Small Area Development," *Alabama Business*, University, Ala., Jan. 15, 1969.

Figure 16-1. Rural people look increasingly to agribusiness not only for economic development in the form of jobs but also in the form of tax revenues. (Courtesy, Midcontinent Farmers Association, Columbia, Mo.)

"heart," it must be able to compete successfully for markets in other areas. It must be able to produce and sell its goods at a lower price or convince likely customers that it produces a higher quality product than other producers, or both. For a community to be in this position, it must enjoy *comparative advantage* in production relative to other areas, as was discussed earlier.

Comparative advantage can result from different factors. Some communities have natural advantages because of their location near sources of raw materials or because of favorable climate or good supplies of power or water. Some enjoy transportation cost advantages because of their location along harbors, rivers, railroads or key high-ways. Industries located near their principal markets usually enjoy marked transportation cost advantages over distant producers who sometimes may have other kinds of advantages such as in raw materials.

Some of the major factors affecting the comparative advantages of industries are man-made. For example, most agribusinesses require considerable amounts of labor. A large well-trained labor supply often provides the incentive for locating new industries in a community.

Adequate supplies of investment capital, credit, water, utilities, transportation and land for future expansion also affect location decisions.

From the standpoint of government, a number of factors, such as state and local taxation policies, business regulations, zoning ordinances and provisions in community plans for industrial parks, can also play important roles. Many industries, particularly the small ones that gradually expand, are located more or less by accident, but more and more, large industries consider carefully what a community has to offer them before they decide to locate there. Communities with farsighted leadership can often do much to provide a type of comparative advantage that makes them attractive sites for basic agribusiness industries.

THE MULTI-STAGE NATURE OF PLANT LOCATION DECISIONS

Smith has outlined the multi-stages of plant location decisions as follows:

> The first stage of the selection of a broad region is based on aggregate factors. What is implied is that types of industries tend to be limited or tied to regions which possess the industry's basic economic requirements. For example, processing industries requiring large amounts of raw materials tend to be tied to those regions where such materials are located, and those industries which use large amounts of unskilled, low-wage labor in their production process locate in regions where large pools of such labor are available.
>
> These generalizations lead to the classification of industries into four general categories—each possessing certain location factor requirements:

INPUT ORIENTED INDUSTRIES.—The pulpwood industry, for example, tends to be tied to its source of raw materials.

MARKET ORIENTED INDUSTRIES.—The traditional example of a market oriented industry is bakeries. The perishable nature of bakery products is such that their production site must be adjacent to their consumer market.

INTERMEDIATE LOCATION ORIENTED INDUSTRIES.—These industries have a combination input-market orientation and maximize their advantage by selecting locations which are a compromise between market and input-cost advantages. An example often cited is that of animal feed processing industries which balance the cost advantages of locating near their source of unprocessed materials against the service requirements of a widely dispersed market.

FOOTLOOSE INDUSTRIES.—These are industries whose production activities do not have specific orientation. The traditional example of a footloose industry is the apparel industry which tends to be labor oriented, but which is highly mobile due to the small proportion of final product value represented by transport costs.[2]

Attracting Agribusiness

A community may do several things to attract agribusiness:
1. Maintain an up-to-date survey of the labor force in the community.
2. Investigate and obtain help to study possible development opportunities for various agribusiness industries.
3. Organize agribusiness and industrial development councils to prepare facts and give counsel to businesses seeking location sites.
4. Encourage the expansion of agribusinesses already established in the community.
5. Provide adequate community assets, such as business sites, utilities and water, transportation facilitites, educational facilities, cultural and recreational facilities, lodging and housing facilities, industrial and business location inducements, health and hospital facilities, adequate labor force, waste dis-

---

[2]Smith, D. K., "Industrial Plant Location Decisions," *Virginia Agricultural Economics,* Virginia Polytechnic Institute and State University, Blacksburg, Mar. 1975, p. 2.

posal facilities, police and fire protection, communication facilities, financial and credit services, equitable tax programs and a favorable public and governmental attitude toward all business.

Figure 16-2. A Rural Areas Development (RAD) program for a community or area is a step in the right direction. (Courtesy, Springfield Bank for Farmer Cooperatives, Springfield, Mass.)

RURAL AREAS DEVELOPMENT (RAD)

The location of new agribusinesses or the expansion of existing ones entails not only a knowledge of local economic factors but also the desire to accommodate agribusinesses.

Although there are many different types of *rural areas development* programs, only two are discussed here, namely, the Economic Development Administration (EDA) program and the Farmers Home Administration's (FmHA) 90 per cent guaranteed loan program.

The EDA Program

The EDA provides both technical and financial help to designated redevelopment areas. Technical assistance includes the services of area field coordinators, technical information services and publications and the financing of technical contracts designed to provide new information.

Financial aid to new or expanding business enterprises is provided in the form of low-cost, long-term loans. Loans and grants, or combinations of both, are made available on similar terms for expansion and improvement of public facilities which will clearly enhance the community's ability to attract new industry or expand existing establishments.

Another key element is the provision for training and retraining programs for unemployed workers. This provision, administered through the U.S. Department of Labor, makes funds available for conducting courses that train redevelopment area workers in skills which are, or are expected to be, in short supply. It also provides subsistence allowances for the trainees for the duration of the training period.

Farmers Home Administration (FmHA) Business and Industrial Loans

Business and industrial loans are made to any legal entity, including individuals, public and private organizations and federally recognized Indian tribal groups, for furthering business and industrial development in rural areas or cities of up to 50,000 population with preference given to those with less than 25,000 people. Credit is provided through two channels. For private organizations and individuals,

FmHA guarantees loans by private lenders, and for public bodies, FmHA can make and service the loan. Interest rates for guaranteed loans are determined by lender and borrower and are consistent with market rates. For private entrepreneurs, if the loan must be made by FmHA, interest is computed on cost of Treasury borrowing plus an increment to cover administrative costs. For public bodies borrowing to install community facilities for business and industrial development, the rate is 5 per cent. Grants are made to public bodies to help finance development of industrial sites that will result in the establishment of private business enterprises.

Loans are made to public bodies and private nonprofit corporations for rural development projects including irrigation, drainage, other soil and water conservation facilities and for grazing associations. Loans are amortized up to 40 years at 5 per cent interest. Financial assistance is available for community facilities, including water and waste disposal systems, and for public use in rural areas and towns of up to 10,000 population. Maximum term is 40 years and interest rate is determined periodically. Development grants may be made to pay up to 50 per cent of the cost of constructing water and sewer systems.

The Farmers Home Administration can make Youth Project loans to individual rural residents under 21 years of age for the purpose of establishing and operating income-producing farm or nonfarm enterprises of modest size.

Each project must be part of an organized and supervised program of work. The project must be planned with the help of the organization supervisor and operated under his guidance, must give indication that it will produce sufficient income to repay the loan and must provide the youth with practical business experience. Loans can finance nearly any kind of income-producing operation, including: (1) crop production, (2) livestock production, (3) repair shops, (4) woodworking shops, (5) reupholstering and refinishing furniture enterprises, (6) mobile machinery repair vans and (7) roadside stands.

OTHER AIDS TO ECONOMIC DEVELOPMENT

Each of the 50 state governments has a department or division concerned with economic development. The names and functions of these agencies vary greatly from state to state, but all provide valuable services to local communities. These services include supplying statistical data, arranging contacts with prospective industrialists and investors, assisting in promotional efforts and counseling on a wide range of area development subjects. Many states also provide financial assistance through agencies such as state development corporations, industrial development authorities and lending institutions.

Most utility companies have staff members specializing in problems of area redevelopment and willing to advise local groups concerning their problems, plans and methods.

Most railroads and a few of the larger truck and air lines likewise have staff specialists engaged in community planning and economic development.

Most banks are similarly prepared to provide technical advice in the areas they serve.

A number of colleges and universities have service and research bureaus interested in area development and redevelopment, with staff members available for field visits.

For additional details on financing agribusinesses consult Chapter 13.

FACTORS IN LOCATING AGRIBUSINESS IN RURAL AREAS

Agribusinesses which may more profitably locate in small cities and towns and in rural areas are those which:

1. Require fewer skills at the outset.
2. Are willing to train a large part of their work force.
3. Are more oriented to the assembly of purchased parts than to the fabrication of those parts.
4. Are faced by necessity with low-profit margins in their industry and hence must keep out-of-pocket labor costs down.
5. Use mostly catalogue-ordered or standard raw materials.
6. Are able to keep inventories on hand for production runs, rather than rely upon hand-to-mouth purchasing.
7. Deliver to customers largely at either end of the one or two main rail, truck, water or air routes which serve the area.
8. Have customers who do not normally visit the plant.
9. Have utility requirements which are not unusual in any way.

10. Do not find it necessary to have professional men, such as engineers, physicists and mathematicians, attached closely to the manufacturing facilities (major exception: a university town).
11. Can profitably sign up for a long-term lease or a lease-purchase program.
12. Prefer the benefits of hiring employees who live close to their work and have more free time than can be provided in a large city.[3]

It is the preceding types of agribusinesses which smaller communities should attempt to attract.

VALUE OF AGRIBUSINESS LOCATION OR EXPANSION

The development of an *integrated broiler chicken* production-marketing complex, for example, can generate the following in a given community: (1) 206 new jobs with a $1.5 million annual payroll, (2) $11.5 million annually in purchases of all inputs and (3) $3.7 million in fixed capital assets.[4]

Many related examples could be provided.

DETERMINING PRIORITIES FOR ECONOMIC DEVELOPMENT

One approach to the study of economic development in local areas is shown in a study by Klindt and Guedry to determine the economic interrelationships that exist among the different sectors in a local economy.

The analysis was conducted using West Carroll Parish, Louisiana, to represent a rural economy. Fifteen economic sectors were identified in the parish. The proportional expenditures made outside the parish economy and to each sector within the local economy were determined for each sector. This information was then used to compute the total

---

[3]McMurtry, Gene (ed.), *Strategy for Community and Area Development,* API Series 47, N. C. State University, Raleigh, Mar. 1970.

[4]Roy, Ewell P., and others, *Economic Feasibility of Establishing an Integrated Broiler Chicken Production-Marketing Complex,* La. Agr. Exp. Sta. DAE 501, Baton Rouge, May 1976.

effect on local output and income of increased economic activity by each of the sectors.

The direct expenditures per dollar of·increased output showed a wide range in the propensity to consume locally among the identified sectors. A low propensity to consume locally was found for sectors which purchased products for resale such as the grocery (.0954), automotive (.1551), agricultural supply (.1733), construction (.1875) and retail and wholesale (.2049) sectors. Alternatively, a higher propensity to consume locally was found in sectors such as government (.8587), agricultural products (.7948) and professional services (.7210). The proportion of purchases made locally had a direct bearing on the amount of additional output and income generated (by indirect and induced effects) in the economy from increased economic activity by a given sector.[5]

A study for a state economy was conducted in Oklahoma. Firms that produced goods and services within the state were separated into nine sectors. Multipliers were computed for each sector. The *sector output multiplier* measured the dollar value of total new output generated by a $1 change in final demand for products produced by firms in the sector. (Final demand means the product is purchased for use as is, without additional processing.) Output multipliers for Oklahoma are listed in descending order as follows:

Sector	Output Multiplier
Agricultural processing	2.50
Livestock and livestock production	2.20
Manufacturing	2.15
Services	1.76
Mining	1.65
Crop farming	1.55
Real estate, finance and insurance	1.54
Transportation, communication and public utilities	1.46
Retail and wholesale trade	1.46

The agricultural processing sector had the largest multiplier at 2.50. This sector included, among others, cattle slaughter plants, grain mills

---

[5]Klindt, T. H., and L. J. Guedry, *Economic Interrelationships in a Rural Community of Louisiana*, La. Agr. Exp. Sta. DAE 461, Baton Rouge, Nov. 1973.

and dairies. If the demand for products of this sector increased by $1, total output in the state would increase by $2.50. The additional output above the new demand was due to the interaction of firms in the agricultural processing sector with those in the other sectors. Agricultural processing firms purchased large quantities of goods and services from firms in other sectors.

The multiplier for the livestock and livestock products sector was 2.20. There was considerable interaction among producers of livestock and livestock commodities and other firms in the economy. For example, these producers obtained most of their feed from the crops sector and sold their output to the agricultural processing sector. The manufacturing sector had the third largest multiplier at 2.15. Again, the interdependence among firms in the other sectors was high. The multipliers for the other sectors were considerably smaller than the preceding three multipliers.

The results from the comparison of the multipliers are heavily dependent on the existing economic base. Over time, the base will change, which may change the ordering of the multipliers. However, given the present base, induced change for economic development should be in the sectors with a large multiplier.

An investment in the agricultural processing sector would generate more new economic activity than the same investment in another sector. The indication is that investment to induce economic development should be concentrated in this sector. The livestock and livestock products sector had a relatively large output and income multiplier. Expansion in this sector would generate considerable new activity and supply raw material for the agricultural processing sector.[6]

INTERLOCAL AND REGIONAL COOPERATION

Cooperation among units of government has been suggested as a desirable means of providing services not otherwise available. For rural areas, it seems especially useful for overcoming difficulties caused by small and scattered populations, inadequate financial resources and areas that are too small for administrative efficiency.

---

[6]Little, Charles H., and Gerald A. Doeksen, *An Input-Output Analysis of Oklahoma's Economy,* Okla. Agr. Exp. Sta. Bul. 666, Stillwater, 1969.

A community that wants to attract new residents and new businesses may find it beneficial to cooperate with other towns and have them furnish services it cannot provide by itself. Rural communities work together in a variety of ways. Mutual aid is one way. Such an approach is often used for fire and police protection. A second approach is for one community to sell a particular service to another. Still another method of cooperation is joint action, especially for large projects such as building and operating a hospital or an airport. Various methods of dividing costs and creating joint committees or governing boards are worked out for such projects.

Many counties in the United States find it beneficial to join hands in forming multi-county planning districts. These districts vary in size from 2 or 3 counties to as many as 10 or 12.

POLICIES FOR RURAL ECONOMIC GROWTH

Edwards has reported on a USDA study which dealt with the best economic strategies to employ in achieving balanced rural-urban growth. Analyzed were seven types of development strategies directed at achieving U.S. rural-urban balance by 1990:

1. Stop outmigration
2. Reduce natural increase of population
3. Expand labor force
4. Create jobs
5. Increase productivity of resources
6. Expand capital stock
7. Expand markets

Each strategy explored had some potential for raising nonmetropolitan (rural) income; but each in isolation displayed undesirable side effects on migration, dependency, unemployment, wages or the level of general business activity. A multi-faceted problem requires a mixed strategy. A mixed strategy which promotes joining the labor force, creating jobs and increasing resource productivity can stimulate nonmetropolitan growth with few undesired side effects. Strategies which enhance capital accumulation and expand markets have limited benefits. Those which directly influence migration or natural population increase are not required under the assumptions of the study.[7]

---

[7]Edwards, Clark, *Strategies for Balanced Rural-Urban Growth*, AIB 392, U.S. Dept. of Agriculture, Washington, D.C., Mar. 1976, p. i.

• • •

In the next chapter, job opportunities in agribusiness are considered.

TOPICS FOR DISCUSSION

1. What is comparative advantage?
2. How may communities best attract agribusiness?
3. Discuss the EDA and FmHA programs.
4. Which types of agribusiness fit better in small towns or rural areas?
5. Present an example of the value of the location of an agribusiness to a community.

SELECTED REFERENCES

1. Douglas, L. H., and Scott Shelley, *Community Staying Power*, Kans. Agr. Exp. Sta. Res. Publ. 171, Manhattan, Feb. 1977.
2. Edwards, Clark, *Strategies for Balanced Rural-Urban Growth*, AIB 392, U.S. Dept. of Agriculture, Washington, D.C., Mar. 1976.
3. Edwards, Clark, and Rudolph De Pass, *Alternative Futures for Nonmetropolitan Population, Income, Employment and Capital*, ERS, Ag. Econ. Rept. 311, U.S. Dept. of Agriculture, Washington, D.C., Nov. 1975.
4. Ford, T. R. (ed.), *Rural USA—Persistence and Change*, Iowa State University Press, Ames, 1978.
5. Klonglan, G. E., and others, *Social Indicators for Rural Development*, Iowa Agr. Exp. Sta. Sociology Rept. 132, Ames, Nov. 1976.
6. Michaels, G. H., and Gerald Marousek, *Economic Impact of Farm Size Alternatives on Rural Communities*, Ida. Agr. Exp. Sta. Bul. 582, Moscow, May 1978.
7. Nelson, James, *A Rural Development Policy Simulator*, Okla. Agr. Exp. Sta. MP–100, Stillwater, Feb. 1977.
8. Nelson, James, and Joel Hamilton, *Economic Effects of Population Changes in Rural Small Communities*, Ida. Agr. Ext. Serv. Bul. 564, Moscow, Mar. 1976.
9. Parker, Carrie G., and others, *A Bibliography of Rural Development*, S. C. Agr. Exp. Sta. AE 391, Clemson, Jun. 1976.
10. Staff, *Communities Left Behind: Alternatives for Development*, Iowa State University Press, Ames, 1974.
11. Staff, *Getting Into Country Living*, Mich. Agr. Ext. Serv. Bul E-1140, East Lansing, Mar. 1978.
12. Staff, *Rural Development Literature: An Annotated Bibliography*, Rural Development Service, U.S. Dept. of Agriculture, Washington, D.C., Jan. 1976.

13. Staff, *Rural Industrialization,* Iowa State University Press, Ames, 1974.
14. Tweeten, Luther, and G. L. Brinkman, *Micropolitan Development: Theory and Practice of Greater Rural Economic Development,* Iowa State University Press, Ames, 1976.

17

Agribusiness Jobs and Employment

Agribusiness is a broad field with fascinating opportunities, needing trained persons to process and distribute agricultural products, to give special services to people who actually produce these products and to do research, teaching and extension that will make agricultural production and distribution even more efficient.

It is expected that agribusinesses will increase in number and relative importance. The trend toward fewer persons engaged in farming but more persons employed in supplying farmers and in marketing, processing and distributing farm products will no doubt continue. In view of these expectations, farm youth, as well as nonfarm youth, should seriously consider a bright future in agribusiness. However, the jobs that can be performed by persons with little education are disappearing or growing at a slow rate. Unskilled and semiskilled jobs, both on the farm and in the city, will be unable to absorb the large number of young people entering the market. By contrast, most of the jobs that are growing at a fast rate will require more education skills and training.

TYPES OF JOBS IN AGRIBUSINESS

In Table 17-1 are shown general types of agribusiness employment.

Table 17-1. General Types of Agribusiness Employment

Accounting	Maintenance
Administrative	Managerial
Advertising	Marketing
Agribusiness development	Mechanical
Appraisal	Merchandising
Auditing	Operational
Bookkeeping	Organizational
Brokerage	Packaging
Clerking	Personnel work
Communications	Price analysis
Community development	Public relations
Conservation	Purchasing
Consulting	Quality control
Consumer information	Recreational
Credit extension	Regulatory and enforcement
Consumer relations	Research and development
Data processing	Sales
Designing	Sanitation
Educational	Service
Engineering	Statistics
Exporting	Storage
Finance	Supervisory
Foreign service	Taxation
Grading	Teaching
Importing	Tourism
Industrial development	Trade association
Inspection	Trading
Insurance	Transportation
Labor relations	Veterinary
Laboratory	Warehousing
Law	

In Table 17-2 are shown more specific types of employment by job titles for several different levels of skill and training.

We now proceed to the sources of job training programs and facilities for agribusiness employment.

SUPERVISED AGRIBUSINESS OCCUPATIONAL EXPERIENCE IN VOCATIONAL AGRICULTURE

How may agribusiness training become implemented in high school vocational agriculture programs? It appears that a "team" effort involving the high school departments of vocational agriculture and office occupations or commerce, together with the cooperation of distributive education personnel and owners of agribusinesses, holds the most promise for successful development.

During the ninth and tenth grades, all students in vocational agriculture are taught elementary aspects of agribusiness and related occupations as part of their general agribusiness instruction. During the

Table 17-2. Selected Job Titles in Agribusiness Employment, by Level of Job Skills and Responsibilities

PROFESSIONAL

Accountant
Administrator, agricultural
Agronomist
Animal husbandman
Attaché, agricultural
Bacteriologist
Banker, agricultural
Biochemist
Biologist
Botanist
Chemist, agricultural
Computer specialist
Conservationist
Counselor
County agent
Curator
Dairy scientist
Economist, agricultural
Engineer, agricultural
Entomologist
Food scientist
Forester
Geneticist
Geographer
Geologist
Home economist
Horticulturist
Journalist
Landscape architect
Lawyer, agricultural
Librarian
Nutritionist
Pathologist
Plant breeder
Plant physiologist
Poultry scientist
Professor
Rural sociologist
Soils specialist
Statistician
Surveyor
Veterinarian
Vocational agriculture
  instructor
Wildlife preservationist
Zoologist

TECHNICAL

Airplane pilot
Artificial inseminator
Broker
Computer programmer
Conservation technician
Credit analyst
Credit examiner
Dairy herd supervisor
Draftsman
Engineering technician
Farm finance representative

Field representative
Field serviceman
Florist
Food technologist
Forest technician
Grader
Herdsman
Inspector
Insurance specialist
Job counselor
Laboratory technician
Land appraiser
Loan analyst
Marketing specialist
Park ranger
Pest controller
Radio technician
Realtor
Regulatory officer
Sampler
Sanitarian
Seed analyzer
Seed technician
Surveyor
Veterinary nurse
Warden, game
Warehouse examiner

MANAGERIAL

Administrator

Executive: President
           Vice-President
           Secretary
           Treasurer
           Controller

Manager, Assistant
         Branch
         Business
         Cooperative
         Credit
         Department
         District
         Division
         Elevator
         Export
         Farm
         Field
         General
         Marketing
         Merchandise
         Office
         Parts
         Personnel
         Plant
         Procurement
         Production
         Retail
         Sales
         Service

(Continued)

Table 17-2 (Continued)

MANAGERIAL (Continued)

 Shop
 Store
 Traffic
 Transportation
 Truck
 Warehouse
 Zone
Officer, Loan
 Trust

SUPERVISORY

Field overseer
Foreman, Construction
 Erection
 Field
 General
 Job
 Machinist
 Maintenance
 Mill
 Parts
 Plant
 Processing
 Route
 Shipping
 Shop
 Warehouse
 Yard
Superintendent, Farm
 Field
 Line
 Manufacturing
 Plant
 Procurement
 Production
 Quality control
 Sales
 Storage
 Warehouse
 Wholesale
 Yard
Supervisor, Area
 Department
 General
 Landscape
 Manufacturing
 Plant
 Production
 Quality control
 Route
 Sales
 Service
 Shift
 Shipping
 Transportation
 Warehouse

PURCHASING AND SALES

Agent, Manufacturer's
 Purchasing

Broker
Buyer, Cattle
 Livestock
 Poultry
 Produce
Merchandising aide
Sales, agent
 analyst
 clerk
 consultant
 correspondent
 counterman
 demonstrator
 dispatcher
 engineer
 liaison
 office worker
 representative
Salesman, Advertising
 General
 Inside
 Lot
 Outside
 Retail
 Route
 Telephone
 Truck
 Wholesale
Trader

OFFICE

Accountant
Adjuster
Auditor
Bookkeeper
Business analyst
Cashier
Clerk, Administrative
 Area
 General
 Office
 Payroll
 Personnel
 Program
 Receiving
 Sales
 Service
 Shipping
 Stock
 Telephone
 Typist
Collector
Interviewer
Investigator
Note teller
Office assistant
 clerk
 receptionist
 reporter
 scaleman
 secretary

(Continued)

Table 17-2 (Continued)

OFFICE (Continued)	Butcher's helper
stenographer	Candler
worker	Equipment operator
Telephone operator	Feed miller
Ticket writer	Fieldman
Timekeeper	Forest towerman
Weigher	Grader
Weighmaster	Landscape gardener
	Machinist's helper
SKILLED	Maintenance man
	Mechanic's helper
Adjuster	Night watchman
Appraiser	Order packer
Auctioneer	Packer-shipper
Baker	Produceman
Blacksmith	Pumper
Butcher	Repairman
Cabinetmaker	Serviceman
Carpenter	Tree surgeon
Decorator	Truck driver
Designer	Veterinary aide
Draftsman	Warehouseman
Electrician	Weighman
Estimator	Welder's helper
Forest ranger	Worker, Plant
Lineman	Shop
Machinery operator	
Machinist	
Market reporter	UNSKILLED
Meat cutter	
Mechanic	Attendant
Nurseryman	Caretaker
Operator, Derrick	Deliveryman
Equipment	Driver's helper
Key punch	Field worker
Machine	Gardener
Plant	Greenhouse attendant
Radio	Groundsman
Painter	Laborer
Serviceman	Maintenance helper
Surveyor	Nursery helper
Taxidermist	Park attendant
Tester	Plant helper
Welder	Porter
Well driller	Potter
	Sampler
SEMI-SKILLED	Veterinary attendant
	Warehouse assistant
Apprentice	Yardman

Source: Mondart, C. L., and others, *Selected Job Title Descriptions for Nonfarm Agricultural Jobs in Louisiana*,
Dept. of Voc. Agr. Educ. Rept. 21, Louisiana State University, Baton Rouge, Jun. 1967.
Staff, *Employment in Agricultural and Agribusiness Occupations*, ERS – 570, U.S. Dept. of Agriculture,
Washington, D.C., Aug. 1974.

eleventh and twelfth grades, students may pursue either one of two
options: (1) enter supervised work training in an agribusiness either
during or after school hours, under the auspices of the distributive
education program or (2) pursue a supervised agribusiness occupation
program in which the students prepare reports on some type of ag-

ribusiness under supervision of their vocational agriculture instructor. These options are conducted similarly to the supervised farming programs traditional in vocational agriculture education. The utilization of the high school commerce or office occupations department is supplementary to either option selected. Suboptions in supervised agribusiness training may include: (1) agricultural machinery sales and services; (2) forestry, wildlife, conservation and recreation; (3) ornamental horticulture; (4) farm supply sales and services; (5) agricultural construction services; (6) agricultural marketing and services; and (7) farm credit activities.

Arrangements usually can be made with local or area agribusinesses for some type of cooperative work-study arrangements during the regular school term and/or during summer periods. In cases where no agribusinesses are located within the school's geographic area, several possiblities exist for agribusiness endeavors: (1) the vocational agriculture department may create its own agribusiness ventures and/or (2) individuals or groups of students may initiate agribusiness ventures on their own guidance.

AGRIBUSINESS AND YOUTH ORGANIZATIONS

The FFA, 4-H Clubs, the FHA and other youth organizations provide a potential for agribusiness leadership through various programs. In these organizations it is conceivable that programs can be further developed that accent agribusiness interests and opportunities.

In some areas, the junior chambers of commerce sponsor business-type programs for youth interested in entering the world of business.

AGRIBUSINESS AND DISTRIBUTIVE EDUCATION

Distributive education is practical training, given by both school and business, in the retail, wholesale and service fields. The student works part time in an approved place of business, gets credit for this experience, is supervised by both the employer and a distributive education coordinator and receives the same wages as any other beginner.

The objectives of distributive education are: (1) to raise the occupational efficiency of distributive workers through planned vocational training; (2) to increase the skill, technical knowledge, understanding and judgment of management and workers and to provide them with occupational information; (3) to prepare workers in distribution to transfer to another distributive occupation or to move in higher-level positions in a given occupation. These objectives are met by placing distributive education in the local public school system's curriculum. The program is financed by local, state and federal funds.

AGRIBUSINESS TRAINING IN JUNIOR COLLEGES

Many junior colleges in the United States offer agribusiness training. Their number is increasing steadily.

Basically, courses are geared to provide training for high school graduates with a farm background. However, a high school diploma is not necessary for enrollment, nor is the farm background absolutely essential.

Students taking these courses are not enrolled in regular college classes. Instead, a separate curriculum has been developed to provide specialized training.

Graduates receive an Associate of Applied Science degree. Students are assisted in securing jobs through their college's employment placement service.

Training in mathematics, communication skills, salesmanship and business management is worked into the curriculum.

Actual on-job training may make up about half of the course of study, each student receiving both classroom and practical instruction. Of course, junior colleges may also offer agribusiness instruction for college credit leading toward a baccalaureate degree.

An example of an agribusiness curriculum offered in junior colleges is in Table 17-3.

AGRIBUSINESS TRAINING IN COLLEGES
AND UNIVERSITIES

Nearly all the land-grant colleges and universities in the United States offer a curriculum in agribusiness leading to the Bachelor of Science degree. The same is true for many private and state colleges and universities. In addition, many of the universities offer an agri-

Table 17-3. A Junior College Agribusiness Curriculum

FIRST YEAR
First Quarter

	Hours
Agronomy (Soils)	1
Seeds	2
Animal Nutrition	1
Feeds	1
Farm Credit	1
Salesmanship I	2
Elements of Distribution	1
Occupational Relations I	3
	12

Second and Third Quarters

Soil Chemistry	2
Animal Science	1
Agribusiness I	3
Agribusiness Accounting I	3
Warehousing and Transportation	1
Occupational Relations II	2
Work Experience I	2
Project I	2
	16

Fourth Quarter and Summer

Soil Physics	1
Processing	2
Livestock Rations	2
Crop Management	1
Agribusiness Accounting II	2
Retailing and Retail Merchandising	2
Business Principles and Management I	2
Work Experience II	2
Project II	2
	16

SECOND YEAR
First and Second Quarters

Microbiology	3
Farm Chemicals and Supplies	3
Retail Advertising	2
Business Law I	2
Business Principles and Management II	2
Work Experience III	2
Project III	2
	16

Third and Fourth Quarters

Grain Marketing	1
Advanced Animal Nutrition	3
Agribusiness II or Agricultural Economics	2
Salesmanship II	1
Federal Regulation of Business	1
Market Management and Research	1
Financial Records Analysis	1
Business Law II	2
Work Experience IV	2
Project IV	2
	16

At the end of the first quarter, the students are divided into two sections and begin a rotation cycle of nine weeks in the classroom and nine weeks at a training station for practical work experience.

Source: Feed and Farm Supplier, Mount Morris, Ill., Mar. 1966.

business curriculum leading to the Master of Science and the Doctor of Philosophy degrees.

In many cases, colleges of business administration will permit their student majors to elect some courses in agriculture, culminating in an agribusiness-type degree.

Another possibility for creating an agribusiness-type major is to combine strictly agricultural technology courses in one college with business and economics courses in another college within the same university.

It is customary in offering an agribusiness curriculum in colleges to require that about one-third of the courses be taken in fields such as mathematics, English, history, biology, sociology, chemistry and political science. Another third in the field of technical agriculture, such as dairy, animal and poultry science; horticulture; agronomy; forestry; and vocational education. The remaining third in the business field, such as accounting, agricultural economics, economics, finance, advertising, real estate and transportation.

There is usually considerable flexibility in college agribusiness curricula so that students have an opportunity to specialize within certain areas of agribusiness if desired.

In recent years, job opportunities for agribusiness college graduates have expanded rapidly to the extent that very often several jobs await each graduate. Also, starting salaries have become attractive and will continue to increase.

AGRIBUSINESS TRAINING IN VOCATIONAL, TECHNICAL AND TRADE SCHOOLS AND INSTITUTES

These types of schools and institutes are increasing the number and extent of their agribusiness training programs. Some have instituted training programs for jobs in all phases of supermarket operations, from meat cutting to managerial positions. One school offers a *supermarket management* training program, including material on display, packaging, warehousing, stock handling, store layouts and personnel management.

Another school, a trade school, offers a two-year course that includes training in feed and farm supply sales; farm produce, grain and livestock marketing; farm chemicals selection, use and application; seed selection and use; farm equipment sales and service, both retail and wholesale; managerial positions; and business data processing and computer technology.

Course work includes the study of economics, accounting, feeds and feeding, soils, livestock management, retail merchandising, farm management, mathematics, communications, credit and finance, etc.

Trainees put in between 25 and 30 class hours per week for 36 weeks each year for two years. Field laboratories, seminars and observations are an integral part of the curriculum, as are professional guidance and placement services.

An increase in the number of this type of trade school for agribusiness occupations is anticipated in view of increasing federal support for all types of vocational training.

Job training and retraining funds of the federal government provide further stimulus to vocational training in both agribusiness occupations and other trades under various legislation.

COMPREHENSIVE EMPLOYMENT AND
TRAINING ACT (CETA)

Training courses are offered under CETA to persons who are unemployed or who are working below their skill capacities, working substantially less than full time or faced with unemployment because of skills that have become or are becoming obsolete. The federal government bears the total cost of all training, subsistence and transportation allowances paid within the state. The maximum time for which allowances may be paid is 104 weeks. The federal agency administering this program is the Department of Labor, Washington, D.C.

WORK-STUDY PROGRAMS

Financing is available under the work-study programs to provide useful work experience for unemployed young men and women, ages 16 through 21, so that their employability may be increased or their education resumed or continued and so that public agencies and private nonprofit organizations will be enabled to carry out programs which will permit, or contribute to, an undertaking or service in the public interest. Financing is available under the work-study programs to promote part-time employment in institutions of higher education of students who are from low-income families. The grants are made to the institutions. The work must be related to a student's educational objective or be in the public interest. No student can be employed for more than 20 hours in any week in which classes in which he is enrolled are in session.

Under cooperative work-experience programs, high school juniors and seniors usually go to school part-time and work part-time on jobs approved by the school. The time in school usually includes a class concerned with the theory of the occupation or business in which the student is employed.

There is a difference between a cooperative work-experience program which has job training as its basis and a work-study program which has financial need as its primary purpose. Many feel that work-study programs are less satisfactory than work-experience programs, since employment in the former may not be typical nor related to the education and career goals of the student.

AGRIBUSINESS TRAINING IN SPECIALTY SCHOOLS

Some agribusiness-type jobs are so specialized that they require training in specialty schools; for example, land appraisal, auctioneering and electronic data processing. Although tuition is charged, costs are modest in relation to the income opportunities.

AGRIBUSINESS TRAINING THROUGH SHORT COURSES AND ON-THE-JOB TRAINING

Many professions, trades and crafts provide short courses for training employees already on the job which are aimed specifically at upgrading employee skills. Fields such as banking, credit and insurance are prominent in their use of short courses.

In other cases, agribusiness companies will have their own on-the-job training programs. The federal government has some programs which financially aid companies providing on-the-job training programs.

AGRIBUSINESS TRAINING IN VOCATIONAL
BUSINESS SCHOOLS

Office occupations are prominent in agribusiness employment. These involve bookkeeping, accounting, clerking, selling, typing, business law, data processing, credit extension, advertising, etc. Business schools are an important source of training for these jobs.

Many high schools also offer vocational courses in office occupations for both boys and girls.

AGRIBUSINESS TRAINING THROUGH
CORRESPONDENCE SCHOOLS

Agribusiness employees and prospective employees may further their training and advancement through public or private correspondence course offerings. These offerings are more prominent in the areas of cooperatives, accounting, salesmanship, business law, real estate management, insurance, credit, finance, economics and business administration. Many colleges and universities as well as private correspondence schools offer such courses. In many cases, school dropouts may be helped through correspondence courses to complete their high school education.

APPRENTICESHIP PROGRAMS

Apprenticeship programs offer training for crafts or trades requiring a wide range of skills and knowledge as well as maturity and independent judgment. The apprentice receives instruction and experience in practical and theoretical aspects of a skilled trade.

Programs generally last from 2 to 6 years, depending upon the trade or skill to be acquired. The apprentice divides his time between on-the-job training supervised by a skilled craftsman (journeyman) and "related" classroom training usually provided by vocational-technical schools in evening courses. Apprentices are paid a percentage of the prevailing rate for journeymen.

METHODS FOR LOCATING EMPLOYMENT

Following are some suggested procedures for locating agribusiness employment:

1. Accept suggestions and help from friends and acquaintances.
2. Register with a job placement bureau or an employment agency.
3. File an application with a plant or firm personnel office.
4. Seek the help of a school counselor.
5. Answer classified ads in newspapers and trade journals.
6. Request help from a U.S. employment service office.
7. Enter into various local, state and federal agency programs for job training and placement.

THE VALUE OF EDUCATION

On the average, a person with four years or more of college will earn $235,000 more over a lifetime than a person with less than eight years of schooling will earn and about $136,000 more than a high school graduate will earn. Even if a college education were to cost from $5,000 to $10,000, the return on investment would range from $18 to $32 per dollar invested. Besides, the value of education extends far beyond any monetary return.

TRENDS IN EMPLOYMENT AND JOBS

In general, if one analyzes the job opportunity projections into the 1980s, it is estimated that the demand will be for 40 per cent more professional and technical workers and for 22 per cent more proprietors and managers. For most jobs, the educational requirements will be at least a high school diploma and for many, at least a college degree. All communities and school districts should do all they can to motivate youth and prepare them with the ability to pursue advanced education and job training.

Many youth do not have the ability, the motivation or the financial resources to complete college. What about these people? The labor market projections show a need for approximately 30 per cent more clerical and sales people by the late 80s. The projections are for 27 per cent more skilled workers, 20 per cent more semiskilled workers and 28 per cent more service workers. These same projections show no need for additional unskilled workers.

If those rural youth (both town and farm) who will not complete college are to compete effectively and if they are to fill effectively the projected clerical and sales positions, the skilled and semiskilled jobs and the service jobs, most of them will have to complete some type of vocational training that will prepare them for these types of employment.

For future agribusiness employment, the total number of farmers and farm workers is not expected to change much (may even decline) from present levels, although there will be a considerable need for replacement since the average age of the farming population is quite high.

Farm supply, machinery and service employment will grow steadily, although the total number of jobs in this sector is not so large as in processing, marketing and distribution.

Government jobs related to agribusiness are not expected to grow very much in total, although the replacement rate will accelerate as many such workers retire.

The agribusiness sector likely to have the greatest growth in total job numbers is projected to be food and fiber processing, further processing, wholesaling, marketing, retailing and distributing agribusiness products.

● ● ●

In the next and final chapter, the future of agribusiness is considered.

TOPICS FOR DISCUSSION

1. Name and discuss some types of agribusiness jobs according to job skills and responsibilities.
2. Quantify the value of education, and discuss how employment might be located.

3. Discuss how training for agribusiness jobs is being developed in high schools, junior colleges, universities, trade schools and other types of schools.
4. Discuss some of the more prevalent job trends in our economy.

SELECTED REFERENCES

1. Fritsch, C. F., and L. R. Lorenz, *Employment and Training Needs in Texas Agribusiness,* Tex. Agr. Exp. Sta., College Station, Dec. 1973.
2. Hardy, W. E., Jr., and J. L. Adrian, Jr., *A Computer Program for Determining the Expected Rate of Return on the Investment in a College Education,* Ala. Agr. Exp. Sta. Q. E. 26, Auburn, Aug. 1976.
3. Hoover, Norman K., *Handbook of Agricultural Occupations,* The Interstate Printers & Publishers, Inc., Danville, Ill., 1977.
4. Staff, *Dictionary of Occupational Titles,* U.S. Dept. of Labor, Washington, D.C., Not dated.
5. Staff, *Employment in Agricultural and Agribusiness Occupations,* ERS–570, U.S. Dept. of Agriculture, Washington, D.C., Aug. 1974.
6. Staff, *Occupational Outlook Handbook,* U.S. Dept. of Labor, Washington, D.C. (issued every two years).
7. Staff, *Occupations in Demand at U.S. Job Service Offices,* U.S. Dept. of Labor, Washington, D.C. (monthly).
8. Staff, "Women as a Managerial Resource," *Atlanta Economic Review,* Atlanta, Ga., Mar.-Apr. 1976.
9. Stone, Archie A., and others, *Careers in Agribusiness and Industry,* The Interstate Printers & Publishers, Inc., Danville, Ill., 1980.
10. Wirth, M. E., and others, *Farm Employment-Student Attitudes and Expectations,* Wash. Agr. Exp. Sta. Bul. 825, Pullman, Jun. 1976.

18

The Future of
Agribusiness

ROLE IN U.S. ECONOMY

While agribusiness will continue to expand, its share of the total GNP and total employment is expected to decline slightly. This is because the remainder of the economy will expand at a somewhat faster rate.

AGRIBUSINESS ASSETS

Assets held by farmers amount to about 68 per cent of all agribusiness assets. Land accounts for much of the farmers' assets. If inflation continues and land values hold or increase, farmers will continue to hold two-thirds of the assets. It is expected that proportionally more of the farmers' assets will be devoted to off-farm investments. Also, investment per worker in agriculture will continue to increase as mechanization and automation develop.

FARM SUPPLIES

Farmers will accelerate their dependence on purchased inputs and, therefore, will become even more commercial. Machinery will continue substituting for labor, as will capital for land. Product and service innovations will become even more widespread. Distribution channels between factory and farm will be shortened. Services to farmers will increase as one-stop farm supply centers become more numerous and more vertically integrated.

FARMING

Farmers will decline in number. Capital and acreage per farm will increase. The farm population will continue to decline as a percentage of the total population. The farm problem will become more neatly divided between *commercial* and *low-income* farmers. The former may receive less attention from the federal government; the latter, more. The efficiency of U.S. agriculture will continue to increase. Living standards among commercial farm families will approximate those of nonfarm families. Rural and urban differences will become fewer. Hired farm labor will continue to decline as mechanization advances. Credit and managerial needs of farmers will increase. As contract farming expands, the need for bargaining associations will become greater. Farmers will increasingly rent farm machinery and land and hire custom services.

PROCESSING AND MARKETING

Processing outlets will be fewer but larger. Total marketing costs will continue to rise. The farm-to-retail price spread may widen still further. Exports and imports of farm products will increase unless trade barriers are erected. The development of "convenience" and synthetic foods, quality control and product innovations will continue. Processors will buy more directly from producers and production areas, using more specification contracts. Assemblers of farm produce will decline in number and importance. Management will become more complex. Inter-regional competition will accelerate.

WHOLESALING

Wholesalers will become fewer, larger and more integrated. More will attempt to control retail outlets in some manner. Some wholesalers may integrate backwards into manufacturing to offset manufacturer-operated sales branches. Agents and brokers will become fewer and larger and represent more product lines. In general, wholesaling will be squeezed on both sides of the distribution chain both by manufacturers and by retailers. Wholesalers will tend to offset this by increased physical and economic efficiencies through larger, automated, centrally operated facilities.

RETAILING

The growth of corporate chain and affiliated grocery stores will continue, while unaffiliated stores will practically disappear. Convenience and food discount stores will make further gains. Specialty food stores will decline. Automatic food vending will increase. Eating places and institutional markets will become more important outlets as more consumers eat out.

Nonfood agribusiness retailing will increase proportionally more than food retailing because of the greater discretionary income among U.S. consumers.

In general, retailers will seek greater innovations and improvements in their physical handling and distributing of goods, including more computer-assisted operations.

CONSUMERS

The U.S. population will become more concentrated in suburban and rural areas with a decline in the concentrated urban areas. White-collar workers will continue to increase relative to blue-collar ones. Per capita incomes will rise substantially, and leisure time will increase. Better educated and more affluent consumers will have more sophisticated product, recreational, cultural and service preferences. More females will be in the work force. As incomes rise, less proportionally will be spent on food, but convenience foods will gain. Consumer desires and preferences will receive more attention from agribusiness and the government.

GOVERNMENT

Consumer protection laws will increase in number and scope as the whole economy becomes more consumer-oriented. Regulatory agencies will become more important in supervising and regulating agribusiness, particularly food processing, packaging and retailing. Efforts at obtaining better market price reports will accelerate.

MARKET COMPETITION

Markets will become generally more concentrated in terms of firm numbers and volume of business. Smaller firms will survive only if they band together under some type of cooperative or coordinated structure. Product differentiation and promotion will increase unless legislation is enacted to the contrary. On the whole, however, the market system will continue to function favorably, providing consumers with abundant and economically priced food and fiber, both foreign and domestic.

ORGANIZATION AND FINANCE

Considerable amounts of credit will be necessary to finance new or expanding agribusiness and to replace many obsolete facilities with more modern, efficient ones. Communities, states and regions will compete aggressively for new agribusinesses and the relocation of existing ones. Various inducements will be offered to attract new businesses.

Equity capital is likely to become a smaller share of total required capital. More agribusiness firms will sell equities to the investing public. Government sources of borrowed funds may continue to be important to smaller agribusinesses. The management of credit extension and accounts receivables will become more acute.

MANAGEMENT

The need for competent, aggressive management will become more evident. Computers will revolutionize management decision making in varied ways. A total production-marketing system concept of management will be one of these. Emphasis on efficiency and cost reductions will continue. Management development of corporate directors and employees also will be emphasized.

EMPLOYEES

Employee education and training programs will accelerate as automation proceeds. Employees may need to train and retrain for several different jobs over a life span. Agribusiness jobs will be plentiful but more so for persons with training and skills. A wide variety of education and training programs in agribusiness will be available from both public and private sources.

WORLDWIDE IMPORTANCE

Not only is agribusiness basic to the U.S. economy but also it is a key to world food needs. If population predictions materialize, U.S. agribusiness may represent the difference between starvation and survival for many parts of the world.

LOOKING TO AGRICULTURE AND AGRIBUSINESS IN THE YEAR 2020

Various experts have attempted to project what agriculture and agribusiness will be like in the year 2020. Computer-controlled machines may plant the crops, apply fertilizer by prescription, determine when produce is ready for market, harvest on order and grade and package the commodities for delivery by helicopter to fully automated warehouses. Agricultural machinery units will be much larger than at present and many will be operated by computer tape, buried wires or sensoring devices. Farmers will use electronic sensors to monitor soil, crop and livestock conditions. Remote control devices with lightweight, portable radio transmitters will enable farmers to monitor irrigation pumps and other equipment. These and other operations such as radar will be conducted from an electronic farm control center to monitor or regulate certain farm operations.

Each farm will have its own computer with appropriate software to help optimize rations, crop plans and livestock and poultry feeding; keep cost, income, tax, wage and other records; and plan meals and menus. Each farm will have access to data telephones, television or direct microwave circuits to obtain needed information on prices and markets.

Closed-circuit television will enable farmers to monitor crop and livestock operations. When larger computers are required, farmers will have access to them by telephone. Huge computerized information centers will be available to provide data and other information on all phases of agribusiness provided by national and international experts.

Marketing and pricing mechanisms will be electronically based with computerized price information and selling techniques, such as electronic auctions, where crops and livestock will be sold at farm through these electronic auctions and will not move to market until after being sold for the highest price possible.

Space satellites also will help farmers monitor soil, crop, forestry, insect, disease, drought and weather conditions in other parts of the world.

Gasoline and diesel-powered farm machinery will be replaced with electric or fuel cells or alcohol fuels made from crops, crop residues, wood, wood wastes and other plants.

The use of helicopters in hauling livestock from farm to market will be prominent.

Most of today's crops still will be grown—but each cornstalk will produce multiple ears, and cotton plants will grow with all of the bolls clustered on the top branches for easy harvesting. Yields per plant will increase significantly. Crops will need only a fraction of the water required by present varieties; they will be far less susceptible to drought. Plants will grow and mature much faster than now and more dwarf-sized plants may be bred. They will have been redesigned with sturdy stems and with all leaves exposed to the sun for maximum use of light. Plastic domes over land in crops may provide the opportunity to control moisture and light and increase yields significantly. Plants will be bred for disease and insect resistance as well as for other specific purposes such as higher protein content. Plant population per acre will increase with close spacing and less tillage.

Weeds may become laboratory curiosities. Harmless chemicals may keep weed seeds from germinating, and chemical spraying may be done with aircraft such as helicopters as well as with newer types of aircraft such as Hovercrafts.

Livestock in the year 2020 will be raised in environmentally controlled shelters. Cattle, hogs, and sheep will grow to market size on a third less feed and in a third less time than now. Hens, kept on an 18-hour cycle, will lay not 250 but 350 eggs a year. Reproductive capacity of animals will be increased providing for multiple births.

Animals may be kept in high-rise feedlots and milking parlors where feeding, watering and other chores will be automated and moni-tored. Waste disposal will be automated with animal wastes converted into fuel and organic residues to be added to soils.

Animals will also be bred to computerized specifications resulting in less fat and more lean meat. Unconventional feed ingredients will be used such as algae and other plants now considered of little value. All feed rations will be computer-formulated.

All farm inputs will be obtained from a one-stop shopping center where orders will be telephoned in, computerized and then delivered immediately, probably by helicopter or with large trucks. Mechanical services also will be available from that one center as will farm and home credit funds.

Technical service companies and agribusiness consultants will pre-dominate and will be available by telephone, closed-circuit television and computer to provide quick and accurate information.

All seed, feed, fertilizer and chemical inputs will undergo drastic changes and will be geared to less environmental damage and be more specific to crop and livestock needs.

Most farm output will be on an advanced contract basis to ensure stable input-output operations.

Farmers will organize into groups and work with government and consumer interests to plan agricultural production and stabilize crop and livestock output.

Americans of the year 2020 will never see—much less swat—a housefly or a mosquito. Combinations of biological and specific chemi-cal methods will have eradicated the dozen insects that cause half of our agricultural losses today and will control the 100 or so other crop-damaging bugs.

Water will be conserved and reused. Whole hillsides of uproduc-tive land will have been treated to shed rainfall and deliver it to reser-voirs serving small towns and recreation areas. The surfaces of reser-voirs and lakes will also have been treated to eliminate loss of water by evaporation. Irrigation will be completely automated and controlled by computers.

Woodlands will be more beautiful and more productive. New methods of timber harvesting will save billions of cubic feet of timber once wasted in harvesting. Wood wastes will be converted into motor fuel.

The long-time migration from countryside to city will have come to an end. Instead of 70 per cent of the American people living on 1 per cent of the land, as at present, the 300 million people will be dispersed across the nation. Many of them will live in new towns and cities of planned, manageable, healthy, and esthetically satisfying proportions. Economic opportunity will abound in rural America because agriculture, agribusiness and industry will be coordinated for optimum business and living conditions.

New foods will be developed involving mostly plant-animal blends such as soybean-beef meats or, in some cases, plant protein (soybean) replacements for meats. Plants of low value will be converted to high-value, edible foods.

The fishery industry will become a controlled farm-type industry with catfish, fish and shrimp farming replacing river, lake or ocean fishing.

In the world at large, agricultural satellites will detect differences in soil; identify the various crops and kinds of forest trees; determine damage by diseases, insects and drought; assess crop stands and predict production; and provide better weather forecasting. Crop disasters will be minimized by weather modifications.

The hungry nations of the present will have learned to feed themselves and to stabilize their populations. The soils of the world will have been inventoried. Crops will be grown either on the soils best suited for them or on soils chemically modified for maximum productivity. World population and food supply will be in much better balance than it is at present.

Much of the world's agribusiness will be conducted by multinational profit-type corporations and cooperatives linking farmers and agribusinesses of different nations together. International commodity agreements will abound attempting to mitigate ups and downs in production, marketing and prices on a global basis.

Food and fiber policies throughout the world will achieve a better balance between producer and consumer interests.

TOPICS FOR DISCUSSION

1. Summarize the future of agribusiness in terms of farming inputs, farming, marketing and distribution.

2. What is your evaluation of some of the projected trends in agriculture and agribusiness by the year 2020?
3. How do you see your future in the agribusiness era of the early 21st century?

SELECTED REFERENCES

1. Ferris, John, *Rural Michigan and the Year 2000: A Delphi Analysis,* Mich. Agr. Exp. Sta. Res. Rept. 194, East Lansing, Apr. 1973.
2. Staff, *The 21st Century,* Ford Motor Co., Detroit, Mich., 1968.

Index